# Under Dark Shadows

GW00758984

# Under Dark Shadows

## Peace, Protest, and Brexit in Northern Ireland

## Roz Goldie

### *With a Foreword by Peter Shirlow*

PETER LANG

Oxford • Bern • Berlin • Bruxelles • New York • Wien

Bibliographic information published by Die Deutsche Nationalbibliothek. Die Deutsche Nationalbibliothek lists this publication in the Deutsche Nationalbibliografie; detailed bibliographic data is available on the Internet at http://dnb.d-nb.de.

A catalogue record for this book is available from the British Library.

A CIP catalog record for this book has been applied for at the Library of Congress.

Cover image: Irish Tricolour, EU, US and Union flags. Public Domain.
Cover design by Brian Melville for Peter Lang Ltd.

ISBN 978-1-80374-007-2 (print)
ISBN 978-1-80374-008-9 (ePDF)
ISBN 978-1-80374-009-6 (ePub)

© Peter Lang Group AG 2023

Published by Peter Lang Ltd, International Academic Publishers,
Oxford, United Kingdom
oxford@peterlang.com, www.peterlang.com

This publication has been peer reviewed.

# Contents

# Acknowledgements

I mention individual people in order of their appearance in the book rather than implying their relative importance. Each person has had a much-appreciated role in helping me produce the end product – though none is responsible for my interpretations of fact or conclusions. I am indebted to Professor Peter Shirlow, Director of the Institute of Irish Studies, Liverpool University for writing the Foreword and his continued collegiate and friendly support. Gerry Robinson, who played a key part in finalising the research for my last book, took me on that challenging tour of the Belfast interfaces and continued to challenge, correct and encourage me to the end of this journey. His knowledge, experience and wisdom in this field equals that of any academic or professional.

Dermot O'Kane, Director of Planning and Building Control, Belfast City Council, generously gave his time, answered some very naive questions, read a number of early drafts and patiently guided me through the labyrinth of planning strategy and regulation – communicating complex issues with the ease of a skilled communicator.

Dr Paul Gallagher, Trauma Education Officer at Wave, has been an inspiration for many years as one of the seriously injured who rose above all the challenges in his life and campaigned for the 'Troubles pension'. He was charming and generous with his time in helping me write about that aspect of the legacy of the conflict.

Brendan Murtagh, Professor of Urban Planning, Queen's University Belfast, was truly enthusiastic about my book and shared his own work, tactfully made suggestions on some first draft chapters and restored my then-flagging confidence in the project.

Professor Richard English is the Director of the George Mitchell Institute for Global Peace, Security and Justice, Queen's University Belfast, where I have been a visiting scholar for over two years. He gave me advice on a number of key issues in the book – and read it – and reassured me that, should I need it, he would support a request for an extension of my time at the Institute.

Professor, Lord Paul Bew generously agreed to peer review the book when House of Lords business on legislation on the legacy and Northern Ireland Protocol was demanding a great deal of his time. Lauren Van Metre, Director, Peace, Climate and Democratic Resilience at the National Democratic Institute, Washington DC kindly agreed to read and endorse the book – for which I am grateful.

Commissioning editor, Tony Mason of Peter Lang Group, International Academic Publishers, has been exceptionally helpful, professional, patient and encouraging throughout the entire publishing process. No matter how much a writer wants to be read it takes the backing of a publisher and editor to make that happen – thanks.

# Pictures

# Foreword

PETER SHIRLOW

Roz Goldie has been and remains one of Northern Ireland's shrewdest but most modest commentators. Her role in the peace process, social justice developments and the capacity to communicate, especially when speaking truth to power, has been impressive if not inspiring. The theme of Roz's writing both within this book and elsewhere is replete with the objective analysis of material and other realities. This is the work of examination, analysis and the questioning of a society that can enable significant shifts, such as the near ending of violence, but is less capable in achieving a system to provide the flexibility, litheness and capacity to end conflict in a manner sufficient to deliver an all-encompassing peace dividend. The problematic of a two-speed peace process is indicative of what the author contends – political vision. This we are correctly informed is due to competing nationalisms or ethno-sectarian constructs that deliver a political system that replicates the hybridity of identity and pluralism emergent within society.

Within this book, we encounter the realities of situations in which civic best provides for meaningful social outcomes when Northern Ireland's political parties cannot locate 'discernible political gains or losses....'. In essence, when votes do not matter the role of inter-community partnership thrives. It is that level of sharpness that is located throughout this account in which we encounter cold, hard and sober comment. Whether it is the Home Office, the Democratic Unionist Party or Sinn Fein, Roz steers us through their gaffes, ideological confrontation and the immiserations of their actions and policy failures. Yet Goldie reminds us that these various machinations cannot unravel the embedded nature of what has changed post 1998. Sectarian and conflict-related violence have declined dramatically, inter-community partnerships have emerged and the desire to engage in armed conflict has receded.

Incisive writing provides a robust and critical review of the contestations and their various discourses around space. Regarding neo-liberalism, the author questions the new economies place within the spaces within communities that were burdened most by conflict. She questions models of community relations that are moralising and far from reflective of the effects of capitalism upon how people experience change and legacy. Challenging the often-nonsensical claim that interfaces are sites of poverty as opposed to questioning how the system reproduces poverty in such places. As with the failings of rights-based discourses that steer away from the social injustices of austerity, elitist education and the rejection of class politics. It is within this account through a range of approaches and data collection that we locate much needed analytical explanation of not merely the description of outcomes but the more important causes. Circuits of power here are understood as both neo-liberal assault and the ethno-sectarian politics of spatial inequality.

As this books reminds us, if one positions their politics around nationalists and ethno-sectarian sentiments they undermine the capacity to build and locate the conditions necessary to deliver meaningful change. As Roz reminds us within this account, it is the political entrepreneurs and their adherents who lack breadth of approach and who determine funding strategies that facilitate interfacing and segregation. After decades of peacebuilding, the shaping of space and place is held tightly by a political elite in order to reproduce their own power, place and even electoral privilege.

Professor Peter Shirlow FAcSS
Director
The Institute of Irish Studies, University of Liverpool

# Introduction

The seeds of this book began when the National Democratic Institute in Washington asked me to revisit my work from the early years of this century. That was in late 2019. At the end of an extensive interview with Lauren Van Metre of the National Democratic Institute, I recall saying *The shadow of Brexit is the footprint of the constitutional struggle*. As with many off the cuff remarks, it now seems appropriate, although that was just where our conversation led. It was a short contract, but it led me to review the rest of my work, after some years of absence, which began a journey – interrupted by the pandemic – that restarted in April 2021.

The Covid-19 pandemic, the global climate change crisis and now the war in Ukraine may dwarf the seemingly small issues of Northern Ireland. However, the history of Ireland and the relatively recent history of the peace process demonstrate the longevity of hostilities, the tenacity of bitter memories and the fallout of unresolved war crimes. This book is a view from the places where peace in Northern Ireland has not reached. It starts with a tour of the Belfast 'peace walls' – the sectarian interfaces that serve as a magnet for violence – in the days after the April 2021 rioting that the world's press and media saw as the re-ignition of the Northern Ireland conflict.

The truth is that Brexit, or the Northern Ireland Protocol which came from the Brexit EU-UK Withdrawal Agreement, was misrepresented as a constitutional struggle – but conveniently so for the then dominant Democratic Unionist Party (DUP). Perhaps it was instinct and many years' experience of local political posturing but it seemed that the DUP had made such a huge mistake in pushing Brexit that the fallout could only be hidden in a manufactured crisis. Sadly, this was accurate. This book is about that and the other aspects of the peace process that rarely preoccupy people living outside the interface areas until violence occurs.

In the *constitutional struggle* Unionism has never before faced the electoral supremacy of nationalist-Republicanism. This poses questions and challenges which have never presented themselves. The will of the people was to remain in the European Union. The vote for the liberal, constitutionally nonaligned Alliance Party – dubbed crypto-nationalist by the far right TUV leader Jim Alllister – has increased to where they have 15% of Assembly seats. Fractured Unionism has clustered around the right wing leaving little space and even fewer votes for a less fevered pro-British mandate. How did we get here? And, is the peace process being destabilised?

This book is written for the general reader as well as academics. It combines the findings of new and old studies, interviews, books, media and press coverage of the peace process in Northern Ireland to support the view that, however seemingly unstable, and apparently under threat, the peace process endures. For the interested reader there are references to follow up. However, the book is an attempt at telling a complicated story as simply as possible – and to an audience who may not be familiar with the history of this small part of the world. It is all the more poignant as we witness war in Ukraine.

The discussion aims to paint a full picture of why, after a quarter century, flags, culture, 'identity' and rights remain so controversial, as does the legacy of the conflict. In writing this book I have taken advice from renowned academics, public officials and people who have lived through the conflict and suffered enormously over the past half century. In this I have been challenged – sometimes very directly – but no more than I challenge the groupthink, the polite avoidance of underlying hypocrisy and the entrenched antagonisms that shape daily life in this part of the world.

At the beginning of 2020 the Northern Ireland Executive resumed operations in Stormont after the longest period of any democratic western state without government. For over a thousand days Northern Ireland had no government – from either Stormont or Westminster. No sooner had the parties agreed to resume their responsibilities than two major events overshadowed the peace process. Firstly, there was the Covid-19 pandemic. Then the deferred realities post-Brexit Northern Ireland Protocol threw everything up in the air. Lockdown recurred as the makings of another political deadlock emerged in the form of the Irish sea border.

Medical emergencies and social fallout from Covid-19 dictated a radical change in people's lives, restricting movement even more than during days of the bombs and bomb-scares that paralysed parts of Northern Ireland for thirty years. At the same time, the UK decision to leave the European Union had serious repercussions for the Democratic Unionist Party (DUP) which had pushed for Brexit. Northern Ireland, like Scotland, had voted to remain in the EU but the UK plebiscite swung the decision the other way. It had implications as the promised freedom of trade between Great Britain and 'the Province' was clearly fictional rather than frictionless. So began the pretence of a popular uprising against the Northern Ireland Protocol which the UK government had negotiated with Europe. Electoral losses in the previous parliamentary election had given the DUP fair warning. The DUP Minister for Agriculture agreed to boycotting checks at some ports on the grounds of alleged paramilitary threats to officials – threats which the police declared as non-existent. By Easter 2021 the political temperature had risen and 'spontaneous' rioting occurred at a Belfast interface.

Discussion about the importance of this rioting, and its implications for the peace process, follows the path dictated by questions from a tour of the interfaces in north and west Belfast, where I listened to my guide, and then asked questions about the particular conditions in 2021. What could be learned from a quarter century of research, theorisation and practice in peace-building? As I walked around the streets of Belfast, it felt a lot safer, despite the apparent imminence of 'renewed conflict', than in decades previously.

Why had urban development failed to generate the promised improvements from 'peace'? Away from the clean streets and shining glass of the commercial city centre, there were obvious signs of division in the flags, painted kerbstones and place names along the stretches of derelict land and huge imposing walls. Far from the sense of safety in the leafy suburbs – some even abutting the interface flashpoints – these working class areas had the literal markings of sectarianism, sometimes explicit threat, and separateness. These were the spaces where *Flags, Identity, Culture and Tradition* made brutal sense, shaped the daily lives of residents and expressed the otherwise unspoken truth; the symbolism of division and contested 'cultures' remains a source of potential violence, and provides the space and places of orchestrated conflict.

I invite you to join me on a journey that looks at some of the opportunities which still await the transition from a negative peace to a sustainable civic society.

# CHAPTER 1

# A personal tour of the interfaces – April 2021

After a weekend of rioting and violence at Lanark Way in Belfast, I went on a tour of the interfaces in the north and west of the city, adopting the role of someone who knew little or nothing about these places – despite my previous research experience. I took guidance from Gerry Robinson, a community resident with decades' experience of living in north Belfast, community activism and lobbying for interface transformation.

We weaved our way through the main roads into side streets and into the heart of north and west Belfast on 12 April 2021 after the rioting in previous days.

ROZ: I read an article in the Irish Times this morning about the interface riots, by a 22-year-old who acknowledged the deprivation issues and said that's why we need the peace walls – and I thought No, that's why we need to take the peace walls down!

GERRY: Now that's a question in itself. Do we need to take them down or do we need to transform them – because if you ask people about taking them down, they say *No we're not taking them down* – but what about something different?

ROZ: You'd know it's not Loyalist here [referring to Irish flags on the way to North Queen Street].

GERRY: See the top of that block of flats – the new flats – look at the roof [built at an angle – where the old flats had a flat roof]. You can't put a flag up like before. Years ago, I said to them – why do you do that? [Fly a huge Irish Tricolour from the top of a 12-storey building] because people in the flats can't see that – you can't see it unless you're far away.

ROZ: So, it's just there to annoy the Prods then?

GERRY:   Aye.

   In North Queen Street the old wall is being replaced in front of homes facing the road.

GERRY:   See they put up a nice soft wall here. (See Picture 1 North Queen Street new wall)

Picture 1. North Queen Street new wall.

ROZ:     And how high was the original wall?

GERRY:   Up to the roof of the houses.

ROZ:    Now I remember that! You couldn't even see those houses from the road!

GERRY:    It's beneficial for the residents and transforms the wall. ... This is where all the rioting takes place – just ahead at this junction [at Duncairn Gardens] so those houses were vulnerable from rioting here. They decided to take the wall down – which is good – it transforms the place – there's a sense of normality – you come out and have a bit of a garden [instead of being permanently in the shadow]. This is the focal point – you'll always hear it on the news *rioting in North Queen Street and Duncairn Gardens*. Now the question that has to be asked, of the authorities, is *what can be done to minimise this area becoming contested*?

ROZ:    Why would people gather here [to riot]? These are all working places.

GERRY:    These are the areas where Unionists and Nationalists compete. This is Tiger's Bay [Unionist/Loyalist] and there is New Lodge [Nationalist/Republican]. This is an interface – the police are caught in the middle – all the time – and this is where the rioting is orchestrated – Loyalists in Tiger's Bay and Dissidents [Republican] in North Queen Street. So, how would you soften this and make something different? What they did was build this business centre [stretching hundreds of yards from the junction].

ROZ:    And has that helped? f

GERRY:    Oh, absolutely – minimised it all.

ROZ:    That's social enterprise. Where are the sports facilities? Where's the John Lewis [i.e. retail outlet shops] and the ice rinks?

GERRY:    In itself it's good but it's not enough for the number of jobs needed in these communities – one man and his van companies.

ROZ:    Where to next?

GERRY:    Up the Antrim Road to Allie [Alexandra] Park and take a
          look at the peace line through the park. ... We're coming
          to a new development but the building seems to have
          stalled for whatever reason. The flashpoints here – and it's
          not often you get it – are where they're facing each other
          on Halliday's Road. ... [Some distance further] This is
          Newington. It was an interface area at one time as well.
          When you turn at Mountcollyer and the Limestone. It's all
          changed. These are all new homes now. The area has been,
          for want of a better word, greened [Catholics moved in].
          It's all social housing.

          We're now at the end of the Nationalist area and into
          a Unionist area. Did you notice all that property is void?
          [Moving on he points forwards.] This used to be an inter-
          face area and you can see how it's all changed, it's nation-
          alist. Now, down this wee street and you can see all this
          land is vacant here. There used to be homes here – all gone
          [now fenced-off derelict land in a 'Unionist' area] – they've
          done nothing with it. This type of space [approximately
          two acres] you'll not see in a nationalist community. (See
          Picture 2)

          What's to stop something being done? You have to ask,
          why is nothing being done?

Picture 2.  Derelict ground adjacent to Mountcollyer Street on Unionist side.

ROZ:       There must be two or three acres here!

GERRY:     Yes.

ROZ:       You could probably build a hundred houses here!

GERRY:     Yep.
           In front is open park land.

ROZ:       There's a barrier in this park, you say?

GERRY:     Yes, we can go round the other side and see that, but this
           is for the Protestant community. You've got a [children's]
           play park here which is not used. You see this – [pointing
           to the vast derelict space behind] it's more like a land grab.

So, they put this physical barrier around the community and all this land here is lying waste. There is no need for housing here because these areas are in decline – whether we like it or not, that's the reality. People have voted with their feet and moved out.

ROZ: So, this land lies derelict while in the Nationalist community there is a huge housing need?

GERRY: Yes, absolutely.

ROZ: But has it been designated 'Protestant'? And do the [government] Departments know who owns it? It's to do with joined-up thinking – not acting in silos.

GERRY: It's owned by the DOE [Department of the Environment] and they're not going to build on it because it's contested space.

ROZ: This is lovely! How big is the whole park?

GERRY: It's huge – this runs from North Queen Street right up to just short of the Antrim Road.

ROZ: There is plenty of green space [natural/park land] in North Belfast.

GERRY: Yes, yes.

ROZ: This is lovely. Why is it that if you built the right sort of houses people wouldn't want to live here? Is it because it is now working class?

GERRY: It's that mentality. You can see it when you go up to Lower Old Park. It's a siege mentality. This is ours – and people start coming in – and they start reacting. It's hand in glove. They create the fear and the insecurity – paramilitary ones, politicians – that's where it all is. They have their captive audience. Those votes will always be there. Now, you start diluting that ...

ROZ: And they'll vote Alliance?

GERRY: Again, all this land and all that land – all lying derelict. This used to be housing all along this street on both sides. That was Gainsborough Drive and this is Alexandra Park Avenue – and they just stopped building houses because there's no demand for them – no need. And all this here is just lying waste – huge land, potentially could be used for industrial units. ... Government chose to abandon it and then they wonder what the problem is.

This Covid thing has exposed that the government can throw money – whatever it wants – when it deems it necessary. They gave all the business community rates relief for a year. Could they not have made this an industrial zone and give the call centres or whatever a rates-free for five years to create employment here? So, there were options for them to do things – they chose not to do it. We're left with this – and they want to know why.

ROZ: These are such vast areas of sheer emptiness!

GERRY: Yes. What other city in Europe would do that?

ROZ: And this is the other side of the [Alexandra] park?

GERRY: Yes, and that's the Grove playing fields – it's huge – a beautiful place. I bring my grandsons here. And there were protests about kids wearing Celtic tops – what's that about?

This is Alexandra Park again – the other side of it [2-3 kilometre round trip from the first entrance]. This is the interface wall – all down here.

ROZ: This is a beautiful place. I'm choked. I feel quite emotional about this – it's a desecration of space. And those youngsters [background sounds of children playing and laughing] are going to grow up for the third, fourth generation with this!

GERRY: These children are going to grow up knowing there must be something bad on the other side of that. That wall keeps me safe. I told a fella that one day. He went away and a few days later he said to me, *you're right. I never thought of it like that. It's just fear – fear, we're handing on to young children – don't cross that 'cos it's dangerous. Why? Cos they'll do you harm.* So, that's the reinforcement – and it becomes absolutely natural, except that it's not natural.

And here they open the gates to let people through. And that was hailed as a great success.

ROZ:      So, what we see there is the other side of the park – with the play park that's unused? And there's a play park here? [on this side of the dividing wall the play park is full of children].

GERRY:   Yes, they duplicated it.

ROZ:      The whole landscape is divided! The wall is so neglected. What is this for!!

Picture 3.  Interface wall in Alexandra Park.

GERRY:   There was rioting in the park years ago. They came to deliberately have riots. An alternative way of dealing is to have planted it up after.

ROZ:     I know – just look at this!! I'm sorry, I find this ....

GERRY:   I know – it's shocking when you see it for what it is.

ROZ:     There must be a quarter mile of wall! [The structure in Alexandra Park is officially 120 metres long and 3.5 metres high (Belfast Interface Project, 2017).]

It's a desecration of beautiful space. It's just outrageous! [Birdsong in the background and children playing.]

We walk in silence until we reach the gate.

GERRY:   And here, we've arrived – the gate.

ROZ:     But it's such a beautiful park!

GERRY:   Isn't it? The natural resources we have here are phenomenal. This land comes from North Queen Street to the Antrim Road. And you have the Grove [playing fields] next door to it and next door to that is the Waterworks which is amazing, and then Belfast Castle and the Cavehill Country Park just at the top. We live in a paradise here and we don't know it.

It's a sad reflection on our society and political leadership that they don't want to see our lives making the most of this.

ROZ:     It is understandable, that, in the early 1970s, at the height of things. I remember you always carried a folding umbrella in case it threw the shadow of a gun. But that's a military response to a civilian problem.

GERRY:   This is a soft policing response – just stick a fence up and then we don't have to go through it again. It's the same for both communities. It [the interface wall] is the red line you'll never cross.

ROZ:      In the early '70s I can understand the level of fear and vio-
          lence – and since then – but we're now nearly, no, actually
          50 years on.

GERRY:    Yes, but this red line mentality [of Unionists] is that
          N*ationalists will never cross over and we're safe*. That's what
          they used to say to us – *You're are waiting on the other side
          of the fence with a suitcase packed to come in, to steal our
          houses and take over.*

ROZ:      Is this the lived experience of the interface? Not all inter-
          faces can be taken down but this could be such a good
          place to live.

GERRY:    That used to be the old Dunmore Greyhound Park – all
          knocked down for new housing.

ROZ:      Nationalist.

GERRY:    They'd all be. So – as somebody said to me – it's like cancer
          they're [Nationalists] spreading all over the place [he
          laughs, sardonically]. Yet the demand for homes is phe-
          nomenal and they're just expanding and expanding. And
          that's what the fear is – it's just fear.

ROZ:      Where next?

GERRY:    Up to Clifton Park Avenue – we'll see that one. ... There's
          the Waterworks and the Limestone Road – so it's all very
          compact. It's like a patchwork quilt. Literally a stone's
          throw from each other.

          You wouldn't be challenged to identify what sort of
          area you're in around here [referring to street decoration,
          symbolism and flags].

ROZ:      Lots of signifiers – aside from flags.

GERRY:    Oh aye – names – all the Seamus's.

ROZ:      I am revisiting work I did on interfaces with all due
          humility. ...

GERRY:    Well, I've become very disillusioned with it all. ... Here we come to Girdwood – a former military barracks and on one side Crumlin Road Gaol. You see the Girdwood site – it's huge. This is a contested space. For years and years, we were negotiating with them to do something here. But would they build any homes for Nationalists? That was seen as Nationalists encroaching.

         The compromise was, I remember well, that they got £11 million of European funding to build this [Girdwood Community Hub] and that was hailed as a great success. One thing that's missing in there – there's no swimming pool. There are facilities but this is more of a land grab. Look at all this space [pointing beyond the football pitches to the swathes of grassland around the site].

ROZ:      Is it [Girdwood Community Hub] used?

GERRY:    It is but not to the extent it could have been. Look at all the land around it. They ran out of ideas and just stuck a fence around it.

ROZ:      It's like a manicured lawn but it's still empty. What about the football pitches? Are they used – are there lots of matches?

GERRY:    It's used for training not matches. All the kids come here to train. It is well supported and well used by football teams but I have to say they'd be more on the Nationalist side – that would be all 'green'.

         They built houses down at the very bottom and stuck this in the middle. Could you not build a big swimming pool here? They didn't want it. Why?

         We walk around the perimeter of the site.

ROZ:      There is all this space and it's just fenced off – cutting off your nose to spite your face?

GERRY:    I remember all the consultants [in the public consultation processes and planning applications over years] and I said

what are you going to do with it? And this is the salami-
styled development. Do a wee bit. In itself you can't argue
it's bad but, in reality, what it could have been [could have
brought in everyone].

ROZ:      It is good but I see that it's cherry picking – choose a few
things but nothing that will open up the space to both
local communities and the wider population. They don't
have a strategic approach.

GERRY:    Absolutely! There's no vision here about what we're going
to create or what we're going to do. Salami-style development – isn't this good? Yes. I can't argue it's a bad thing but
if you do the joined-up thinking there are massive opportunities – it could be transforming – but that's not in their
thinking.

ROZ:      So, who made the decisions – was it Departmental or the
City Council?

GERRY:    There was a photo shoot here and all the political parties there and we weren't allowed to speak. The decision
was made.

ROZ:      Ah, City Councillors – and it was really a policing-styled
decision.

GERRY:    Now what they're saying is a*h, there's land – we're going to
build a swimming pool.* I said if you put in a bog-standard
swimming pool it's green – has to be 'cos for the Nationalist
community there's none. [Loyalist/Unionist districts]
Ballysillan has one, Shankill has one – so it's going to be
green. You need to put an Olympic sized pool in. Put it
up there where it creates a buffer zone and there'd be such
a footfall of people coming in that you wouldn't know
where you were. It's never going to happen – so what are
we left with? Now again if somebody says *is that a good
thing – putting a swimming pool in?* You can't argue against
it – you have to say it is.

This is a huge site. If you were a builder you'd start at the edge and work inwards. You'd not start at the centre, build something and leave all this ground lying.

ROZ: Now why are all these fences so high? They are prettier than some of the walls but do we need two metre fences?

GERRY: There's no reason for it – it's just a fancy fence but look at this green [empty] space we're looking at. It's huge! (See Pictures 4 and 5 of Girdwood) When you see the amount of land here can you not visualise an Olympic sized swimming pool? Of course, you can – so why hasn't it been done?

Picture 4. Girdwood facing onto space in front of Unionist housing.

[Walking around the site on the Crumlin Road side.] And there's the gaol. When I used to go to meetings, I'd say you can't develop this [Girdwood] in isolation from that [the Crumlin Road gaol]. This should be all integrated – the Gaol, the Courthouse, Girdwood. It's like a necklace that runs into the city centre – you've got Clifton House, historical buildings – everything. You're talking to a wall as they just don't want to know. They have their vision – and nobody knows what it is because it's a secret – and they don't want to deviate from it.

Picture 5.  Land adjacent to Mountcollyer Street.

ROZ:      Does this gate [to Clifton Park Avenue] close at night? I see the kids playing on the road – is it closed to traffic?

GERRY:    Yes. You can drive in, to get to the Girdwood Hub but you can't drive down this road – they put barriers up.

Another thing – you could have put a clinic in here and people have to come to it – like the one at the Holywood Arches, with nurses, doctors and physios so everyone would be forced to come here – nobody knows what you are and it stops being an interface. They didn't want to know about it.

ROZ:     It's not rocket science. Not everybody would think of that, but once those sorts of suggestions are put forward, at least they should be on the agenda. What I don't understand is that there is no appetite for that thinking.

GERRY:   They didn't want to think about it – talk about – it was just No. You go to meetings and you talk to politicos – they don't want to know.

Look at the massive stretch of land between the houses and the interface wall [in the Lower Oldpark, Unionist/ Loyalist area] and when we go down there [Nationalist area] we see the houses are right up at the interface. Look at the huge swathes of green open space – this is all Lower Oldpark.

If you build something you can transform the interface – I'll show you an example further on. Build something other than houses that provides services, jobs – nothing to [create fear]. If it stays like this it'll never change.

ROZ:     This is all Unionist?

GERRY:   Yes, and see how far it goes up [the broad stretch of empty space between the houses and the wall] right up there. And it continues right up to the Oldpark Road [at least 500 metres]. It's a colossal amount of ground. Are you telling me it's beyond their capabilities to build across that line and bring in services, jobs or whatever? And, then, that interface is gone.

The question I ask is *when does an interface cease to be an interface – and what is going to be done to remove them?*

The opportunities were there and they lost them for want of political motivation.

Moving on to the Crumlin Road.

GERRY:   You see the potential we have here. I want to give you a sense of what's on this side of the fence and what's on that side. All these huge tracts of land are lying derelict. These were all houses at one time and were demolished.

ROZ:   This is acre upon acre of prime city land – and they talk about 'shared space'!

GERRY:   Look at this – it's unbelievable! The waste land. This was all homes at one point and then the Protestant community moved out. They voted with their feet. So, this area is in decline. I want to give you a sense of the void that is in the PL [Protestant/Loyalist] communities and you can't justify it any more.

ROZ:   Why not put something there that is useful to everybody – not just one lot.

GERRY:   The people who are in control, these politicians, have this red line [the peace line] and they won't go beyond that. They think this is securing their votes. And yet it is the fear they instil within these communities that secures that vote and keeps them as they are, because these communities will never be transformed. Now you see that blue wall that is the continuation of the wall we saw at Girdwood – it goes all the way round here.

ROZ:   That is miles!

GERRY:   Yes. It is difficult to comprehend. People think a peace line is only a wee small thing. There are business units on the road here – blocking that end of the Unionist community area. We are heading to the Lidl store on the Crumlin Road. It's another interface area but they've transformed it with the new Lidl. See that black gate there? That's the entrance to that estate – in Flax Street. Now they've opened that so in theory you can drive down there from Ardoyne through Flax Street, into that car park and down the Crumlin Road (See Picture 6: Flax Street Gate).

However, that's not the gate we're talking about. That's the Mill – potentially they're all being turned into flats. So, you can see the sheer volume of people going to move in there (See Picture 6: Mill development at Flax Street). That's just directly facing the Protestant community here. So, you can see where Catholics are moving right up to the peace lines as the demand for housing is so high. The Protestant community see this as a threat.

Picture 6. Mill development at Flax Street.

ROZ:     They don't see it as something positive? Do they see it as Nationalists coming over the wall?

GERRY:    Correct. That message is reinforced all the time by poli-
          ticians – not overtly said but they all know how to give
          a message. Yet this development is fantastic. It really has
          transformed this part of the Crumlin Road and Lidl store
          is very well supported. Other units are going to open up
          and they're talking about a MacDonald's or Burger King
          over there.

ROZ:      Was it just derelict before?

GERRY:    All derelict. So, that's good use of land. That used to be
          called the Dunnes' site – there was a Dunnes' there, wasn't
          very well thought through and it closed as it wasn't well
          supported. Lidl is taking off and with the new units
          coming in it'll be a real success.

          Remember North Queens Street where they were
          transforming the street furniture [reducing the wall to 3-4
          feet]. They've done it up here in The Ardoyne and it's again
          in isolation. Is it a good thing? Yes, it is because it trans-
          forms it, but it has to be part of an overarching strategy
          on how to transform this city and it's all piecemeal salami-
          style development.

          Now we're at the interface I was talking about. Flax
          Street (See Picture 7).

Picture 7. Flax Street gate.

ROZ: And that's been there for how long – forty or fifty years?

GERRY: Something like that – this is the Crumlin Road. This was put up by the army to stop people driving bombs into the city centre – it hardly needs to be here now.

And this whole frontage [the units under the mill development] hasn't been open for years – since somebody was killed in it.

They've agreed to open the gates – like in Lanark Way – [at stated times] and that takes a lot of pressure off the people in Ardoyne.

Now some of the walls here have been replaced – softened – and that one is beautiful, now they've scaled it back an awful lot.

GERRY:    We're going to go down Alliance Avenue and show you something positive that can be done. This is Twaddell Avenue at the top of the Shankill. That used to be a bus depot.

ROZ:      It's huge and derelict.

GERRY:    See the big cameras? This was Holy Cross. I want to show you. This peace line runs all the way at the back of those houses all the way down. Now there's nothing much you can do about that. You see the green fence? That separates houses [of Unionists and Nationalists] so we recognised you can't do much about that. There is no access as streets are blocked off. The interface here used to be all waste ground and then they built houses and this [the Grace Family Centre]. If they had lifted this and moved it back feet twenty then the interface is gone.

          What you see here [facing onto the street]. We're going to see the opposite, Protestant side. This is transformative – it really is. Yet, look how close it is to the fence! It could have had an entrance on the other side. Absolutely madness! So, they nearly got it.

          [We take the long circuit onto the other side of the wall.]

          What I want to show you here is the same theme that runs through all these Protestant communities – where there are huge stretches of land that are void. This is Glenbryn which is Unionist. When this first happened, this was a land grab. [Nelson] McCausland was involved in all this. Look at all the bungalows here. This is beautiful. Look at all the land. That goes all the way up to Ballysillan – that's all void. And there – all semi-detached houses. In a Nationalist area you'd never get this because this is low density housing. You wouldn't be allowed to build them like that anymore – as for every two bungalows you could build three houses.

Now look at this – it is the back of the Grace Family Centre (See Picture 11: Back of Grace Family Centre). Isn't that crazy? You understand – what's stopping them coming six feet across and transforming it? [There is plenty of space to accommodate an extension.]

Picture 8. Glenbryn side of interface at Alliance Avenue, with Grace Family Centre on the other side of the wall.

GERRY:    That whole space could have been taken away. Now you see how all those bungalows are a land grab? They are all at the periphery of the area [and the centre is derelict].

That really annoyed me when I saw that happen and I thought 'shame – a missed opportunity'. And these are homes that have been up since just after Holy Cross [the dispute] and nobody wanted them. Now some are taken but other than that they've been left for years.

These are new homes – it's only in the last couple of years they've been finished and these are at the back of that interface. In the years between, the land has been derelict.

Do you see what I'm getting at?

ROZ:      Yes, they build on the edges to secure territorial boundaries – and the middle or at least part of it is empty. In that sense you could talk of a land grab. Certainly, those houses face the road – no front garden.

GERRY:   That mentality – this is the red line. This is ours.

ROZ:      So, they'll put young families at the interface just to protect their boundaries?

GERRY:   Yes – because if that space becomes available it might be taken. And you can't allow others to creep over because that shrinks your footprint – and if that shrinks people move out – in a domino effect.

Straight down the Shankill to Lanark Way.

GERRY:   Look at all the land here – and demolished houses on Lanark Way. You turn this into an industrial zone and do something there. Lanark Way is open again and the peace line is open.

ROZ:      It's open in the day, so why is it shut at night?

GERRY:   Security – but sometimes it doesn't close until ten o'clock at night. So, yet again they built houses down here and left that – so this is the periphery. And there's another stretch of land -void. Houses on the periphery. (See Picture 9: Lanark Way interface from Shankill side)

Picture 9. Lanark Way interface from Shankill side.

GERRY: When they were rioting [in Lanark Way] if they'd turned down here [parallel street] ...

ROZ: Which is literally 20 yards away.

GERRY: Yep. This is the interface – and that is Clonard [Nationalist community on the other side of a wall 20-30 metres high, metal fencing and grilles]. If they'd thrown fireworks and missiles that would really have sent things up – wouldn't it?

ROZ: But they didn't?

GERRY: No, so they were told not to. It's a huge peace line, isn't it?

ROZ: That must run a mile and half way into the city.

GERRY: Aye.

ROZ: Why is it so high?

GERRY:     Because people could throw things over – Clonard is on
           the other side of that. Again, we see this is all land that's
           derelict – on the Shankill – that's what it's all about.

ROZ:       And this is all Cupar Way? (See Picture 10)

Picture 10. Cupar Way peace wall.

GERRY:     [On the mile to the next peace wall the dereliction is evi-
           dent.] My God! Look at that!

ROZ:       Is that bomb damage – any of it?

GERRY:     No, it's vacant ground.

ROZ:       Where housing could be developed.

GERRY:     Unfortunately, yes – but there's no demand for that in this
           community.

ROZ:       Demographic shifts are complicated. There is never one
           reason but Belfast has been 'greened' since the 1970s.

GERRY: This is Agnes Street on the Shankill Road and there is the Gaol. They built these houses on the Crumlin Road as a land grab. This is a main arterial route. See over there [void land off the main road] empty. These are here to say you won't cross over to Agnes Street – this junction is ours.

You have to ask why did the planning authorities allow that? Why not say No the main road is for commercial premises.

ROZ: It's much healthier for people to be living off the main arteries.

GERRY: Yes. It's not healthy to live on the main roads with all the lorries and traffic going up and down. The main road should be the main focal point where communities come together to meet and shop.

ROZ: There is mile after mile of so-called peace wall in this compact area.

GERRY: Aye. People don't really appreciate the extent of these interfaces and the extent of the civil unrest that generated it.

ROZ: It is the architecture of war – there's no easy fix – no easy way to take them all down.

GERRY: No, not the ones like this – no. These walls run down the back end of people's houses [in 'opposing' communities] so people don't want them down.

* * * * *

The conversation covered many issues, not least of which was the link between the interfaces and the very high levels of deprivation in these communities, violent political protests over more than two and a half decades of the peace process, the gentrification of other parts of the city, and the gap between the reality of life in parts of the city and the intentions of the Belfast Agreement (the law which enshrined its principles and promises).

Another sharp observation from my guide was the lack of political leadership and the will to change. It was not until the end of that year the report of the Commission on Flags, Identity, Culture and Tradition was finally published and its comments on leadership are worth noting – despite the fact that 'the dogs in the street' knew this and were more likely to act on it.

*The Commission recommends that all those in positions of leadership – political, civic and in public agencies – seek opportunities to publicly declare their commitment to the following vision and ambition for our community:*

- We are committed to creating an open, tolerant and respectful society, which seeks to increase and deepen understanding of differing cultural identities.
- Our ambition is to become a community in which everyone's cultural identity and its expression is both respected and respectful.
- We will do our utmost to build a society in which everyone feels welcome and entitled to express their cultural identity, in a way that respects others, within the rule of law.
- We wish to see our society move to a place where the development of diversity is seen as contributing to our collective cultural wealth.
- It is our responsibility to undertake this task within a culture of lawfulness, in which everyone sees the mutual benefits of complying with the framework that govern how identity and cultural expression is marked.
- We recognise the importance of good relationships in our communities and institutions, and that our words and actions will impact, positively or negatively, on developing and maintaining those relationships.
- We will seek to develop and protect shared public spaces, where no area is seen as belonging to any one section of the community. (FICT report, 4.27)

These are worthy sentiments, but are not reflected in the outcomes of the Commission's work. Indeed, the final report would seem to imply that sectarian division in politics is so entrenched that the peace process is constantly undermined – if not destabilised. It was with this in mind, and some key questions about urban development that the investigation proceeded.

# CHAPTER 2

# Good Friday, 1998 – the end of peace walls?

Having considered the reality of Belfast interfaces in 2021, the immediate and striking question is why these places seem virtually untouched over the years of the peace process. The 1998 Belfast Agreement was the peace settlement to end the thirty-year conflict in Northern Ireland. It was endorsed by referendum and strengthened by the involvement of the US Administration and co-guarantor governments in London and Dublin. This was to be the promised Northern Ireland peace process in action.

In law the 1998 Northern Ireland Act (NIA) underpinned the Agreement, providing a comprehensive set of legally binding solutions to the key issues of inequality, discrimination and electoral gerrymandering, and it contained new governance arrangements. Although it was renegotiated in the 2006 St Andrew's Agreement,[1] the Belfast Agreement – or Good Friday Agreement as many call it – remains the anchor and reference point to this day.

In 2021 the press, broadcast and social media – and many politicians – foresaw the return of conflict in the wake of sporadic but escalating violent Loyalist protests at the post-Brexit Northern Ireland Protocol and the Irish sea border. Some academics echoed this pessimism. The purpose of this chapter is to critically review key aspects of more than two decades of the

---

1   Key elements of the agreement included the full acceptance of the Police Service of Northern Ireland (PSNI) by Sinn Féin,,,,, restoration of the Northern Ireland Assembly and a commitment by the Democratic Unionist Party (DUP) to power-sharing with Irish republicans in the Northern Ireland Executive. This included the devolution of policing and justice powers within two years from the restoration of the Executive. The parties were given until 10 November 2006 to respond to the draft agreement. The first and deputy first minister would be appointed on 24 November 2006. The target date of 26 March 2007 for a new executive, after a general election in March 2007 was met.

peace process, and why a return to widespread violence, if not outright conflict, was feared in 2021.

## What peace-building was supposed to be

The notion of peace-building was developed by the United Nations following the 1992 report *An Agenda for Peace* and the 2000 Brahimi Report on UN peace operations – in tandem with the passing of UN resolution 1325 on women, peace and security. Three decades later, the extensive literature on peace-building provides important insights, although Meehan's 2018 review of research on post-conflict stabilisation demonstrates the limitations of the research in this field – as later discussion shows.

Jarman (2016) cites The Brahimi Report, which noted six features as crucial to peace-building.

> *(1) actively engaging with local parties and creating quick-impact projects designed to have a real impact on quality of life; (2) holding free and fair elections; (3) reforming policing and justice systems based on international standards; (4) establishing a culture of human rights in the new institutions; (5) disarming, demobilizing and reintegrating former combatants; and (6) developing a co-ordinated strategic framework for all aspects of peace building. UN Resolution 1325 expanded this approach by highlighting the need for gender perspectives in all aspects of post-conflict peace building, including 'the need to support local women's peace initiatives and indigenous processes for conflict resolution' [...] that involve women in all of the implementation mechanisms of the peace agreements. ... [and fail because] hoping that securing agreement among the political elites would prove sufficient to end the violence. (Jarman, 2016: 131)*

The Northern Ireland peace process addressed each of these and yet the instability of politics, and the frequent civil unrest, with breakdowns in law and order have characterised most of its history. An elite deal was agreed, a free and fair electoral system has operated, and both the police and judiciary have undergone reforms since 1998. Equality and human rights have been enshrined in law and in the then new institutions of the Human Rights Commission and the Equality Commission for Northern Ireland. Although it remained problematic there was some progress in disarming, demobilising and reintegrating former combatants (McEvoy & Shirlow, 2009). Yet, despite attempts to develop a co-ordinated strategic framework for all aspects of peace-building, this process has often lacked credibility and efficacy.

Jarman gives a judicious account of the limitations of peace-building Northern Ireland and the UN strategic approach at the start of this century – concluding that progress has been conflict management rather than conflict transformation. He says,

> *The British Army is no longer seen on the streets, military infrastructure has been removed and the reform of policing is widely regarded as a model to be aspired to in many other places. But many of the paramilitary organizations continue to exist, and they retain a power base through a mixture of threat and admiration in many working class communities. In some areas they are still called upon to dispense forms of rough justice, and they are also deeply involved in forms of criminal activity. ... The scale of segregation in housing and education, plus similar divisions in sport and socializing, helps ensure that the patterns of division remain and are continually being reproduced. These divisions, in turn, help to ensure that identity politics remain prominent, and, while the 1998 Agreement allowed everyone born in Northern Ireland to hold both British and Irish citizenship, most Protestants still consider themselves British, and most Catholics regard themselves as Irish. ... **It remains more of an example of conflict management or of conflict resolution rather than one of conflict transformation.** (Jarman, 2016: 144. my emphasis)*

Brewer's study was one of the first sustained attempts to provide a coherent sociological analysis of peace processes in a comparative perspective. Rather than understanding peace as a mere absence of war, he sees peace processes as highly dynamic, complex, diverse and inherently fragile. His analysis includes key social variables, such as civil society, gender, emotions and collective memory – arguing that Northern Ireland's efforts have been among the most innovative and well-funded in the world. Discussing Northern Ireland's Consultative Group on the Past, Brewer includes their recommendations in full and remarks: *They are worth noting at length because of their potential value to other post-violence societies* (Brewer, 2010: 182). Yet, as if to illustrate the difficulties of societies coming to grips with how to remember the past, events have moved on in Northern Ireland since his book went to press and it is unlikely that any of the Consultative Group's recommendations will ever become policy.

His later study (Brewer, 2022) extends his understanding of peace, and *goes beyond vague notions of reconciliation, to constitute the restoration of moral sensibility, from which flows social solidarity, sociability and social justice. These concepts form the basis for a moral framework outlining what peace means sociologically* (Brewer, 2022).

Waller (2021) describes the peace process in *A Turbulent Sleep*, as if we are about to awake to renewed conflict because hopes of successful results from community relations practice signally failed to appear since the cross-community play schemes in the 1960s, through to the 'good relations' policies after 1998 and into this decade. Cochrane's *Fragile Peace* (2021) more accurately points to age-old hatreds and entrenched sectarianism in Northern Ireland as matters of considerable concern. Yet, however much Northern Ireland is fractured by sectarian hatreds, the focus must be on if, and how well, the post-1998 reforms have been implemented. Overall, then, it is fair to describe Northern Ireland as Murphy (2020) does as a liminal society – existing between conflict and peace. It is not sufficient to attribute this to sectarianism, or as some do, the legacy of colonialism.

The uncomfortable truth of the peace process in Northern Ireland is that it has co-existed with constant protest, violence and sporadic civil unrest. When rioting at a Belfast peace line on 7 April 2021 threatened *chaos to last all summer* and *No end in sight*, there were fears of renewed conflict.[2]

As Murphy (2020) argues cogently in relation to Bosnia-Herzegovina, the Basque Country and Northern Ireland, in the wake of peace agreements the end of conflict produces insufficient change to allow us to speak of peace in an entirely meaningful sense.

> *We may speak about war and peace, violence and its cessation but in reality all of our case studies sit between these cumbersome dualities. This is liminal space and those managing through and organising in, environments of transition, are operating within that space. They are no longer in the midst of war or conflict, but neither are they yet in a framework of positive peace (Galtung, 1969). (Murphy, 2020: 172)*

2    Headline reports in the Belfast Telegraph, News Letter, and Irish News, 8 April 2021.

Treaties produce change but not sufficiently to resolve old hatreds, divisions and the problems of managing these – for the public sector in particular. These difficulties remain alongside the other great challenges like climate change that cannot be ignored, leaving a vital role for Peacebuilding Entrepreneurship. Post-conflict societies must be understood in terms of *organisational* as well as *political* processes. Murphy instances middle management taking the initiative and driving policy to mitigate if not transform conflict during times of violence – and specifically, in the Belfast context, with the example of local government after the peace agreement. This is a delicately managed peace-maintenance process, mitigating the risk of instability. It does not prevent hatred and hostility.

So, was rioting in 2021 any different to events in past 'peacetime' decades? Perhaps it was the fact that Unionist-Loyalist factions combined both political and paramilitary interest groups in this protest about the Irish sea border. However, this 'combined interest' was also evident in the violence and disruption surrounding protests about contentious marches, flags and emblems throughout the peace process. Indeed, such struggles need not and did not become outright war. Previous disturbances had been more widespread and longer lasting. The question, arising from the 2021 protests about the Northern Ireland Protocol, was whether it was, in truth, a constitutional issue and if so whether it would destabilise the peace process – and the detail of the Protocol is examined in Chapter 8. So, was the political settlement of 1998, the elite bargain and popular support in a referendum, about to crumble?

In Northern Ireland the context of peace-building and maintaining stability is paramount. This context is political and organisational and sits beneath the shadow of a bitter legacy. Reforms were planned, policies drafted and a wide ranging set of changes envisaged for public administration, planning and post-conflict regeneration. In all these areas opportunities were missed or at the very least slow in coming to fruition.

Each of these will be discussed at a later point. The important issue at this point in the discussion is the continued existence of sectarian 'peace lines', their expansion after 1998 and the fact that they continuously attracted and accommodated violence. After a quarter century they were supposed to have been dismantled – a date was set for this to happen by

2023. So has there been any progress? To answer this question we must first be clear about what is meant by the term 'interface'.


## What are interfaces?


Interfaces have been extensively researched, counted and described since the peace agreement (Belfast Interface Project, 2017; Byrne, 2006; CRC 2008; Department of Justice, 2019; Donnelly, 2006; Gaffinkin et al., 2008; Heatley, 2004; Jarman 2004, 2006 and 2008; Shirlow & Murtagh, 2006). The public policy implications have been enumerated (Bell et al., 2010; CRC, 2009; O'Halloran et al., 2004). Belfast City Council commissioned research *Improving Connectivity and Mobility in Belfast* which noted that

> *the inner city areas with more socially deprived and segregated populations ... continue to suffer from high unemployment and low education levels. These problems have been exacerbated by the sectarian divisions between the residential areas, resulting in low travel horizons and poor access to certain types of goods and services. (Boujenko et al., 2008: 30)*

Interfaces are defined by Jarman (2004).

> *The conjunction or intersection of two or more territories or social spaces, which are dominated, contested or claimed by some or all members of the differing ethno-national groups.*

> *It ... is important to recognise and acknowledge that interfaces are not a static phenomenon, nor a purely historical legacy of the Troubles, but rather they are a dynamic part of the social fabric of a community that is highly polarised and extensively segregated. ... localised attempts to reduce violence in established interface areas may only serve to displace the violence to other locations, which may be less easy to manage. (Jarman, 2004: 22)*

This is accurate. Interfaces are not simply the result of the latest conflict, and as already noted, Lanark Way has been the site of violence for 150 years. Interfaces are flashpoints where violent sectarian confrontation happens – some going back for decades, but others are more recent, and emerged after 1998 as society became more polarised.

## Change since 1998

In 2005, there were forty-one identified barriers erected by the Northern Ireland Office (responsibility for which now rests with the Department of Justice), half of which had been built since the first cease-fires in 1994. These were 'official' barriers, and did not include security walls, such as those built by the military and the Northern Ireland Housing Executive. By 2007 eighty-three peace walls had been confirmed. Other physical barriers which are not technically 'walls' are similarly constraining, including the architecture of some redeveloped housing constructed to face away from contested routes, creating long stretches of permanent impenetrable wall on major roads; reflecting the implementation of a *de facto* policy of segregation-for-security (Jarman, 2008; Murtagh, 2017). This is clearly at odds with the rhetoric of 'shared space'.

By 2012 only one of eighty-three had been partially opened – and only during the day time – despite attempts by the Alliance Party who tabled a motion in 2011 in Belfast City Council to remove these barriers (BBC, 3 September 2011).

In some cases, interfaces might be temporary, lasting for only a few days at the time of contentious marches, demonstrations and counter-demonstrations which generate bitter hostilities and violence.

> *A comment by BCRC illustrates the impact of the contentious marches especially around the Twelfth of July. 'The shop fronts on the Crumlin Road are shared space – except five days a year.' Clearly there are areas where shared space exists for most of the time but parades-related disputes can create division. SLIG [Suffolk Lenadoon Interface group] said 'There are some parading issues and there is ongoing sectarian violence from young people who target houses in Suffolk (for example, window smashing on a regular basis).' Indeed, unresolved issues about contentious parades, associated bands, parades-related protests, and abusive language were all said to fuel violence at interfaces in Forthspring, Springfarm, and North Belfast in general. (Goldie and Ruddy, 2010: 30)*

There have been cosmetic changes to some Belfast interface structures and one even removed in 2020. They were examined, photographed and described in detail by the Belfast Interface Project in 2017 (Belfast Interface Project, 2017) as part of a regional study – under the title

*Interface Barriers, Peacelines and Defensive Architecture.* In this report 'defensive architecture' includes more than the sites of sectarian interface violence, and rather obscures a more positive picture – however belated and relatively minor the progress made towards the policy objective of removing interfaces by 2023.

Indeed the 2017 study interprets structures such as a raised flower bed with young trees as an interface where it is not defensive – as anyone could step over it – and appears to be for the purpose of separating homes from road traffic. A tall fence in Everton is, I was informed by a resident, not an interface but the curtilage of a private business site. Also, the tall fencing around a West Belfast medical centre is, like that in many areas, erected to protect the pharmacy from attempted robbery. On the other hand, the bulk of actual interface structures remain in place, which poses questions around the development of sites where these have been altered or removed.

The Department of Justice (DOJ) Framework Document is clear and there are signs of a strategic approach being taken – or at least proposed, finally.

> In considering options for change, four main alterations are usually possible, these are: – Remove – complete removal of interface structure and reinstatement of the affected site; – Reduce – partial removal or reduction (in the scale, height or nature of the interface); – Re-classification – the formal re-designation of an interface fence for an alternative purpose, such as use as a perimeter fence by a local landowner; – Re-image – interim changes to the interface structure. (DOJ, 2019: 12)

Although the framework Document pre-dates the new government policy, it gives a sense of government working beyond the silos of individual departments and public authorities.

> DoJ will look to complement and enhance such work through the T:buc Interfaces Programme. Consideration will be given by other Government Departments and agencies on how their programmes and funding interventions will impact positively on the potential to secure community consent for interface reduction or removal work. In this regard, we will seek to align with the broad good relations agenda progressed by The Executive Office – under T:buc-and work with DfC, NIHE, DfI, local Councils and other parts of the public sector to ensure that their plans for community development, job creation, housing, health provision and schooling have a positive bearing on meeting the needs of interface communities, whenever appropriate. Significant programmes of work

*and investment such as Neighbourhood Renewal, Early Intervention Programmes, Peace IV, Social Investment and the Tackling Paramilitarism Programme offer the prospect to change interface communities. (Department of Justice, 2019: 13)*

The Department of Justice also provides a list of plausible criteria for evaluating changes to interface structures.

These walls and gates are physical barriers, erected with the purpose of preventing connectivity – some to prevent car bombs reaching the city centre and others at the behest of residents to stop drive-by sectarian murders – in the most deprived wards of the city. However, events changed in 1998 with the Belfast Agreement and later demilitarisation of the city.

*Sectarian interface rioting over many years necessitated building security gates and walls, and acted as an obstacle to connectivity and free access in Belfast. The negative impact of these physical barriers was reinforced by the symbolism of territory marking, with hostile sectarian displays of graffiti, flags and emblems. And yet, for some residents, the key safety issues around removing interface walls and barriers are more about unwelcome road traffic than fear of violence. (Goldie and Ruddy, 2010: 9)*

*NIO officials consider that, for some residents, the key safety issues around removing interface walls and barriers are more about unwelcome road traffic than fear of violence. (Goldie and Ruddy, 2010: 31)*

There was an expectation that the Belfast Agreement would bring peace by ending sectarian violence, particularly at interfaces – and that these places would be transformed if not eradicated in the years that followed. Quite the reverse happened. Against optimistic expectations, residential segregation, hostility and ethno-political polarisation increased after the 1998 Belfast Agreement so that '*the capacity for normalised social relations remains, in the short to medium term, unlikely*' (Shirlow and Murtagh, 2006: 227).

Importantly, however, it should be noted that in Belfast and Derry/Londonderry the existence of interfaces has attracted organised and funded practitioners because these places are the outcome of the most recent thirty-year conflict. Indeed, it was expected that the peace process would see an end to these interface structures – but the number noticeably increased after the Belfast Agreement.

In 2009 the City Council funded the Belfast Interface Project to commission research on Belfast interfaces. In *Crossing the line: Key features of
effective practice in the development of shared space in areas close to an interface* the authors found common issues on the reasons for the continuity
of interface structures.

> *The Chill factor: The greatest impediment is the chill factor that comes from fear, distrust,
> and reluctance to use space that is identified as 'belonging to the other side'. It reinforces
> the poor inter-community relationships that characterise some interface communities.*

> *Youth thrill seeking behaviour and parades related disputes: Other challenges to shared
> space are youth-led thrill-seeking behaviour and parades-related disputes, reinforcing
> rather than challenging segregation. These are overwhelmingly linked to areas which
> lie close to interface areas throughout Northern Ireland and are both the product and
> outcome of interface issues. (Goldie and Ruddy, 2010: 9)*

Community and interface practitioners also cited lack of qualifications
and employment skills alongside poverty and educational disadvantage
as core to the problem – as well as the need for community ownership
and community development approaches to transforming interface areas.
    The 2010 research findings appeared to signal positive progress with
the key practitioners recounting examples of good practice in promoting
shared space and the reported giving an optimistic set of conclusions.

> *The conclusions are that core ingredients in promoting shared space, of a physical, social
> or organisational nature, include successful mobile phone networks, effective long-term
> (inter-community) dialogue, strong local/community leadership (and political support
> for this), a robust and agreed vision for transforming interfaces that integrates inter-
> faces into the wider strategic redevelopment agenda and implementing CSI, and shared
> knowledge of good practice. (Goldie and Ruddy, 2010: 63)*

> *There are three approaches to promoting shared space, which must be used together.
> These are the adoption of a community-based conflict transformation approach, stra-
> tegic multi-agency working and decision-making with local communities in an inclusive,
> participative process, and the development and use of a sound evidence-base for future
> practice and policy. (Goldie and Ruddy, 2010: 64)*

However, as later events would show these conclusions were overly optimistic, and lacked voices other than from those who worked on interfaces

or officials who were tasked to provide 'solutions'. Firstly, the mobile phone networks did not operate quite as interface workers had reported. More than a decade after the 2010 research report I spoke to a community activist who was not employed as an interface worker, asking about the mobile phones network. It was hailed as a massive breakthrough, I said.

He laughed out loud – with anything but humour and replied. *I got a phone call one day saying, 'If you don't get those kids away from the interface in the next fifteen minutes, we're going to open fire.' That person's well up now.* 'That person' was the paramilitary commandant in the area and an elected representative.

Secondly, when the dispute over regulating the flying of the Union Flag at Belfast City Hall arose in 2012, violence in the city centre and at key interfaces was neither mediated nor in any way moderated by interface workers or the mobile phone network. It was perhaps naive to take practitioners at their word.

The 2009-2010 research for the Belfast Interface Project was hemmed in by its remit and the adherence to the then-government policy of Cohesion, Integration and Sharing – and for all its sound methodology its deficiencies lie perhaps in the Council's underlying community relations discourse. The way in which interfaces are understood – that is, the discourse – determines how the problem(s) and any proposed solutions are shaped.

Murtagh (2017) provides an incisive critical review of six distinct discourses of contested space – whether neo-liberal, moralising community relations, emotive-pathos, rights-based, bureaucratic-logical and policy- or security-oriented. Each has a narrative suited to the professional or political orientation of the adherent. He calls for an alternative to these and contends there is a need for

> *... stronger analytical explanations of the causes and consequences of ethnic violence, surfacing different circuits of power and how they work together and independently from each other in the reproduction of spatial inequalities. (Murtagh, 2017: 20)*

This insight into the way in which interfaces are described, theorised and thus captured in the framework of different professional interest groups is one of the most important advances in our understanding of contested space. It opens up a lens through which we can see the perspective of the viewer – in whatever job or either side of the 'divide' – and pinpoint the possible predisposition to ghettoise what is already a virtual ghetto. Each has something to offer – although some have proved signally lacking in effective outcome. Each focuses on one or more important parts of the problem but none encapsulates the full solution.

Belfast City Council invested in a broad range of research and planning strategies over the past two decades addressing the interfaces and yet – because of the long delay and partial implementation of the 2002 Review of Public Administration – urban planning powers were not transferred to local government until 2015. It must be asked whether the Council has exercised these powers since then and made inroads into solving the intractable problem of interfaces.

However, before that discussion the extent of this seemingly intractable problem merits our attention. Why has violence and rioting persisted, almost unbroken, in times of peace?

# CHAPTER 3

# Politics, protest and sectarian violence

Interfaces are only found in working class districts and where the people living there experienced the worst intensity of the conflict (Fay et al., 1999). In these districts the levels of poverty, unemployment and educational underachievement have remained stubbornly high. These places have been contested in large part because of historical competition for scarce resources, and housing in particular, for decades when there was discrimination against the minority of Roman Catholics in employment, housing and education (Bew et al., 2002; Harvey, 2000; McEvoy et al., 2003; Palley, 1972; Whyte, 1983). This was *a very real cause* of the conflict (Cameron Report, 1969: para. 127). It was not until the end of the 1960s that there was universal franchise in local government elections.[3] The Northern Irish state, and its government, were Unionist, partisan and anti-Catholic. In 1934 its first Prime Minister said the Stormont regime was *a Protestant Parliament for a Protestant People* (Bew et al., 2002: 7).

The fact that the Protestant and Catholic working- and non-working classes lived in similarly unfit housing was not recognised on the twentieth-century political landscape – where favouritism only meant that working class Protestants could have more access to virtually slum housing than their Catholic neighbours. Northern Ireland's political status quo was Unionist. Institutionalised segregation occurred as early as the post-war housing development of social housing, with Catholics moving into the west of the city and Protestant into the east.

---

3  Although there was universal franchise for Westminster elections, it was not until 1969 that this included local elections (Whyte, 1983). Before that only rate-payers had a vote. In addition the system gave two votes to persons paying rates for business premises as well domestic rates. Graduates of Queen's University Belfast had an additional vote.

In 1998 it was assumed that these divisions would heal somehow and interfaces come down. That optimism did not result in change.

Just as violence in 2021 in Lanark Way attracted international attention, so too have other 'peace-time' territorial disputes – and some from before the Belfast Agreement. Among these was the Drumcree protest, the Holy Cross confrontation and, at the long-derelict former army barracks at Girdwood, the use of interface and other public space for violent 'recreational rioting' at the interfaces. These need to be seen in terms of the purpose of interface violence, and its refraction in other violent protests in public spaces. The social and political implications, and the enormous costs of policing these protests, are addressed in the later chapters – as is the stand-off at Twaddell Avenue 'freedom camp'.

## Drumcree

The political importance of marching parades increased if anything after the first IRA ceasefire of 1994, as Unionists strove to maintain symbolic supremacy through Orange Order (and Loyal Order-related) demonstrations of 'Britishness' in the context of perceived 'threat' of the ongoing peace negotiations. There have been no such Catholic-nationalist marches since the late 1960s when the Hibernian Order stopped all their marches.

Drumcree was one of a number of high-profile violent Unionist/ Loyalist protests. In the case of Drumcree it was a protest demanding the right for contested Orange Order marches to proceed through a Nationalist/Republican district against the wishes of residents.

There had always been a strong sense of 'identity' and 'tradition' in retaining the unchallenged right of Loyal Orders to march with their bands, irrespective of the wishes of local residents. For Unionist-Loyalists in the mid-1990s this claim to 'march freely' became bitterly entrenched. Indeed, the word Drumcree became a watchword for the violent struggle for recognition of the right to march on 'the Queen's highway'. The battle lines were set with Loyal Orders and their supporters on the one side, and the 'concerned residents' and their Nationalist and Republican supporters, assisted by Sinn Féin, on the other.

> *The name Drumcree conjures up images of pitch battles between supporters of the Orange Order's fight to walk a route it claims it has taken for over two centuries through the town, while security forces implemented the determination of the Parades Commission by blocking their way. Orangemen have been banned from walking Obins Street in the town for the past quarter of the century, an area which had formed part of the outward route previously. However, boiling point was reached in the 1990s over the 'walk home' from their hour-long church service via the nationalist Garvaghy Road, culminating in the banning of Orangemen from the route in 1998. (Kilpatrick, 2010)*

The summers of 1995 and 1996 saw massive disruption across Northern Ireland with protests against Orange Order marches on the Garvaghy Road from Portadown to the church at Drumcree. The parade was banned by the police in 1996 after previous years of unrest. The murder of the three Quinn brothers in July 1998 was the result of *one of 137 loyalist petrol bomb attacks on Catholic homes in that week alone*, followed by widespread rioting and the threat of extensive community violence well beyond the Portadown district.

This atrocity was worsened by the Rev Ian Paisley's public statement that the murder of the three young children was a drug-related incident – an assertion quickly refuted by the police and disproven by the subsequent three life sentences given to the main perpetrator. The judge described the attack as a *shameful outrage* and said it was carried out by the UVF – *its motive was sectarian* (Murphy, 1999). UUP leader David Trimble condemned the murders and called on *the brethren of Portadown ... to distance themselves from these murders... [and] leave the hill at Drumcree church* (Morris, 2021a).

At the time, as the IRA bombing of Omagh town centre would be just weeks after the Belfast Agreement, this outrage caused massive public revulsion. In 2021, the sudden death of the only perpetrator convicted of the Quinn boys' murder was covered in a full page article in the *Belfast Telegraph* – in which the sense of collective unionist shame was apparent.

The annual disruption at Drumcree went on for some years after 1998 with a broad swathe of political and paramilitary Unionism taking part. Perpetuating an increased sense of threat, it was asserted that unionism

suffered 'losses' in the new equality agenda and power-sharing government. The broad Unionist view was that the 'equality agenda' was a victory for Nationalists and therefore was a loss for Unionists (Hayward &
Mitchell, 2003).

Following the years of violent unrest surrounding Drumcree, The
Parades Commission for Northern Ireland was established, on the recom-
mendation of the North Report in 1996, under the Public Processions (NI)
Act 1998. Its remit was to consider disputed parades and demonstrations
where no resolution could be reached. It was neither successful nor lasting.

In 2010 government attempts to replace the Parades Commission were
thwarted as the Orange Order would not agree to the suggested alternative.
Indeed, the Parades Commission was critical of both the Strategic Review
of the Parading Body and its response to the Draft Public Assemblies,
Parades and Protests (Northern Ireland) Bill was a cogent critique of a
shoddy piece of draft legislation. Aside from the fact that these proposals
would potentially restrict freedom of assembly far beyond the relatively
few Orange Order parades (99% of which were wholly uncontested), the
Commission gave a useful analysis of the faulted discourse of *rights-based
approach* that the DUP and Sinn Féin had employed in respect of a new
parading body. Their response points out that:

> *This is not new and it may be misleading to suggest otherwise. The Commission has
> been working to promote and balance human rights since its inception. It was inspired
> to do so by its genesis in the North Report and required to do so under Human Rights
> Law. ... The Commission has never been found wanting by any judicial review in its
> interpretations of its obligations under human rights or its application of those rights
> in its decision makings. (para. 2)*

The two main parties appeared to interpret 'human rights' as a way of
vindicating their ethno-political – and sometimes overtly sectarian – position to their own electorate, and assumed they would automatically have
*a card to trump the card of other players.*

> *We should point out, however, that protagonists too often and too simplistically believe
> that if there is a robust adherence to a human rights framework and principles, then
> this will mean 'inevitably' that their 'position' must win through. They believe it because
> they understand that they have human rights and expect to see a vindication of those*

*rights in the face of challenge or opposition from the 'other side'. Both 'sides' claim that they want decisions to be made which **are** firmly based on a recognition of human rights. Unfortunately, they also tend to believe that the application of any rights based approach translates into an almost exclusive focus on 'their' human rights. In this context human rights is not part of a discourse which seeks to promote tolerance, respect and understanding but rather a card to be used to trump the cards of the other players. (para. 3)*

The proposals for a new Parades body showed a lack of transparency (para. 7) and a measure of arbitrariness in that Clause 37 permitted the prosecuting authority some discretion, but failed to provide either criteria or guidelines (para. 8). The power of OFMDFM to give exemptions might have been argued to run counter to the independence of the existing Parades Commission; as might also the fact that decisions made by the Department of Justice require the approval of the First and Deputy First Ministers' Office (paras 9-10). The Commission was robust in its declaration that freedom to parade and protest are *fundamental to the vitality of a democracy and stand as its very cornerstones* (para. 5). A fair point was made, referring back to the North Report that there is little of value in parading issues being *politicised or being brought into local politics*. Their formal response to the Draft Code of Conduct: Public Assemblies Parades and Protests Bill was similarly critical noting that it lacked a *transparent, open and accessible 'Code of Conduct'*.

It would appear that, if the dominant parties of the DUP and Sinn Féin realised their ambitions, the politics of parading and freedom of assembly were to be regulated by the rules of 'ethnic poker' rather than a genuinely rights-based framework that stated clearly what might constitute prohibited activities and thus criminal behaviour.

By 2010 the regional press reported that at Drumcree *the only thing police were battling back was a gale-force wind* (Kilpatrick, 2010) and that what had been sufficient to bring Northern Ireland to a virtual stand-still had faded to nothing of consequence. The restriction remained and the mass protest ended but a symbolic demonstration continued until 2020 (Kula, 2020).

## The Holy Cross dispute

After three decades of conflict, the start of the peace process and significant population shifts in Belfast, social housing had become more segregated along sectarian lines. Holy Cross, a North Belfast Catholic primary school for girls from Ardoyne, was sited opposite the Loyalist Glenbryn area. These two areas are divided by a 40-foot-high wall, which is the interface at Alliance Avenue. On 21 June 2001 Loyalists began picketing the school, in protest at what they claimed as Catholic intimidation, attacks on their homes and the denial of access to facilities such as shops and playgrounds. Catholics made similar claims about attacks on their houses by Loyalists. The police received intelligence that UDA (Ulster Defence Association) members (Loyalist paramilitaries) were planning to *exploit community tensions* to kill Irish nationalists, Catholics and/or police officers. The violence was severe, widespread and the threats real.[4]

These pickets resumed in September with the new school term, lasting until late November as hundreds of protesters tried to stop the (primary level) schoolchildren and their parents from walking to school through their area.

Every day the little girls and their parents had to be accompanied by riot police and British soldiers through these hostile demonstrations with protesters throwing stones, bricks, fireworks and urine-filled balloons, and hurling sectarian abuse and obscenities at them. As Heatley (2004) recorded there were *scenes of frightened Catholic schoolgirls running a gauntlet of abuse from loyalist protesters as they walked to school captured world headlines*. The Loyalist paramilitary Red Hand Defenders made death threats against both the parents and school staff. Even what was considered appropriate for early evening television news caused disbelief, revulsion and public repudiation.

---

4    Three Protestant families left their homes in Alliance Avenue, saying they were
     afraid of a nationalist attack. During the evening and night there were serious
     disturbances in the area around the school. Loyalists fired ten shots, and threw
     six blast bombs and 46 petrol bombs at police lines. Two Catholic homes were
     attacked with pipe bombs, and a child was thrown against a wall by one of the
     blasts. Twenty-four RUC officers were hurt.

However, the world-wide shock and horror at the 9/11 attacks in the US forced the Holy Cross dispute off the international media's headline news.

It was only after a promise of a redevelopment scheme guaranteeing housing and greater security for the Loyalist Glenbryn area that the picketing stopped. As is clear from my tour of the interfaces this housing was neither needed nor would it be occupied when it was eventually built.

Both the schoolgirls and their parents were severely traumatised by these events – and security forces remained outside the school for several months after.

As if to summarise the case for 'their' working class people, Loyalists argued they had seen no 'peace dividend' and felt they were being 'ethnically cleansed' from the area. The Protestant population of Glenbryn had declined significantly during the 1990s. Some believed they were being driven out. Others alleged that the IRA was using the children's journey to-and-from school to 'gather intelligence'. Heatley quotes a community worker engaged in the protest.

> *Protestants felt they weren't getting a fair deal under the Good Friday Agreement. People in Glenbryn kept telling the Government about attacks on their houses and how vulnerable they felt but we weren't being listened to. That is why people protested on the Ardoyne Road, the focus wasn't so much the school itself [...] The community in Glenbryn is in decline and it is fearful of Ardoyne. That does encourage a siege mentality.*

There is more than a little irony that Catholic Irish Nationalists welcomed the protection of both the police and British army from protesting mobs who were allegedly loyal to the crown. The vehemence of this protest, its longevity and the trauma it caused to the primary schoolgirls and their families was publicly condemned by all politicians and church leaders. It had a lasting effect as a former senior police officer said almost twenty years later.

> *I think it's fair to say ... you don't have to scratch too far below the surface till you get to people's memory of [events] ... people can draw back into their previous memories pretty easily. The best example I have of that is the Holy Cross dispute. I was there ... I met with community representatives on both sides. The residual sores or hurts are just beneath the surface. It would have been a constant factor as we try to deliver policing. ...*

*just for the fact that it's all gone, or however many years ago it was, for the people living there it's still a living memory.*

It may be coincidental but, as the Holy Cross dispute was ending, power-sharing in the Stormont Assembly was under increasing strain and collapsed the following year – not to return until April 2007.

Despite the talk of the 'disconnect' felt by Loyalists, events at Holy Cross produced no positive outcomes for the demonstrators. PUP (Progressive Unionist Party) Loyalist politician and former paramilitary Billy Hutchinson said that *The protest was a disaster in terms of putting their cause forward but it was a genuine expression of their anger and frustration and fear over what is happening in that part of North Belfast* (Heatley, 2004).

However, it was more than simply events in north Belfast that had generated the paramilitary-orchestrated Holy Cross dispute, because it happened in 2001 when the long-running Drumcree dispute over Orange Order marches appeared settled – although without granting the Orange Order permission to march through the Garvaghy Road.

In the years after the 1994 ceasefire, Drumcree had been the most destructive Unionist-Loyalist response to the peace negotiations and the Agreement, threatening Northern Ireland's economy as well as bringing violence, injury and death to the streets. The Holy Cross dispute was a resounding echo of that.

## The functions of violent protest and destabilising the peace process

Meehan's typology may explain these protests, and the political landscape of protest and violence both at interfaces and the wider public space. Meehan (2018) categorises *three broad types of large-scale violence: competitive, embedded and permissive violence* is useful.

### Competitive violence

*Violence aimed at contesting underlying political settlements (both at the national and subnational level). ... This may be violence deployed by actors excluded from the existing elite bargain or by actors within an existing elite bargain looking to renegotiate their position and power. This kind of violence may be deployed by actors with a relatively limited aim to improve their position and power, or by actors aimed at fundamentally challenging the political settlement.*

This might well be a short description of the much talked of 'disconnect' between Loyalism and the formal politicians – first with the UUP, who brokered the elite bargain of the 1998 settlement, and then the DUP. The Unionist population in Belfast was in steady decline over decades as the Nationalist population rose. Unionist-Loyalist actors could be said to be *fundamentally challenging the political settlement* that was the Belfast Agreement. And some two decades later, there came the threat of Loyalist paramilitary violence in protest against the Irish Sea Border resulting from the post-Brexit Northern Ireland Protocol.[5]

However, since the Unionist elite, and particularly the DUP, have kept regular contact with working class Loyalism and paramilitary Combined Loyalist Command, the reality in 2021 was more complicated – not least as the Westminster government also entertained the Loyalist Communities Council.[6] While it is impossible to verify all the details of these connections it could be seen as implicitly devolving of *the 'right' to use violence* – embedded violence as Meehan calls it.

*Embedded violence: Violence directly embedded in how a political settlement works. The privileges that elites are awarded in order to strengthen their loyalty to the state are not only economic (e.g. control over certain resources, import licences) or political (government positions) but may also include the 'right' to use violence. These 'violence*

---

5   BBC NI TV News 'Newsline' and ITV Regional News 19 May 2021.
6   The Loyalist Communities Council (LCC), which represents the Ulster Defence Association (UDA), Ulster Volunteer Force (UVF) and the Red Hand Commando, met the Independent Reporting Commission (IRC) on 19 May 2021. James Ward, Violence Not Ruled Out in Battle against Protocol, Loyalists Tell MPs, *Belfast Newsletter*, 20/05/2021, p. 8. John Malley and Connla Young, Alarm as loyalist's Westminster Warning of Protocol Violence, *Irish News*, 20/05/2021, p. 1.

*rights' determine who has the 'right' to enact violence, upon whom, for what reasons, and with what level of impunity.*

*These 'violence rights' may subsequently be used to secure material interests (e.g. land grabs) but the point is that the 'limited access orders' which underpin many political settlements may be founded upon who has the right to use violence, rather than only the explicit apportioning of material benefits. These kinds of state-sanctioned violence should alert policymakers to the fact that violence may not only be driven by state fragility and (41) failure but may also be embedded in the bargains made to forge order and stability. A stable political settlement may expose populations to significant levels of violence. (Meehan, 2018: 37-38)*

It is possible to classify violence at interfaces and in Loyalist-Unionist protests as embedded – as appears to be the case during the 2012 Flags Dispute. Another explanation of this violence as permissive is at least plausible. This was persuasive and it certainly created instability.

*Permissive violence: Violence that results from the state's inability to monopolize control over violence ... This kind of violence occurs because the state is unable or unwilling to monopolise control over violence and has instead made selective decisions of how and where to allocate the limited coercive resources at its disposal. This creates opportunities for 'permissive' violence in the sense that a government 'allows' violence to happen in certain places because it has chosen to focus its limited coercive resources (i.e. police and military deployment) elsewhere. This may include violence used by actors to control places where state authority is weak or non-existent but which is not aimed at destabilising the overarching political settlement. It may also encompass forms of criminal activity in which violence is a key component, but where such activities are not aimed at challenging the government. Indeed, violent criminal actors may have a vested interest in upholding the status quo since it is within this system that they are able to operate. (Meehan, 2018: 38)*

Using the threat of widespread Loyalist street violence in 2001 at Holy Cross was seen as 'successful' because new social housing was built and allocated to Unionist/Loyalists – and in 2021 it was sufficient to push the post-Brexit Northern Ireland Protocol to the top of the UK government agenda. It could be characterised as violence including *forms of criminal activity in which violence is a key component, but where such activities are not aimed at challenging the government.* More coincidences of sectarian street violence and the political convenience of this disruption are described later.

Indeed, as Meehan acknowledges, competitive, embedded and permissive violence overlap and intertwine.

> *These various types of violence are often closely interlinked and can mutate over time. Groups that accumulate power and wealth through permissive violence may then look to challenge the state to demand greater inclusion into a political settlement. The informality governing embedded and permissive violence may make the 'rules of the game' surrounding these types of violence unclear and volatile. Governments may periodically seek to crack down on such forms of violence due to international pressure, efforts to improve their legitimacy, or fears of the growing power of potential competitors. (Meehan, 2018: 41-42)*

Can the interface violence – and associated disruption – in early April 2021 be understood in this way? It is certainly the case that this dispute made the *'rules of the game' surrounding these types of violence unclear and volatile.* Existing research findings provide a useful starting point but need the addition of credible information on the current situation, since it may reveal something beyond headlines of horror. We shall return to Meehan's framework later but continue with the theme of interface and protest-related violence – and the key actors involved.

## Key actors in community settings

The need for community ownership and community development approaches to sectarian interfaces has been asserted throughout the years. Yet, even in 2010, amidst claims of good and effective practice at interfaces there was some scepticism about the role of community leaders and 'activists' as sometimes-paramilitary members were euphemistically called.

> *Community ownership of the process of building shared space in interface/ community work was a significant theme in interview responses. Despite very positive opinions, however, there was an underlying suspicion that some community leaders acted as gatekeepers, manipulating views about removing barriers for example. This compounds already poor communication between the community and statutory agencies, and a possible lack of new interface workers. (Goldie and Ruddy, 2010: 9)*

Indeed, the role of paramilitary personnel, all apparently 'former' combatants, was seen as a positive development in the peace process during
the decade following the peace agreement.

McEvoy and Shirlow (2009) held an upbeat view of the role of former
combatants a decade ago employing *a perspective which encompasses the
strengths or skills that former prisoners may bring to their own reintegration
as well as their potential contribution to their families or community* (McEvoy
and Shirlow, 2009). Their goal was to persuade those in both policy implementation and practice to see *prisoners and former prisoners as 'subjects
rather than objects'* (McEvoy and Shirlow, 2009).

The authors made a strong and credible case for the importance of
ex-combatants in tackling legacy issues and the ugly realities of the sectarian conflict.

> *In community organisations, housing associations, neighbourhood regeneration pro-
> jects, youth diversionary projects, community education projects and many more types
> of organisation – one finds ex-prisoners acting as managers, staff or volunteers across
> the spectrum of civic and community life in Northern Ireland ... In particular, such
> individuals have been at the forefront of local debates within Loyalist and Republican
> communities on truth recovery and 'dealing with the past' in Northern Ireland. (McEvoy
> and Shirlow, 2009: 38)*

Certainly, former combatants were involved in interface work and many
in paid posts – and their former status gave them a great deal of street
credibility which was presented as a positive development in the peace
process.

> *They have been involved in painstaking relationship building and coordinating with
> other ex-combatants and community leaders on either side of the divide in order to calm
> sectarian tensions at interface areas or during contentious marches (Jarman, 2002, 2004;
> Shirlow and Murtagh, 2006).*

> *In this and other work, the work of ex-prisoners represents genuine, measured and prac-
> tical efforts at transforming communal attitudes to violence in communities where it has
> long been a default option. (McEvoy and Shirlow, 2009: 48)*

Some ex-combatants and other community activists did take considerable risks and, without the support of formal political leadership from the

wider Unionist family, they were engaged in shaping an embryonic vision of sustainable civic space (Shirlow et al., 2010; Shirlow, 2012) – albeit with notable failures and occasional insincerity.

Nevertheless, although they may have negotiated safe personal mobility around their local area, they did not transform the fixity, community stasis and political stagnancy which are the signature of these contested spaces, about which Cresswell (2010) speaks. Indeed, there remains the long-standing underlying suspicion that some community leaders are gatekeepers, misrepresent resident's views about removing barriers, compound already poor communication within neighbourhoods, and between community and statutory agencies. This was evident in my conversations with Gerry Robinson before and during the tour of interfaces. Also, it has been noted that public servants can act as gatekeepers. Indeed, an independent consultant said, '*the security industry and civil service have their own turf wars*'. (Goldie and Ruddy, 2010)

In response to the idea that the interface work was and maybe remains, 'a nice industry' a former very senior police officer had this to say about community leaders and interface workers in 2019.

> *They emerged within what they called their particular authorising environment. They can only go so far. At the end of the day, on both sides of the main divide here, [there are] three types of people. Some, throughout the period, with a lot of money knocking about the peace process and I don't think they were in any shape or form moving on. There are some, at the other end of the spectrum, I am absolutely convinced, are people who absolutely made the journey. And then there are people in the middle who kind of fell in the middle and struggled – they got it but were operating within an authorising environment that had limitations. At Short Strand [in 2012-13 during the Flags dispute] there were people who were trying to do good stuff but people who didn't – things had got to an extent where actually it had to be allowed to vent before it could be wound back in. It's a complex thing.*

The reference to Short Strand relates to one of the key sites of interface violence during the Flags Dispute. Seven years before that 2019 interview, and more than a decade after the Belfast Agreement there was a growing sense that the peace process was not unfolding on the streets, around urban interfaces, or materialising as the government had hoped.

The need for mainstream government intervention – or funding as the growing interface industry saw it – was presented as something positive.

> *There is some scepticism about the accountability of community work at interfaces, with several external commentators questioning the lack of specific outcomes to measure success to date. 'Showing the outcomes' is an important issue. In that connection a DSD [Department of Social Development] official gave a very open and honest statement. 'NBCAU [North Belfast Community Action Unit] was set up seven years ago as a temporary measure and we are now being mainstreamed. We probably wasted [some of] our money we handed out at the beginning because we were a crisis intervention, but the [rest] has contributed to a situation where people are slowly but surely beginning to engage.' (Goldie and Ruddy, 2010: 37)*

This 'waste' was confidently justified simply because of the absence of bombing and serious levels of widespread violence, or what Galtung (1969) called negative peace.


## The Flags Dispute


The widespread and violent Belfast flags dispute of 2012-2013 was an orchestrated protest against the City Council's decision to restrict the existing practice of flying the British Union flag at City Hall from 365 to 18 days designated by law for government buildings.[7] This involved violent rioting that contradicted the 2010 findings on best practice at the interfaces.

---

7   Since the early years of the peace process local government had recognised the importance of large displays of flags in public space. For example in 2005 Belfast City Council had to adjudicate on whether the St Patrick's Day Carnival parade merited funding as this was seen as a 'Tricolour day' rather than an inclusive event for the whole of the city's population. Similarly, Newry and Mourne District Council had to decide on means of facilitating a resolution to a highly contentious parade by the (Protestant-Unionist) Black Preceptory in Newry town in 1998 – a parade that threatened widespread protest, rioting and civil unrest (Goldie, 2008).

What might have been a symbolic struggle became a serious public order crisis and demonstrated how precarious, if not spurious, 'good practice' at interfaces turned out to be (Nolan et al., 2014; Goldie and Murphy, 2015). The actors remained the same but the factors had changed – with the political ascendancy of Nationalist and Republican representation in Belfast City Council and the impact of implementing equality legislation and conducting public consultation. The once-solid Unionist Chamber in Belfast saw Sinn Féin and the SDLP in prime position, with the middle ground Alliance Party having the casting vote on issues like flying the Union flag.

Republicans wanted the Union flag taken down permanently, and unionists wanted it to keep flying all 365 days of the year. Republicans had always maintained that the ethos and symbolism of the City Hall was almost entirely British, and that flying the Union flag there every day was an equality issue. The challenge to the status quo, of flying the flag on City Hall every day of the year, with all its political symbolism, divided members along fairly but not entirely predictable party lines. Unionist consensus was that the Union flag was the constitutional flag of Northern Ireland, as enshrined in the Belfast Agreement, the legislation that came from it, and the findings of a judicial review. Alliance proposed a compromise with the flag flying on the then 18 designated days, in line with UK policy on the flying of the flag from government buildings in Great Britain. In contrast, the Nationalist SDLP choice was for no flags or – less preferably – the 'designated days' option put forward by Alliance. Sinn Féin did likewise.

*In 2012 Sinn Féin, which had previously opposed this policy, changed tactics and decided to support it. This news was deeply unsettling to unionists, and in the run up to the vote the DUP and the UUP circulated 40,000 leaflets warning in emotional language that the Alliance Party policy was a threat to unionist identity. (Nolan et al., 2014: 9)*

On 3 December 2012 the Council voted to restrict flying the flag at Belfast City Hall to eighteen designated days. They did so after having taken legal advice, conducted an Equality Impact Assessment (EQIA), held a full public consultation and consulted the Equality Commission for Northern Ireland (ECNI) on the policy before making a democratic decision. The legal advice to Belfast City Council was that a tribunal could find against them, should they fly the flag every day, on grounds of fair employment and treatment, and require an explanation that was *more convincing than citing custom and practice*. ECNI advice in 2003 had stated that it was a discretionary matter for local government decisions. *The Commission has however concluded that it is ultimately for the Council to determine.*

The 'designated days' decision sparked a riot on the night the vote was taken, and was followed by months of street protests. The estimated cost of policing the protests for four months was £20 million.

In December 2012 and early 2013 there were almost daily street protests throughout Northern Ireland. Most involved the protesters blocking roads while carrying Union flags and banners. Some of these protests led to clashes between protesters and the police during riots. Alliance Party offices and the homes of Alliance Party members were attacked and Belfast City councillors were sent death threats. According to police reports at the time, some of this violence was orchestrated by high-ranking members of the UVF and UDA Loyalist paramilitary groups. This coincided with increased numbers of sectarian attacks on Catholic churches by Loyalists. It is worth noting that the Progressive Unionist Party (PUP) – a party with connections to the UVF paramilitary loyalists – was the only Unionist party that did not have a role in distributing the 40,000 leaflets before the vote.

Unionist protesters regarded the decision on flags as *an attack on their cultural identity*. However, the 'rational' arguments put forward did not stack up. This upsurge in violence was a knee-jerk emotional reaction to changes at Belfast City Hall, expressed in visceral sectarian hostility and wanton destruction – and it would last until 2020, although without widespread support or violence for that long.

There are no simple quick answers in building peace and everyday safety in contested space. When experience appears to have produced no workable lessons, the status quo of conflict remains – albeit in the much-reduced form of violence that had characterised a fragile and negative peace.

The struggle for electoral dominance in City Hall, Stormont and Westminster in twenty-first-century Belfast was bitterly acted out by proxy on the streets – reflecting conflicting perceptions about the allocation of social housing – in the Flags dispute and the stand-off at Holy Cross. Meehan's embedded violence states *these 'violence rights' may subsequently be used to secure material interests (e.g. land grabs).* Land grab is how Gerry Robinson described the function of interfaces carving out 'Protestant' areas where there has been little if any demand for housing. Needless to say, it is votes rather than land which play into the electoral plans of the political elites – and derelict land did not protect the Parliamentary seat for the DUP sitting member Nigel Dodds when he lost out to John Finucane of Sinn Féin in 2019.

In north Belfast the potential for both physical and symbolic land-grab existed, in the form of de facto sectarian allocation of social housing and electoral ascendency or defeat.

> *Housing still plays out large from a political point of view. ... They're absolutely focused on where is the next housing going and how does that play into a particular part of the community ... which feeds into the greatest manifestation of all – the peace walls. The Council does a huge amount of work, and the DOJ [Department of Justice] but is slow and painstaking. (Belfast City Council Senior Manager, interviewed 2019)*

Shortages of social housing (in Nationalist areas) and demographic changes in Belfast are vital factors in the dynamics of sectarian interfaces because voting preference is reflected in the shifting balance of power in both local government and at Westminster.[8] Nowhere has this been more keenly felt than in working class north Belfast – which contains the most deprived wards in the entire jurisdiction and whose inhabitants suffered the greatest number of fatalities in the conflict. Yet, large tracts of land lie derelict on the 'unionist' side of many interface walls. In 2019 the electoral head-count delivered a crushing defeat for the DUP when John Finucane replaced the sitting MP after eighteen years in the seat.

Although the factors involved are more complex than social housing alone, the Holy Cross dispute revealed the depth and intensity of violent hostility involved in competition for housing and territory. Nearly twenty years after Holy Cross, parts of north Belfast are marked by void houses and

---

8    In the fight for the DUP seat Banners were erected across streets in North Belfast, Antrim and Ballymena alleging the Finucane family were terrorist murderers and literally have blood on their hands (reported on broadcast media on 18 November 2019 and in the Newsletter, Irish News and Irish Times newspapers, 19 November 2019). Finucane was replaced by another Republican as Lord Mayor of Belfast.

stretches of derelict land. New housing in Unionist areas is low density, and the decline in the Unionist-Protestant population remains a vital factor. However, as a later discussion proposes, there is the potential in new urban development planning regulations for a change in the space, sense of place and use of sites left derelict in the city.


## Demilitarisation and the Girdwood development


Early into the peace process, demilitarisation in Belfast freed up land providing the prospect of development and housing, for both Unionists and Nationalists.

The site of the former army Girdwood Barracks was an opportunity to develop the 'shared space' that was official policy and supposed to be the goal of peace-building and government. However, Girdwood sat adjacent to an interface and was of particular political interest because of the declining Unionist population in north Belfast – and thus the electoral ascendancy of Nationalism and or Republicanism.

Gerry Robinson was involved in negotiations and consultations on the development of the Girdwood site and was on interface management committees for many years. His experience is one of frustration – at a number of levels and is worth repeating.

> Before Girdwood came on scheme I remember talking in meetings with these people in the Department. We were talking about Lower Old Park and Lower Shankill and Cliftonville masterplans. One week I said, 'I want to see the masterplan for the whole of inner North [Belfast].' 'Ah, we can't get that map. It has to go to the DOE to get it.' I said bring the maps so we can see what's planned [and comment]. It never happened.

> As part of the discussion on the development of Girdwood it was once suggested building an Olympic sized swimming pool with a stadium that would host swimming competitions at regional and international level. It would bring in a lot of footfall and help to make Girdwood a neutral venue. ... They couldn't or didn't want to grasp it. In order for this to happen it would require the Shankill leisure centre to be closed but this was seen as a loss – and with no political leadership to guide a conversation like this on its merits it went nowhere.

*When Girdwood opened, Belfast Met was told to move in on a nominal rent. I was working with the met at that time on the delivery of their essential's skills programme within the workplace and community. I can remember having a conversation with them in regard to the delivery of essential skills and asked did this mean they would no longer provide these courses in the Ashton Centre and lower Oldpark community settings. He just laughed and said no, the politicos would not let it happen. Well, if that is the case what is the point of it all? This is another example of a missed opportunity to bring both communities together to break down barriers. If you want to make change then the way we do things will have to change. There is an old saying, 'if you always do, what you always did, you will always get, what you always got, if you want something different, then you have got to do things differently.'*

*I can remember a photo taken of the politicos in Girdwood at the time they made the announcement regarding its development and none of the politicos made any comment on it. At a meeting sometime later, I had an opportunity to have a conversation with one of the elected reps at the photo shoot. During this conversation I asked why none of them made any comment on it and was told they were not allowed. I was also told that all the cross-community work we are doing was great but, in the end, it will be the politicos that will decide Girdwood and that's what happened.*

*Now Girdwood – people say to you 'is it a good thing?' you can't say it's bad because it is good – but could it have been better? Of course, it could – it's carved up. And I remember saying this – 'you're going to develop this and leave this [interface adjoining Girdwood]. You can't develop this in isolation because this is a live interface' ... a salami style development in isolation from a live interface literally across the road from Girdwood.*

The development of the Girdwood site was amply supported by EU Peace funds, filtered through the city Council. A senior local government official talked of ongoing – if low-level – sectarian conflict there.

*We have a huge investment through European money on the Girdwood site – the old army site – which is brilliant, but night on night for the last three or four months we've had a lot of trouble up on that site between kids from both sides. There's an element of [recreational rioting] but the bottom line is it's still a contested site because it not the finished article. There's still a lot of space round that. That area is still very contested ... very divided if you look out the front ... which is Clifton Park Avenue, and you look across you look straight down a peace wall. If you look at the housing there in that space, they haven't seen the benefit yet so that's still ongoing.*

There is a certain irony that, a decade after Girdwood was developed, these ideas have taken hold. Murphy (2020) contends that post-conflict societies must be understood in terms of '*organisational* as well as *political* processes', and points to instances of middle management taking the initiative and driving policy to mitigate if not transform conflict during times of violence. Specifically, in the Belfast context, Murphy instances local government after the peace agreement, quoting a senior Belfast City Council Manager,

> *local government associations (usually local councils) have had to focus on the delivery of services and therefore the reality of division – a common outworking in which staff are unable to work in some locations because of the extension of a paramilitary threat against them. … Existing research on the provision of services in Belfast would also confirm that this is an operational reality. This logistical challenge creates issues in terms of balancing resources in a way that takes account of physical and community nuance and the territorial divides that impact waste collection and management, cleansing, cemeteries, parks and leisure provision. Belfast City Council are attempting to manage the division of leisure services through an innovative strategy in which each service delivery point (such as a leisure centre, sports ground or swimming pool) has a unique selling proposition designed to draw people in from all over the City: 'the rationale behind that is to create movement across the city. We would be fully linked into infrastructure, which is a challenge.' (Murphy, 2020: 121-122)*

Years after Gerry Robinson had made just such a proposal – rejected by City Councillors of all parties – a senior official reported the Council planned to use leisure facilities to improve connectivity in Belfast and increase cross-community contact. The policy and intention, as yet unrealised, seem simple enough. However, it might be noted that there is no mention of these *unique selling points* in relation to interface areas. There were some expectations that the upcoming planning regulations might enable a process of positive change.

# The meaning and purpose of past interface and sectarian violence

Goldie and Ruddy (2010) list reasons for interface violence but, as do other researchers, fail to fully explain its purpose. Meehan's *three broad types of large-scale violence: competitive, embedded and permissive violence* provides a credible framework of explanation for the flare-up of street violence at Belfast interfaces in the Holy Cross dispute, the 2012-2013 Flags dispute and events in April 2021. To repeat and elaborate on Meehan's definition *of* Competitive violence, *it is: Violence aimed at contesting underlying political settlements (both at the national and subnational level).* Holy Cross was as much about Unionist anger after the Drumcree protest failed to achieve its aim, as it was about housing issues in north Belfast. The Loyalist resurgence during the Flags dispute was contesting the Belfast City Council decision to fly the Union flag only on designated days, and the orchestrated interface violence of April 2021 was allegedly a challenge in opposition to the post-Brexit Northern Ireland Protocol and the Irish Sea Border.

Competitive violence *may be violence deployed by actors excluded from the existing elite bargain or by actors within an existing elite bargain looking to renegotiate their position and power.* The DUP always took a pro-Brexit position, despite the fact that this jurisdiction voted to remain in the European Union. It therefore required popular unrest to distract from a political disaster and the falling fortunes of the party arising from Brexit and some high-profile scandals. It suited the First Minister and the party she (then) led to have violence *deployed by actors with a relatively limited aim to improve their position and power, or by actors aimed at fundamentally challenging the political settlement.* In this case the settlement was the Northern Ireland Protocol.

Meehan's definition of embedded violence also fits the evidence around these events – as the informal permission from the Unionist elite, if not encouragement for violence protest, was evident in the Flags dispute – where all but one of the Unionist parties leafleted for the mass protest. When he speaks of *violence rights* Meehan might well be describing the unofficial Unionist stance on loyalist and often paramilitary-led demonstrations. Whether it was to sell the compromises in the Belfast Agreement, or to sweeten the bitter pill of the political ascendancy of Republicanism and Nationalism, embedded violence has been in the very fabric of Northern Ireland politics since 1998. Indeed, the Ulster Workers' Strike of 1974 – in protest at the power-sharing outcome of the Sunningdale Agreement – was the combined efforts of paramilitary and political actors of the time (Bew and Gillespie, 1999: 84-89). It is very much *how a political settlement works* in the history of Northern Ireland.

> *The privileges that elites are awarded in order to strengthen their loyalty to the state are not only economic (e.g. control over certain resources, import licences) or political (government positions) but may also include the 'right' to use violence. These 'violence rights' determine who has the 'right' to enact violence, upon whom, for what reasons, and with what level of impunity.*

> *These 'violence rights' may subsequently be used to secure material interests (e.g. land grabs) but the point is that the 'limited access orders' which underpin many political settlements may be founded upon who has the right to use violence, rather than only the explicit apportioning of material benefits. These kinds of state-sanctioned violence should alert policymakers to the fact that violence may not only be driven by state fragility and failure but may also be embedded in the bargains made to forge order and stability. A stable political settlement may expose populations to significant levels of violence. (Meehan, 2018: 41-42)*

The third type of violence is *permissive violence* and this is a portent of increasing political instability in 2021 Northern Ireland.

> *Violence that results from the state's inability to monopolize control over violence ... This kind of violence occurs because the state is unable or unwilling to monopolise control over violence and has instead made selective decisions of how and where to allocate the limited coercive resources at its disposal. This creates opportunities for 'permissive' violence in the sense that a government 'allows' violence to happen in certain places because it has chosen to focus its limited coercive resources (i.e. police and military deployment) elsewhere. (Meehan, 2018: 42)*

Policing in Northern Ireland and the use of state controls became problematic with Loyalist accusations of 'heavy-handed policing' when violence or mass demonstrations were challenged, and in Republican areas where 'state policing' has not always been seen as legitimate – and thus state authority was weakened.

> *This may include violence used by actors to control places where state authority is weak or non-existent but which is not aimed at destabilising the over-arching political settlement. It may also encompass forms of criminal activity in which violence is a key component, but where such activities are not aimed at challenging the government. Indeed, violent criminal actors may have a vested interest in upholding the status quo since it is within this system that they are able to operate. (Meehan, 2018: 42)*

Certainly, the authority of government and policing in working class areas around the interfaces was weakened further by criminal elements and activities in paramilitary controlled housing estates. The fact that 88 police officers were injured in the orchestrated interface rioting in April 2021 shows a degree of weakness in the state's 'authorising power'. It is also part of a long-standing pattern of violent Unionist-Loyalist resistance to change (Cochrane, 2021).

Meehan acknowledges:

> *These various types of violence are often closely interlinked and can mutate over time. Groups that accumulate power and wealth through permissive violence may then look to challenge the state to demand greater inclusion into a political settlement. The informality governing embedded and permissive violence may make the 'rules of the game' surrounding these types of violence unclear and volatile. (Meehan, 2018: 42)*

Although the factors involved are more complex than housing or alleged ethnic cleansing, Holy Cross epitomises the propensity for violent territorial competition. Nearly twenty years later north Belfast no longer has a Unionist MP. In 2019 the dirty fight for the Westminster seat saw the erection of banners defaming the Finucane family – in a crude attempt to persuade the electorate to vote Unionist. At that time a high-profile Loyalist made the case for supporting these banners – despite their being removed by 'state forces'. Loyalist Blogger Jamie Bryson, who had been the public face of the 2012 Flags dispute, spoke on the Stephen Nolan Show billing itself as *the biggest platform on radio* (BBC Radio Ulster, 18/11/19 9-11 am) expressing *20 years of pent-up anger at a one-sided Agreement*. Bryson was reluctant to speak on the subject of his role in planning, designing and erecting the banners and spoke of an *axis between the Loyalist and Unionist community*. This increased the popularly held belief that the political elite work with unreconstructed paramilitary forces when there is political capital at risk. (Of course, the same could be, and has been said of Sinn Féin.) In 2019, in the absence of a devolved government and with politicians still arguing over how best to address the legacy, this was an open wound that remained to be healed.

> *I think it's fair to say ... and particularly in something like the flag protest. The number of contested issues has obviously contracted and reduced significantly – whether it be the parades, or flags ... but you don't have to scratch too far below the surface till you get to people's memory of them and therefore there are things that can happen. ... things like the current debate around Brexit and what could or could not happen raises a tension there. (Senior Manager, Belfast City Council, 2019)*

## Conclusion

Obdurate defenders of the 'need' for sectarian interfaces often have an interest – professional, political and or emotional – in their retention. A key goal of the government's Together Building a United Community (TBUC) policy was to remove peace walls by 2023, which seemed a long way off back in 2013. Institutional sectarianism reinforced division and not least when government departments and local governments appear to accept and fall into line with the spurious assertions of 'community consultation' and 'stated wishes' of local residents, who want to retain these barriers.

Keeping 'community consultation' in mind, the development of one area along a north Belfast interface wall posed a fundamental question. Why had the multi-million pound Grace Family Centre been built on one side of the interface at Alliance Avenue, serving only the nationalist community?

# CHAPTER 4

# The Grace Family Centre – Progress in planning at interfaces?

The fifteen years following the Belfast Agreement saw violent Unionist-Loyalist protests about the right to march to Drumcree church, the Holy Cross, and the Flags disputes, all of which caused widespread disruption, required major security responses and cost public monies that might well have been better used. Then came the protest at Twaddell Avenue.

Beyond Alliance Avenue is Twaddell Avenue, at the top of the Shankill Road. Its landscape has been altered since the end of the 'Twaddell stand-off', with the extension of an existing interface wall. The area became a flashpoint after 2013 when Orange Order marches were banned by the Parades Commission from returning home by the outgoing route – past the shops in the Nationalist Ardoyne area – after 12th July events. DeYoung describes the protest for an American readership, listening carefully to participants and their strong sense of Loyalist/Unionist grievance.

> *In recent years, the Greater Ardoyne Residents' Collective (GARC) has staged protests and counter-parades on the Twelfth against the Orange parade's passage (Henry 2011). To curtail the rioting which erupted as a result of these clashes, the Parades Commission determined in 2013 to halt the Orange parade so that it could not complete its route at the Ardoyne-Woodvale interface. The contested stretch of road would have taken about seven minutes to walk. A standoff between police and Orange Order members (known as Orangemen), the marching bands, and parade supporters ended in rioting: petrol bombs, bricks, and bottles launched across police Land Rovers, a frenzy of shouting and jeering and the periodic blast of water cannons (BBC News 2013a). (DeYoung, 2016: 181)*

She captures the sense of injustice that Loyalists felt with the peace process and the end of a Unionist state and Protestant hegemony.

> *This camp, sometimes referred to as a 'civil rights camp' or 'protest camp', appropriates public space as an expression of resistance, identity, and territory. It is both a microcosm*

*of broader social, political, and economic issues facing post-Troubles, post-industrial Belfast, and a lens with which to examine contemporary Loyalism. (DeYoung, 2016: 181)*

The facts of demographic change, with a further sharp decline in the Protestant population in north and west Belfast in the first decade of this century, was and is still perceived by Unionist-Loyalists as Nationalists literally gaining ground at the expense of Unionists.

*NISRA has estimated that 95,000 Protestants and 46,000 Catholics died between 2001 and 2011, while there were 89,000 Protestant and 118,000 Catholic births (Nolan 21). During this period, the demographic balance in Belfast city experienced a small but important shift: the Catholic population increased by 4.2% and the Protestant numbers declined by 11.9% (Nolan 22). This is reflected in higher levels of vacancy, dereliction, and open space in working-class Protestant neighborhoods. Nationalists are thereby perceived to literally be gaining ground as boundaries between highly segregated areas begin to shift. (DeYoung, 2016: 184)*

In the Twaddell case, this was also seen as a cultural defeat for Orangeism. The three-year stand-off ended in 2016. Under the headline, *Twaddell camp dismantled as Orange parade past Ardoyne shops in north Belfast passes off peacefully*, the press reported:

*Permission for the contentious procession past the nationalist Ardoyne in north Belfast was granted after an historic deal between the loyal orders and nationalist residents' group the Crumlin Ardoyne Residents' Association. ... A so-called protest loyalist camp in the nearby Twaddell area will now be dismantled as soon as the demonstration reaches its end destination. (Belfast Telegraph, 1 October 2016)*

This was heralded as an 'historic' agreement brokered between the Orange Order and local Nationalist residents. It cost £21 million to police the protest 'camp'. It became a flashpoint for three years, but it was never a peace wall or an interface structure.

At the junction leading onto Twaddell Avenue, cameras were erected after the 2001 Holy Cross dispute and this became a de facto extension of the peace wall–separating houses occupied by Unionists and Nationalists. Along this interface in Alliance Avenue, houses were constructed right up to the interface wall on the nationalist side, and the £2.162 Million Grace Family Centre developed over an eight-year period. This is a case, like the development of the site of the former Girdwood military barracks, that begged the question, how much are changes to the physical structures determined by political leadership or interference, policy and the implementation of law – or the lack of one or all of these?

The physical development in the area around Twaddell Avenue demonstrates how political protest or resistance to change can become solidified, and/or rendered a physical hazard to civic stability and peace. The Grace Family Centre was built in Alliance Avenue and served the Nationalist community on one side of the wall.

On the face of it, the Grace Family Centre was a welcome and much-needed development, in an area with high levels of social deprivation. No one could argue with that. Indeed, evaluations of the operation of the Centre appear[9] to show the service is excellent – and this case study in no way detracts from this commendable work.

However, the facility and services provide for only one side of the interface – the Nationalist side. The Unionist population have no direct access, are not represented in the service providers and would be unlikely to feel at ease if they did choose to use the Centre. This raises a number of issues – from its planning through to its implementation. One has to ask if this was investing in the existing sectarian division in North Belfast – albeit inadvertently. The Centre might have been built with another entrance leading into the Unionist side of the wall – an entrance that could be securely closed if and when deemed necessary. The local residents live in the area where the Holy Cross dispute happened – with Protestant-Unionists on the Glenbryn side and Catholic-Nationalists on Alliance Avenue – so there is a bitter history on both sides and traumatic memories for those who experienced those months of violence on the daily journey to the primary school.

The scale of the development, and its undoubted benefit to the women and families of the area, provided an opportunity to invest in the 'sharing' and 'community cohesion' which were supposedly policy aims of the Belfast Agenda, had this facility served both Nationalists and Unionists. This

9 Evaluations list the services, courses and attendances. They do not include a rigorous service-users perspective.

appears to have been beyond the thinking, planning and vision of the public authorities and political representatives over years – and nearly two decades after the Belfast Agreement.

Planning permission for the Centre was granted in 2018.

> *North Belfast is set to get a new family and women's centre, after a £2m community project was given the green light at Belfast City Council last night. ... Named the 'Grace Family Centre', the new site will provide training and educational opportunities for women and families in the area and construction will begin in September. Situated in Alliance Avenue in the Ardoyne area of the city, the site is currently vacant and was previously owned by the Housing Executive. ... 'The proposal is for a two-storey building which will comprise the community facilities which are sub-divided into three main areas to ensure secure/good management of the child welfare element along with the ability to maximise the use of the community facilities and social enterprise facilities (cafe)', the plans read. ... Sinn Féin,,,, Councillor Ryan Murphy has welcomed the decision by Belfast City Council to grant planning approval to the Grace Women's Development Centre. The Oldpark Cllr said: 'I am delighted to hear that the Grace Women's Development Centre has been granted planning approval last night in council'. 'This £2m investment will take them out of the community centre and give them a home of their own. It will also create much-needed jobs and deliver services in the local area.'[10]*

In May 2020 the building was nearing completion and provided good publicity for the city Council and politicians of all parties. The press noted that the Council invested *£1.464 million in the new state-of-the-art facility, with £553,000 funding coming from the Department for Communities and a further £145,000 investment from The Executive Office's Urban Villages Initiative.*[11]

10  *Belfast Telegraph*, 16 May 2018, Andrew Madden.
11  *Families in north Belfast will soon benefit from the new £2.162 million Grace Family Centre on Alliance Avenue, with construction at an advanced stage. The purpose-built, two-storey centre which is set to open in late summer will provide families with childcare for up to sixty children, a counselling suite, a multi-functional training suite, a café and office space. It will also be the new permanent home for Grace Women's Development Limited, which has provided vital services for women and their families in the area since 1984.*
   *Belfast City Council is investing £1.464 million in the new state-of-the-art facility, with £553,000 funding coming from the Department for Communities and a further £145,000 investment from The Executive Office's Urban Villages Initiative.*

The Centre opened to a fanfare of publicity with plaudits from both Nationalist and Unionist politicians, including the First and Deputy First Ministers. It is undoubtedly a great asset to the north of the city and that is unquestionable. Indeed, it appeared to be a community venture for the benefit of all, as one might well think from reading the official press release.[12]

Aside from observing that the reported cost increased from £2.164 to £2.3 million it should be noted that this facility was open only on the Nationalist side of the interface wall. It may *improve the quality of life for citizens in areas of need* but only in the Nationalist Ardoyne. It is open to discussion how this sectarian division in provision could *build on our vision*

---

*Speaking at a sneak peek preview of the new building, Alderman Brian Kingston, Chair of Belfast City Council's Strategic Policy and Resources Committee, said: 'I'm delighted to see construction work progressing so well on this outstanding new community asset for the city and the north Belfast area in particular. The new facilities will have a huge impact on the lives of local women and their families when it opens later this year, enabling Grace Women's Development Limited to offer a wider range of learning and training opportunities that promote personal development, health and wellbeing. Construction of the centre is only possible due to vital funding through our Belfast Investment Fund (BIF) which aims to encourage partners to co-invest in projects that develop or regenerate facilities for people who live in, invest in or visit our city. To date, BIF has allocated £28.2 million to eighteen projects as part of the council's wider £325 million physical investment programme, which includes over 350 projects across the city. This investment supports the goals of the Belfast Agenda, our local community plan, by making a significant contribution to the city's economy, creating jobs, improving our neighbourhoods and supporting our residents, in particular, those facing challenges.*

*Minister for the Department for Communities, Deirdre Hargey, said: 'As Minister for Communities, my absolute focus is to stand up for and support the most disadvantaged in society. My Department has been supporting Grace Women's Development Limited for many years through the Neighbourhood Renewal Fund to deliver community development and relations programmes, health and well-being initiatives and educational and training opportunities in disadvantaged areas. This new facility will be vital for this community by enabling them to build on their success to date and offer a wider range of services which will benefit local women, their families and the wider community.'* <www.belfastcity.gov.uk/news/new-grace-family-centre-nearing-completion>.

12    <www.belfastcity.gov.uk/News/New-£2-3-million-Grace-Family-Centre-opens-in-nort>.

*of Supporting People, Building Communities, Shaping Places.* There is, at best, some wishful thinking in these attempts at cross-community public relations – and a certain irony since this interface abuts the territory of the Holy Cross dispute.

Could the planning and implementation of a multi-million-pound project have happened without reference to the statutory duties to promote equality of opportunity and good relations – with or without the need for Equality Impact Assessment (EQIA)? This occurred twenty years after the Belfast Agreement, and legislation on non-discrimination and promoting equality of opportunity and good relations. Yet this decision shows no evidence of implementing those statutory duties or the policies that purported to drive for *A Shared Future* (ASF), *Cohesion, Sharing and Integration* (CSI), and *Together Building a United Community* (T: BUC). Without any doubt, the Grace Family Centre is a good investment in terms of improving the *health, wellbeing and life chances* of some citizens – but not for all citizens in that part of north Belfast. Could it be seen as an investment in division? Surely the positive equality duty and the secondary obligation to promote good relations, required of public authorities, would have exposed this problem? Apparently not. Indeed, it seemed that the peace process, and equality and good community relations considerations had no place in planning the development of highly contested space in Belfast.

According to publicly available documentation, the planning permission did not require Equality Impact Assessment (EQIA), so more detailed research was needed. I emailed the City Council and was forwarded to Dermot O'Kane, the official heading up the team working on Belfast's (then draft) Local Development Plan. Planning permission for the Grace Family Centre was granted under existing regulations and, even with the advent of new rules, EQIA would not be required for applications for planning permission. EQIA is necessary for policy – existing or proposed new policy – but not individual projects whatever the public cost of these developments.

Existing planning regulations for Belfast were established in 1990 and would hold until replaced by new regulations which had been in development for some six years. What they will produce will be a sweeping reform of existing planning law. However, in 2018-2020 planning permission was under 1990 rules. So, did these take account of the interface? I put this and other questions to Dermot O'Kane, the Council's Director of Planning and Building Control by email.

> A small point but important to my case study of the Grace Family Centre, I assume that planning permission for this would have required addressing the interface – given the de facto exclusion and inaccessibility for the unionist neighbours.

> *A material change of use or physical works to a non-residential building usually requires planning permission. In terms of addressing the interface, any current or recent planning application would not be tested against interface issues as there is very little by way of incumbent policy on that particular subject. In sensitive locations like this we can seek advice from the police and usually engage quite closely with local political representatives. Obviously, you are aware that the new plan does have provision for such cases.*

> Will that [permission for the Grace Family Centre] continue to be an example of 'meanwhile use'?

> *A meanwhile use is really a nod towards allowing a beneficial use to a local community on a temporary basis for schemes that might not otherwise be acceptable with a view that they could help to stimulate a focal point and shared facility that could contribute to local engagement. It's also seen as a way to stimulate broader regeneration in areas that struggle to attract investment.*

> In any case, who would decide this under new arrangements – Planning professionals or Councillors?

> *Whilst most planning decisions are delegated to officers, larger schemes and those where there is significant community interest can as the behest of members be called in to committee for determination.*

> Is there a due/expected date for the Plan Strategy to be officially adopted? Was it necessary that the process took so long?

> *The Planning Appeals Commission (PAC) who hosted the Independent Examination have advised that they will report to the DfI in later September. We would hope to see their report some time after that with a view to adopting the plan towards the end of the year.*

It seemed the then-draft strategic local development plan (LDP) for Belfast was about to take account of the many essential considerations including problems around sectarian interfaces in the Belfast area. It was late in coming – and too late for the planning determination on the Grace Family Centre – which reflects the slow progress in reforming public administration and implementing statutory duties on public authorities to address inequalities and flawed community (and race) relations.


## Planning powers move from central to local government


Planning was a key aspect of public administration in Northern Ireland and due for reform in 1998, but it was late in the day that the long-delayed Review of Public Administration (RPA) took effect. The intention in 1998 was to implement this reform as quickly as possible but the absence of a Stormont Executive until 2007 made the RPA deadline of 2002 impossible. Although planning was a key part of the reform, these powers did not transfer to local government until 2015. At that stage the planning regulations, already 25 years old, were in force and would remain so until the LDP took effect.

Any and all developments in Belfast were determined by the policy and numerous strategies. However, the only statutory power lay in regulations devised in the 1980s, which came into effect in 1990 and perhaps necessarily reflected the times and conflict of those years, leaving the fingerprints of what might by termed a war plan – although Dermot O'Kane was more than uncomfortable with my use of this terminology.

It would appear that the 'missed opportunity' in the construction of the Grace Family Centre has deeper roots than the development of community and wellbeing services at an interface – or indeed anywhere else in the city. More than two decades after the peace agreement the necessary reforms were only then being implemented in strategy.

The rigorous process of getting these new regulations in place is fully documented on the Council's website. The upcoming LDP is part of the new administrative architecture of peace.

*The Belfast Agenda sets out the framework to support inclusive growth and improve services for residents and businesses. Belfast City Council's Local Development Plan (LDP) will provide the planning framework for the city up to 2035.*

*1.1.3 The combination of deindustrialisation, the troubles, and the massive housing re-development had a profound impact of weakening the city's economic and social base. Consequently, its spatial legacy is evidenced by numerous derelict sites, poor quality environment and segregated neighbourhoods disconnected by 'peace walls' and barriers. The need for affordable housing remains an enduring challenge for many citizens in Belfast and the LDP will provide a spatial land use framework to enable an adequate supply of housing to meet the identified needs.*

*1.1.4 In recent years there has been a transformation with new development in the city centre, enhanced public realm, Titanic Quarter, and Ulster University, which have added vitality, created employment opportunities and attracted new residents, visitors and tourists. However, this is contrasted with the communal territorial disputes, persistent social inequality, curtailing safe access to the benefits of the wider city and peaceful interaction with civic society. It will be critical to tackle persistent social inequality throughout the city and build community cohesion and resilience through collaborative effort to ensure inclusive growth for all. (DPS001: 3)*

This is a substantial move into comprehensive planning and consideration of the core problems of the city – sectarian division, housing shortage, inappropriate housing for the diversity of residents, the need to attract investment for twenty-first-century business, and environmental issues including sustainable transport and air quality, plus physical and virtual connectivity – and notably the intention that urban development strategy and planning regulations *tackle persistent social inequality throughout the city and build community cohesion and resilience.*

Belfast's Local Development Plan has a simple strategy at its core – to have the inner city and Industrial Harbour district as places of economic activity and increased population density with other areas retaining or developing lower density housing and designated green space. Achieving this needed a comprehensive plan addressing the social, economic, environmental and sustainability issues – and the many related policies and procedural obstacles. This required not only a comprehensive range of skill sets but also organisational ingenuity and a process of leadership.

The political and post-conflict context added further dimensions to the process with six political parties represented in the Council's Planning Committee which endorsed the plan, and the ongoing threat of widespread, violent protest against the Northern Ireland Protocol, which came with Brexit creating the Irish Sea Border. The LDP process entailed six years of drafting, public consultations, a Public Inquiry and signing-off by a central government Department before the plan was ready to be adopted. An additional factor complicated the process. As RPA finally happened and planning powers moved from central government to local Councils this did not include powers over infrastructure. This complex context framed the questions about the lengthy process of getting the LDP enacted.

## Leadership and the plan for urban development

Good communications and cooperation from the Council led to a focused interview with the Director of Planning and Building Control, Dermot O'Kane who had steered the process of producing a Local Development Plan (LDP) for Belfast – and answered some key questions about both the substance and, just as importantly, if not more so, the process of creating the new strategic local development plan (LDP) from scratch.

Based on a face-to face interview this analysis of the LDP process is explained in terms of recent contributions on leadership made by Chambers et al. (2010) and Murphy (2020). Chambers et al. use a model that *is a compass to help our leaders navigate through these turbulent times* with a framework of four key leadership capabilities:

- Sense making – seeking many types and sources of data and involving others in the process.
- Relating – developing key relationships within and across organisations.
- Visioning – providing people with a sense of meaning about their work and answering the question, 'Why am I doing this?'
- Inventing – creating new ways of working together, including the processes and structures needed to make the vision a reality.

Getting LDP to the stage of getting departmental approval required all four of the leadership qualities enumerated by Chambers et al. It also shows the four elements of what Murphy (2020) calls Peacebuilding Entrepreneurship: social commitment to conflict transformation; exercise of political skill; exercise of professional, reputational expert or positional capital; and the cultivation of intra- and inter-organisational networks of support.

There is clear evidence of sense-making in the making of the LDP, as it necessitated many types and sources of data and involved others from outside the team in the process. The plan and strategy embrace a very wide range of issues, requiring a similarly wide range of expertise. Team leader, Dermot O'Kane, explained:

> *We've a number of roles, but the primary role is to bring forward the Development Plan and all that comes with it. We are also responsible for conservation in the city, for urban design for the city and for tree protections. ... So I've a conservation officer who works in my team and an urban design officer as well – with the broader spectrum of design. Without doubt the biggest project is this one.*

> *In terms of the structure of the team we have four main themes. The first is housing policy, with the need to improve both the quantity and quality of housing. There is the economy as well so we have to think about employment plans – we've a team who looks after that. We've a team who looks after the environmental side of open space – which could be things like designated protected land – to make sure it's right for development. And infrastructure as well, so that's transport. We're not the transport authority but from a planning point of view we generally take a stand and let the authorities do what they do. It's just to ensure that planning covers their development and availability and that sort of thing.*

And, asked, does the team gel well?

> *We have a very strong chemistry and very different skill sets. We work as a team and everyone is very capable. [One team person] the design officer studied town planning and specialised in design so he contributed to that section of the plan. [Another] picked up the mantle of sustainability. [Another] who worked with me in DOE has taken the portfolio of economic development. So some had skills and some have been acquiring skills but after five years our guys could give most a run for their money in their own field.*

When planning powers were transferred from a central government
Department to Belfast City Council in 2015, was the team new?

> *Yes, almost the entire team, although about four of us came from DOE [Department
> for the Environment]. Everyone in the team is a professional planner, but they will
> have a number of specialisms. While I came from the department one of the things we
> did when we came in was to build the team up – so we recruited quite heavily early on,
> which some other authorities didn't do because I don't think they quite grasped the mag-
> nitude of developing a plan. However, this might simply have been a resourcing issue.*

> *Most of the team would either have worked with [non-NI] Councils before or other au-
> thorities outside the DOE or worked in England, Scotland and as planning consultants.*

> *We've a number of roles, but the primary role is to bring forward the Development Plan
> and all that comes with it. We are also responsible for conservation in the city, for urban
> design for the city and for tree protections. ... So I've a conservation officer who works
> in my team and an urban design officer as well – with the broader spectrum of design.
> Without doubt the biggest project is this one.*

> *In terms of the structure of the team we have four main themes. The first is housing
> policy, with the need to improve both the quantity and quality of housing. There is the
> economy as well so we have to think about employment plans – we've a team who looks
> after that. We've a team who looks after the environmental side of open space – which
> could be things like designated protected land – to make sure it's right for development.
> And infrastructure as well, so that's transport. We're not the transport authority but
> from a planning point of view we generally take a stand and let the authorities do what
> they do. It's just to ensure that planning covers their development and availability and
> that sort of thing.*

This team leader recognised the huge scale of the task from the beginning
and had the authorising environment and vision to recruit appropriately.

For Chambers et al., inventing is creating new ways of working together, including the processes and structures needed to make the vision a
reality. As existing regulations had been in place for thirty years, and governance had changed radically after 1998, creating the LDP was starting
from a blank sheet. This contrasts with the usual situation where almost
all new regulation is produced with the safety-net of a template, read over
from other UK (or until Brexit, EU) law, directives, guidance or policy. This
required new ways of working. The drafting, policy and strategy discussions

and team building that was intrinsic to the out-of-office sessions in a nearby coffee house was inventive. In addition, the leader harnessed the varied skills and expertise of the planning team, in a process that transformed a vast number of policies and strategies – none of which had a statutory basis – into comprehensive regulation.

> *When I studied in the University of Sheffield one of the professors ... used to say that when he was starting a new design he'd prefer to start with even an envelope with writing on it and a stamp – something to work from. He'd never start with a blank piece of paper. Sometimes I think writing policy is a bit like that – with other people about, who are not part of the conversation. It's much better than in a benign lifeless room.*

Taking discussions out of the office was a literal, physical change of landscape and thinking outside-the-box in the process of producing something entirely new in LDP.

> *It is place-making focused and hopefully will provide the tools for the Council to try to achieve this.*

> *We had to rationalise the plan to make it shorter than it could have been. We intentionally rationalised planning policies to avoid repetition and to move away from a check-list approach. The plan has to be read in the round.*

> *We said that what we wanted this book to do was to provide a proper set of tools for planners so they can maximise the public interest. We didn't want to write a plan that made planning a tick-box exercise.*

The process obviously required 'relating'. Developing key relationships within and across organisations was essential from the start. Those relationships were with other planners, and statutory authorities in housing, environmental protection, economic development, social and community cohesion and transport.

Did the process involve people who were experts on social cohesion, interfaces and so on – people other than your very skilled team?

> *We actually had working groups. The officers who were tasked with each of the sections then invited people – in the case of urban design we had architects, the Royal Ulster Architectural Society, and we had heritage groups.*

*They were all involved. When we were drafting the document we consulted ... topped and lopped and it was all done in a collaborative spirit. The Housing Executive – senior officers – all involved – heritage and planning division – all involved. They're the statutory bodies ... [with us saying] it's in your interest as these are all involved in the decision-making. If you want it in, tell us, or if not we can have a debate about why we shouldn't. So we did all that. Then it went out to formal consultation, we went to the people in our working groups as well as the wider public – something like 88 events for our options paper and 66 for this [The draft Local Development Plan]. We did all that.*

The engagement with stakeholders and residents' groups in this process is fully documented on the Council's website. However, it was not as productive as the team might reasonably have expected when it came to the Public Examination stage and an Inquiry.

*And [during the Inquiry] we got all these responses back, which would make you question the level of engagement that actually took place because the comments in the formal responses did not match what was said in the workshops.*

Clarity of purpose is obvious in LDP, with a strategy and plan encompassing 'visioning'. The process gave the planning team, other colleagues, political representatives and those voluntary and statutory organisations, plus individuals involved in public consultations, a palpable sense of meaning about their work or their role in the process – and answered any questions about 'why am I doing/endorsing this?'

*In some ways we started with a blank canvas – but I suppose to go back to my analogy of my university professor, sometimes it's good to work with an envelope with some writing and a stamp already on it. We had to review existing planning policy, and whilst much of it was fit for purpose we took a decision to rationalise it to illustrate how it all emanated from the need to improve our city – which is why there is so much read-across.*

*We've a plan strategy and we did a literature review and looked at plans elsewhere, then a suite of operational policy which is needed to assess the merits of individual planning applications.*

*We had a former chief planner in Scotland on our team who headed up planning at the time of transfer. He said to me 'a plan strategy should be no more than 50 pages long' and I agreed with him. And if you read this document there's a big change that happens at about page 50. So, in effect, that's the strategy but we were then tasked to include operational policies to replace the Department's established policies from the previous regime.*

*So, because we were tasked with all this stuff it went from being 50 pages to being 300 plus – and that's with a lot of compression. But we decided that if we're going to do this we'll still try to make it relate to the big picture. I'm not sure you'll find a plan anywhere on these islands that has the same format. We tried to build around the themes of sustainability, social, environmental and economic – and to see how that one relates [to the others] – that is, we always wanted that read-across. Ultimately even things like telecommunications masts and out-of-town shopping centres all impact on our ability to achieve – and that's our model for Belfast.*

Along the way, over six years, did any colleagues, politicians or others put up resistance to what the planning team was doing? Did the team experience resistance?

*Yes we did. Some said to me that the Council is very good at producing strategies [on a vast range of topics] – The point I made early on was, do you realise that these plans have no statutory basis in planning? It means that when a planning application comes in we cannot consider that master plan when assessing the proposal – views that because it has been out for public consultation it has weight in the decision making process. I explained that whilst many things are material to the decision making process, when it comes to planning policy or guidance the regulations are quite explicit and cannot be bypassed simply because it seems expedient to do so. You can't bypass that by creating others.*

On the subject of Departmental resistance, was it purely a turf war or resistance to reform and change?

*I think there are a couple of reasons for it. As an officer you were a decision-maker there's a lot of responsibility on your shoulders and if people didn't like the decision. So, we did get very much wedded to the position 'well I can defend my decision because the policy says'. There's no doubt that there's a comfort in being wedded to a literal interpretation of policy and sometimes this can come at the expense of the wider public interests.*

LDP, and the process of having it finally ready for adoption, encompassed key issues and what the team leader called *public interest*. There is a vision of a better city meeting the challenges created by decades-old road building.

*The Westlink, I know, has severed Belfast … but there are solutions. … Belfast could have more green space for walking and cycling. Open the Knockmore line. Transport changes could reduce the car traffic in the city.*

*There is a considerable body of evidence that shows that increased dependency on car travel results in much lower urban densities. Lower densities can lead to social fragmentation and decreasing levels of physical and mental health. We know there is demand for bungalows and a nice garden and that's okay but by and large the evidence is that urban density and people living in more sustainable neighbourhoods makes much more cohesive and healthy communities.*

From the protection of trees and the reduction of car traffic dependency to the enhanced community and social cohesion, the planning team in Belfast City Council skilfully addressed collective problems and achieved a remarkable cross-party endorsement from elected representatives. Achieving this amounts to what Murphy (2020) calls Peacebuilding Entrepreneurship. It required the four key factors: social commitment to conflict transformation; exercise of political skill; exercise of professional, reputational expert or positional capital; and the cultivation of intra- and inter-organisational networks of support.

Social commitment to conflict transformation is apparent in both the LDP document with specific mention of interfaces, social and community cohesion, tackling social inequalities and promoting good community relations. The need to address the reality of a city divided by sectarianism and inequality is made clear in the introductory pages of the LDP document.

If LDP is to succeed, as with all policies and strategies, there needs to be a statutory footing or improvements just don't happen. This Plan has statutory powers and is sufficiently comprehensive to make a significant difference to how people live in this city and to their quality of life in the future. It addresses the sites, and the use of space and places where, among other things, sectarian violence happens. It looks at community and social cohesion from the perspective of promoting good relations in tandem with environmental issues, sustainability, economic development, transport and infrastructure.

> *We have compressed a lot in that document. We have further documents – guidelines – which technically aren't statutory – but in UK and Irish law it's normal to supplement that policy with guidance. Some of them have been endorsed by the Planning Committee.*

To achieve endorsement from the Planning Committee was no small victory. That Committee comprises representatives from all six, variously opposing, political parties. Putting forward a case for LDP so that it reached an all-party consensus demonstrates the exercise of substantive political skill. This is in marked contrast to the Commission on Flags, Identity, Culture and Tradition, which is discussed later in this book.

The process of steering LDP through drafting, a six-year process with a series of public consultations, obtaining political endorsement in a politically divided Council Chamber, to the public inquiry took someone who could exercise political skill to a high degree. That long and complex process necessitated the capacity to engage in public consultation and repeated public debate at over 150 events.

> *I would say that document was written in a few months – two or three months. Obviously it's been lopped and topped and it'll be lopped and topped post-Inquiry but there's a question as to how this can be written in a couple of months and takes six years to get to this stage. The process is that we had to prepare an options paper, consult on that – which is all a good thing to get public endorsement and political endorsement. And then there's consideration of responses to the options paper, the drafting of the Plan Strategy and then the Independent Examination of the Plan Strategy which was hosted by the Planning Appeals Commission.*

> *To be fair such an extensive process brings with it endorsement and legitimacy that it is the will of the public and our elected officials. The thing is that it has legitimacy … [and] the people of Belfast have said this is how they want their city developed and developers will be expected to meet those expectations. That's the logic of it. Six years is too long but I suspect the next plan will be much more straightforward – that the next one will be a review of this one – and we'll have learned what works and what doesn't.*

Leadership in creating LDP needed considerable exercise of professional, reputational expertise and positional capital, and the cultivation of intra- and inter-organisational networks of support – and substantial patience. Aside from the broad range of networks involved in the drafting and consultations on LDP, already mentioned, the Director of

Planning and Building Control, and some of his team took opportunities to attend Public Inquiries in Belfast and further afield, networking and seeking advice on their project and the process of reaching a successful conclusion.

> *[The Public Inquiry in Belfast] started in the middle of November and ran for two weeks. Then there was a pause for Christmas and it started again on 18th January this year and ran until the middle of March. It spanned three months – probably [sitting] for eight or nine weeks.*

And the Inquiry's determination?

> *We'd have liked it by now. [Named colleague] and I were at every single hearing so we know what was said and if there are issues to be changed we'd rather get on with that and get finished, published and adopted.*

> *And also [named colleague] and I went to the Swansea Wrexham Local Development plan Inquiries. We got to speak to the inspectors. They advised that plans are so complicated and you've received political endorsement – particularly in a city as complicated as Belfast. And they said 'in a document like that [the Belfast Local Development Plan] the department needs to come at it from the point of view that by and large it's fit for purpose and not get embroiled in dotting i's and crossing t's.*

> *Another expert in her field said that in Wales we handle the matter with kid gloves – if you did that [nit-picking] you'd never get a plan adopted. And I found it really helpful hearing that.*

Professional etiquette, experience of public service in Northern Ireland, with perhaps some well-justified confidence in the product of the LDP process, tempered the wording and some content in the interview responses. Clearly there were hurdles, resistance and what could be construed as a turf war along the way. And, as is abundantly clear in the Review of Planning in Northern Ireland, the process entailed excessive and departmental oversight which appears to have added nothing other than lengthening the process.

Producing LDP shows skilful leadership as processual peace-building in the use of significant professional, reputational expertise and positional capital. The team leader moved from a central government Department at the time when planning powers transferred to Belfast City Council. Predictably, coming from the NI Civil Service to Belfast City Council entailed a noticeable change in terms of organisational culture.

> *I moved quite quickly through the ranks in planning and when power was transferred to local government, and I transferred to Belfast City Council at that time. I certainly found the hierarchy much more obvious in the Council. Maybe that's because where I was based in the Department of Environment, we were largely in individual offices and you didn't meet the chief executive and directors very often – where in the Council they were physically more visible. I found it strange coming from probably making decisions ... and dealing with major schemes, where I would regularly have met with the Minister as an advisor. I did a lot of work on major planning appeals, High Court appearances. I was used to being at the top table and here you're not. It seemed really odd but that's the thing about moving.*

This necessitated tact and diplomacy – as is evident in the language used in the quoted responses – from someone who obviously had a wide professional network across the islands of Britain and Ireland and was respected.

It was not possible to complete the numerous Supplementary Planning Guidance documents that accompany LDP, have these put out for public consultation and later agreed by the Planning Committee, until the Department issued a direction for Belfast City Council to adopt the Local Development Plan. At the time of this interview the Council's planning team had been waiting for over two months for a determination.

> *The Planning Appeals report was sent back to the department in September and we're waiting on the department to issue a direction for us to adopt the plan or make some changes. Once we get that we'll know which policies are going ahead [and can produce] each separate guidance document. ... If you look at what is in half a dozen paragraphs we'll have guidance which goes into a lot more detail to avoid confusion by the reader.*

> *There's a lot of confusion in planning – either the developer deliberately confuses because he or she doesn't want to do something. Likewise the objecting resident will pick up one line and go 'look you can't build this'.*

> *We need commitments on things like SPGs [Supplementary Planning Guidance] – some of them are merged and changed ... urban design ... infrastructure. Transport wasn't*

*included but we've produced guidance on it as well. We've been waiting six years for a transport plan.*

Belfast City Council officials had the expertise, skill and desire to advance what was in the public interest in urban development and planning. That process has produced a firm statutory basis for transforming some if not all contested space in Belfast. This is an instance of leadership as processual and exemplifies what was intended in RPA and the statutory duties to promote equality of opportunity and good relations.

## Conclusions

Although Belfast City Council's Grace Family Centre provided much-needed services for women and families in a deprived area of the city at the Alliance Avenue interface, it was accessible only on the Nationalist side of the wall. Was this urban development for division? Had the statutory duties (to promote equality of opportunity and good relations) been ignored in granting planning permission?

Whatever, if any intention there may have been to tackle division and sectarian hostilities at this interface, planning law had not changed for thirty years. New regulations were in the making with a team at the city Council coming to the end of a protracted six-year process in making the Local Development Plan for Belfast.

This speaks volumes about the politics of public administration and the challenges of implementing progressive law enacted to embed peace in Northern Ireland. The lengthy process of drafting new regulation, with consultation and public scrutiny was further protracted by the need for departmental approval – something that seems to be slow in coming at a matter of practice. This exemplifies the daily operational obstacles to the changes inherent in the long-delayed Review of Public Administration.

# CHAPTER 5

# Narratives on interfaces and a challenge to the planning system

Looking beyond the process of making regulatory change to the wider arena of urban development in contested space, some recent research literature and the Public Accounts Committee report on planning in Northern Ireland are informative about practice in planning.

O'Neill and Murtagh (2021) provide an in-depth analysis of *the implications of equality legislation for spatial planning and in particular how it connects the profession to the territorial legacies of segregation, interfacing and poverty*. They identify deficiencies in professional practice, and a lack of necessary guidance and support from the equality sector for those tasked with conducting Equality Impact Assessment (EQIA).

> *Planners in particular, return to the way in which EQIAs are treated as a procedural necessity in explaining why they make little substantive difference to the design and delivery of policies: 'It would seem that the EQIA is a statutory duty which is then tick boxed after the policy has been prepared rather than beginning with the EQIA. There does not seem to be anybody to ensure that this is carried out.' ... [And on some occasions] equality was reduced to a tactic simply to justify a clientist outcome, often with little or no regard for the evidence of the impact on the Section 75 groups. (O'Neill and Murtagh, 2021: 20)*

Progress in new equality legislation, which went beyond anti-discrimination with a statutory duty on public authorities to promote equality of opportunity and good relations, made no significant difference to the planning process. This was, in some part at least, due to the absence of the necessary guidance and support for planners. EQIA, equality schemes and promoting equality of opportunity failed to impact on practice and decision-making in planning.

*Planners and related professions need better support to interpret the Act and how to make its provisions work in reality. They have been let down by a lack of guidance, workable models and skills support; and some have corrupted the principles of equality in the service of clientism and profit. There is a need for a re-energised ethic for the profession and the need for responsibility in the use and application of knowledge. However, practitioners also need support from the profession, academia and critically the equality sector to ensure that the worthy ideals of good relations can make a difference to the most disadvantaged and deprived communities in Northern Ireland and to other places coming out of conflict. (O'Neill and Murtagh, 2021: 26)*

Effective and sustainable change in the use and development of contested space needed more and much improved guidance on implementing Section 75 and Schedule 9 (of the 1998 Northern Ireland Act), as well as adherence to professional ethics. In Belfast the addition of new statutory planning regulation, policy and strategy may prove to be vital to this change in planning process and decision-making. As noted in later discussion, the Section 75 duty to promote equality of opportunity is an advance on, and deliberately separated from anti-discrimination law – which is Section 76 of the 1998 Northern Ireland Act (NIA). This is an important distinction which was not fully grasped in the early years of this century – even in the equality sector where the practice challenging discrimination was the foundation of all practice, if not the limit of their understanding.

## Narratives and received wisdoms on interfaces

The years since 1998 saw the production of swathes of planning strategies and peace-building agendas in Belfast, all of which lacked statutory power. Finally there was to be a legally binding strategic plan for development in Belfast with the Local Development Plan (LDP). This takes account of the key factors around contested space – but may yet face obstacles from the predominance of group thinking and the partiality of discourses on sectarian segregation.

Herrault and Murtagh note that *once it is established, group thinking is reproduced by a cadre of think tanks, universities, interest groups, NGOs and external funders* (Herrault and Murtagh, 2019: 10). This is clear from comments Gerry Robinson made during our tour of the interfaces. Although elected members of Belfast City Council did discuss interface issues consistently, opportunities to transform contested space and sectarian interfaces were missed or avoided. Importantly, suggestions made by local residents during public consultation throughout the decades fell on the deaf ears of both politicians and officialdom. As Gerry Robinson said:

> *Before Girdwood development took place, I remember meetings taking place with the funders at the time. We were talking about the need to work together in order to create one masterplan for Lower Old Park, Lower Shankill and Cliftonville.*
>
> *At one of these meetings, we asked if we could all be provided with a copy of a map which covered the three area master plans for inner North [Belfast]. 'Yes, but it will have to come from the DOE.' I remember asking for it to be made available for the next meeting in order for all of us to see what was being planned and for us to add our own views and comments. It never happened and that for me illustrated no real desire to do anything which was going to challenge or upset the status quo.*
>
> *... I was also told that all the cross-community work we are doing was great but, in the end, it will be the politicos that will decide Girdwood and that's what happened. I remember saying, is this the legacy you are leaving for us and for the next generation to come, a salami style development in isolation from a live interface literally across the road from Girdwood?*

The received wisdom – backed by interface workers – was that substantial change was always just out of reach. The variation was in the narratives about interfaces. This view is borne out by academic research (such as Komarova and O'Dowd, 2016) and tallies with Herrault and Murtagh's critique of 'encounter' or contact theory.

Gerry Robinson's opinions are widely shared by many informed local residents – if not by the *cadre of think tanks, universities, interest groups, NGOs and external funders*. This groupthink may produce substantial, if unacknowledged or inadvertent resistance to the implementation of LDP in time to come – although its legislative powers should prevent this happening, even with attempted political interference.

After decades of stasis, positive movement is possible – but only if key challenges and 'group thinking' on peace-lines can be overcome. Solutions to the violence, fear and hostility around the city's interfaces take the form of varied and often contradictory narratives about the core of the problem. The brute facts suggest that effective change is a political-economic matter. A central issue is inequality with poverty at its core, and competition for social housing, exploited by politicians seeking votes and paramilitaries holding power and assets (Herrault and Murtagh, 2019; Murtagh, 2017; O'Neill and Murtagh, 2021).

However, this is not universally accepted. In fact the answers to the problems of interfaces are determined by professional experience and the expediency of preferred discourse. For some, the solution is framed by the somewhat tired Community Relations perspective.

> *The focus on mutual understanding, contact and challenging stereotyping, emphasised tropes of forgiveness and trust at the expense of more locally based, community development methods. Once established, path dependency 'locked-in' policy around a narrow form of identity politics and 'locked-out' alternative forms of community activism with more explicit economic and structural aims. (Murtagh, 2017: 8)*

The community relations narrative, fundamentally a hearts-and-minds approach, has shaped both policy and its lack of implementation since 1998 as is clear in later discussion of the 'good relations' duty.

Henry Kissinger's apocryphal phrase *when you have them by the balls their hearts and minds will follow* springs to mind when confronted with community relations solutions to the brute facts of interface violence. In that context, and at times of crisis, the securocratic discourse appears to make more sense than cross-community encounters.

The fact that a security/policing response changes little if anything, and may simply displace 'recreational rioting' or temporarily moderate or-chestrated street violence is understood. However, this does not appear to have impacted on either the security narrative or the various ethno-political entrepreneurs. *In this context, the socio-spatial separation of ethno-religious communities has enabled them to be better policed, managed and ultim-ately de-risked but not reformed* (Murtagh, 2017; 9). Indeed, some of the responsibility for groupthink falls to academics – often constrained by a policy-bound research remit.

> *Moreover, research on interfaces, how it is variously produced, consumed and, in particular, feeds into policy outcomes are critical in assembling discourse. Attitudinal data have been prioritised in understanding walls as artefacts rather than their social and economic performance and their connection with restructuring processes in the wider spatial economy. (Murtagh, 2017: 10)*

Murtagh (2017) also provides a concise insight into peace-building policies and their spatial development priorities over the decade after 2005, citing many of the criticisms of 'shared space' policies that were, at best, constructive ambiguity. One of the most cogent among these policy critiques can be found in the responses from the Committee on the Administration of Justice (CAJ, 2006 and 2020). These publications are recommended for those interested to read further.

The security discourse can be seen as it emerged, literally, in concrete form with the construction of the Westlink motorway. This was built on the recommendations of a 1970 government report (Cunningham, 2014 cited in Murtagh, 2017). It was intended to disrupt previous urban connectivity between areas where the residents were all or mostly Catholic/Nationalist/Republican and Protestant/Unionist/Loyalist. This was wartime thinking and its implementation was seemingly continued in post-conflict developments, although not in 'safe' districts such as the Titanic Quarter in the city. Working class areas with high density social housing in north and west Belfast have not attracted similar investment or improvement.

Suffolk-Lenadoon Interface Group (SLIG) is cited as a very positive example of interface work and with justification. Indeed, it is a model of community development practice and context-specific peace-building. However, this is a Nationalist area of west Belfast where there is no longer a Unionist electoral or Loyalist paramilitary prize to be won. The fact that this group emerged from the cooperation and collaboration of strong local women is laudable – for, had there been any potential gains, ethno-political entrepreneurs would have been involved and taken charge as happened elsewhere in Belfast and other urban sites throughout Northern Ireland. SLIG is a rare instance of courageous local women providing a number

of services, including low-profile community peace-keeping, that resulted
in a decline in interface violence. It is an exceptional model. However, it
is not one that can be replicated easily or where gains are to be made by
politicians or paramilitary criminals.

The frequently overlooked yet vital factor of economic and social inequality in reproducing contested space is well stated.

> *This suggests the need for stronger analytical explanations of the causes and consequences*
> *of ethnic violence, surfacing different circuits of power and how they work together and*
> *independently from each other in the reproduction of spatial inequalities. (Murtagh,*
> *2017: 20)*

In the draft LDP, this is recognised as a serious challenge in the current
and, unless it is targeted, the future realities for parts of Belfast city.

> *1.1.4 In recent years there has been a transformation with new develop-*
> *ment in the city centre, enhanced public realm, Titanic Quarter, and*
> *Ulster University, which have added vitality, created employment op-*
> *portunities and attracted new residents, visitors and tourists. However,*
> *this is contrasted with the communal territorial disputes, persistent*
> *social inequality, curtailing safe access to the benefits of the wider city*
> *and peaceful interaction with civic society. It will be critical to tackle*
> *persistent social inequality throughout the city and build community*
> *cohesion and resilience through collaborative effort to ensure inclusive*
> *growth for all.*

It is encouraging that Belfast's LDP acknowledges that it is *critical
to tackle persistent social inequality throughout the city* as Murtagh's argument suggests.

However, tackling the *reproduction of spatial inequalities* is based on a
particular understanding of what promoting equality of opportunity means.

Unfortunately, promoting equality of opportunity was widely and
mistakenly understood. For egalitarians it seemed the promise of tackling poverty and changing socio-economic inequality. For many of those
tasked to enforce the statutory duty it was seen as being little or no more
than anti-discrimination – understandably among those who had battled

for equality and rights over the decades, including ECNI. Now, as then, the problems of poverty and underachievement remain well beyond the reach of equality of opportunity. Crucially, however, the malpractice of clientelism in planning can be confronted and changed with more clarity around the law on equality of opportunity and anti-discrimination. What is planned – and in whose interest – is the challenge for urban development in Belfast.

## The limits of discourse on urban development

As is clear from the tour of the interfaces, there is plenty of land in Belfast available for development – be that for housing or other purposes. Great swathes of land on the unionist side of the interfaces in north and west Belfast have lain derelict for decades. Where there has been development in areas of deprivation, such as at the former army barracks site at Girdwood, the overwhelming expectation was that the land would be used for social housing and so years of bickering about who would get housing and the votes that followed, prevented progress. There has been no political leadership to match that seen in the public sector, as instanced in the development of the Belfast LDP. Compromise is regarded, it seems, as a mark of political failure when it comes to 'sharing'. This is clear in the lengthy, expensive and fruitless deliberations recorded, only to be discarded, in the report of numerous consultations and commissions – be that on legacy, survivors and victims, *Flags, Identity, Culture and Tradition*, or the development of the site of the former Girdwood Barracks.

Urban development beyond the commercially successful and 'safe' commercial and middle class districts of the city has been subject to *'locked-in' policy around a narrow form of identity politics* and this has clearly *'locked-out' alternative forms of community activism with more explicit economic and structural aims* (Murtagh, 2017: 8). This has been secured – one might even say entrenched – by the different discourses on 'the problem' of interfaces and each of these has served politically and professionally convenient purposes. It is important to recognise that these discourses are partial at best, and each is potentially an obstacle to progress. It is more useful to see the complex and fluctuating nature of contested space – sometimes needing meaningful dialogue and sometimes needing a security response. However, the immediate issue has always been the continued inciting of distrust, fear and hatred by politicians, and exploiting competition for scarce social housing, among those most disadvantaged and most affected by the conflict – and community control exerted by paramilitary factions.

The antagonism reproduced over decades that has engineered a sense of both a symbolic and actual conflict of 'identity' has both fuelled and rewarded the efforts of ethno-political entrepreneurs in Belfast. In this respect, the role of paramilitary control of neighbourhoods is central. Their criminality and extortion rackets make economic development, and even basic retail trading, virtually impossible. As this is a matter of crime and security the security narrative thus gains sometimes undeserved credibility as the entire solution.

While the language of a 'disconnect' between the unionist working class and their representatives continues, and complaints abound that unionists have not benefited from the peace dividend, notions of equality and good relations are regarded as irrelevant at best, and at worst a loss to Unionism. This is the reality beyond the legal arguments, ideological debates and deliberate spreading of disinformation – on equality, the Belfast Agreement and the Northern Ireland Protocol. A peace dividend of social justice doesn't figure in these narratives.

## A very public challenge to the planning system

The adoption and implementation of the Belfast LDP, could significantly enhance planning throughout the city and help transform contested space. Yet, there may be other systemic failures that may pose challenges to progress. The 2022 report of the Public Accounts Committee (PAC) review of planning in Northern Ireland seriously questions the very fundamentals of the entire system.

According to its website the PAC is tasked by the Northern Ireland Assembly to *examine public spending ... to highlight good practice and poor value for money and to recommend improvements to the stewardship of Taxpayers money.* Their examination of planning in that jurisdiction came to some very unfavourable conclusions. *It's official: The planning system in Northern Ireland is broken (in so many ways)* (Hamber, 2022).

On Hamber's reading, there seems little hope of progress that could embed peace-building, social justice or even effective practice into urban planning because the system is fundamentally flawed. Referring to the PAC report, he states:

*Some specific findings include:*

- *the planning system lacks transparency and public trust; the PAC was 'alarmed by the volume of concerns around transparency'*
- *the PAC was 'appalled by the performance statistics'*
- *there is a lack of accountability for poor performance; the PAC was 'alarmed by the Department's misunderstanding of accountability'*
- *the planning system is one of the worst examples of silo-working within the public sector*
- *the Department's leadership of the planning system has been weak*
- *members of the public feel excluded and often believe they have no choice but to launch legal proceedings*
- *the planning committees appear 'to take an interest' in particular developments; the PAC was 'alarmed to hear that lobbying is happening, even though it shouldn't be'. (Hamber, 2022.)*

This accurately reflects the criticisms of the planning system made by the PAC.

*Taken together, the Committee was left with the impression of a system that can't plan for the future; isn't doing well on deciding today's applications; and doesn't appear to be properly enforcing the decisions it made in the past.*

**The planning system in Northern Ireland is not working. The Committee recommends that a Commission is established to undertake a fundamental review to ascertain the long-term, strategic changes that are needed to make the system fit for purpose. This should be led by someone independent from the Department.** *(para. 36)*

This would appear to throw doubt on the likelihood that new regulation in the Belfast LDP will make the intended impact and improvements – or that it will take time to change practice.

The PAC concerns around the planning process, excessive departmental oversight, possible political interference in decision-making and clientelism are of particular interest – and are detailed in the report (Public Accounts Committee, NIA 202/17-22, 2022). The conclusions graphically describe a system with poor governance and procedures that are inappropriately politicised. This defies the fundamental motives of the Review of Public Administration in Northern Ireland which were the intention to improve procedure, enhance practice and increase public accountability and transparency.

Having portrayed the LDP process as exemplary in terms of leadership in reaching its final outcome, the length of time it took was excessive and not least in the long delays before Belfast City Council planning got departmental sign-off after a six-year process. Although the PAC report does not refer to the Belfast experience – and indeed reading the report it may seem as if the LDP does not exist – this is appropriately identified as a serious problem.

> The Committee is also concerned that the Department has implemented an excessive range of 'checks and balances' at either side of the Independent Examination which have contributed to delays, and do not happen in other jurisdictions. The Committee did not get any sense of the value added by these checks and is concerned that this level of interference is symptomatic of the culture within the Department, and its approach to the planning system in general. The system has become so legalistic and bureaucratic that professional planners are tied up in processes, not adding value or placemaking. This is expensive for public bodies and discouraging for staff. (para. 44)

It would seem that there is more than a change of organisational culture needed. When an administration fails to enact reforms in government, implement legal duties and is so legalistic that it is 'adding no value' this holds out against peace-building and effective governance. The LDP experience with the department is a case of excessive 'checks and balances'.

At a more local and practical level in the planning process, the inability or refusal to alter the landscape of interfaces seems to have happened because of continued poor practice, a lack of legally binding rules for development and perhaps also the use of 'call-in' and 'overturns'. PAC comments on these are clear and critical, and demonstrate the need for radical and rapid change.

> *Whilst each planning committee has a Scheme of Delegation setting out the applications to be decided by the planning committee, and those which are delegated to officials, elected members retain the right to 'call-in' applications from the delegated list, for consideration and decision by the planning committee. The Committee was presented with evidence that call-in procedures vary considerably, and it is not always clear, even to members of the same planning committee, why certain applications are called in. Whilst there may be valid reasons for calling in applications, such variation in process and lack of detail leads to speculation and a lack of trust, particularly when planning committees appear to take an interest in particular types of development. In this context, the Committee was especially alarmed to hear that lobbying is happening, even though it shouldn't be. (para. 48)*

The existence of lobbying in planning decisions, raising due concern, has been documented in research (O'Neill and Murtagh, 2021) and flies in the face of transparency and accountability in decision-making. The Belfast LDP provides the appropriate and legally binding criteria for decision-making but appropriate decisions could be undermined by politicians lobbying for individual or group interests – unless robustly kept in check. Indeed, it seems that political interference in planning decision-making happens – and against the advice of officials – which also concerns the PAC.

> *The NIAO's report found that one in eight decisions taken by planning committees was made contrary to the advice of the planning officer. Whilst the Committee understands that planning committees are not expected to agree with official recommendations in all cases, it expects so-called 'overturns' to be supported by robust planning reasons which are publicly available. Witnesses agreed that this was not always the case, and that record keeping processes vary considerably across planning committees. (para. 49)*

Ensuring compliance with planning determinations is also patchy with such a huge variation in council areas that the PAC found *that discretion is being used as an excuse not to carry out enforcement action in some cases.* This adds to the existing criticisms of the system and points to the next area of challenge – the Department. On that subject the report found that *the Department is completely disconnected from the reality of the system, largely as a consequence of its hands-off approach since the transfer of functions* (para. 51). Against such a background it is clear that the Belfast LDP emerged from a process which had strong leadership, tenacity and clarity of purpose. Having got to the final hurdle the Belfast planning team are to be congratulated, especially as the PAC report made the almost unprecedented comment on the Department.

> *The Committee is very concerned, based on the evidence it has heard, that the Department does not grasp the severity of issues facing the planning system, does not recognise the obvious need for change and has little understanding of its role in implementing change. (para. 62)*

In light of the report's dire conclusions it is encouraging to find leadership and best practice prevailed in the process of producing the LDP for Belfast. That being possible, there is great potential for the proposed Commission to address the fundamental problems in Northern Ireland's planning system – and to find solutions. In particular, and of central importance to stability in the peace process, is the legal and administrative framework in the LDP for constructively dealing with the physical architecture and infrastructure that remains a toxic legacy of the conflict.

## Conclusions

Planning powers were belatedly transferred to local government and, even then, the planning system delayed and almost stifled attempts at producing new and vastly improved regulations. Professional practice fared no better as clientelism continued and spatial planning often ignored equality and transparency considerations – compounded by the lack of necessary guidance and support from the equality sector for those tasked with conducting Equality Impact Assessment.

Thinking on the subject of interfaces, and thus any planning or development, is myopic and limited by the narrative employed. From ineffective community relations 'contact' theory through securocratic to identity politics discourses there is widespread groupthink *reproduced by a cadre of think tanks, universities, interest groups, NGOs and external funders* (Herrault and Murtagh, 2019: 10). While commercial and less deprived areas have experienced huge economic and social benefits, interfaces have not – leaving these places and people to inequality with poverty at its core, and competition for social housing, exploited by vote-seeking politicians and community control and intimidation from paramilitaries.

The official verdict, in the PAC report, is an indictment of the entire system holding up the inefficiency, lack of transparency and accountability for public scrutiny.

Interfaces are the architectural legacy of the conflict and have not been transformed as was promised. They have their symbolic counterpart in the use and misuse of flags, identity, culture and tradition, which is the subject of the next chapter.

# CHAPTER 6

# Peace and the symbolism of conflict

When state papers were released in Dublin in late 2021 Bowman commented that the Belfast Agreement *was so complicated that some mocked it as a Heath Robinson agreement, by which they meant a ridiculously complicated machine to achieve a simple purpose* (Bowman, 2021).

The Agreement and the legislation that enshrined its principles and promises was necessarily *ridiculously complicated* because it had to provide just enough compromise to keep everyone on board, and retain the ambiguities of the negotiated settlement. The legitimacy of aspirations to Irish unity, already in the 1985 Anglo-Irish Agreement, were integral to the settlement and 1998 Northern Ireland Act (NIA). Unionist demands that Northern Ireland remain British were secured. However, according to a former European diplomat who was involved in the peace negotiations constitutional issues were not discussed or dealt with in detail (Montgomery, 2021). Somehow this vexed subject was presented with sufficient vagueness to satisfy each of the negotiating parties – which is somewhat ironic in light of the alleged constitutional 'threat' to the Union with Britain in the post- Brexit Northern Ireland Protocol.

Of equal ambiguity was how the Agreement and law tackled the explosive issues of what came under the umbrella of *flags, identity, culture and tradition*. While never far from provoking violence, any or all of these symbolic matters could be exploited to wage proxy battles and figurative conflict – as they had been for much if not all the century of the Northern Ireland state. By 2016 so little progress had been made that a Commission was established to investigate, consult and produce recommendations for the government – as politics descended into what would become a three-year limbo with the suspension of Stormont.

Symbolic ethno-political war and peace-building: Flags and Parades

The symbolism and symbolic action expressed in public displays of flags and emblems, and parades remained the subject of serious contestation during the peace-building process. While there are a plethora of parades and demonstrations, accompanied by numerous flags and emblems of 'identity', it is only a small number of those held by the Protestant-Unionist-Loyalist Orange Order, and the related but separate Black Preceptory, that were most frequently disputed and most likely to result in widespread civil unrest. Discussion of public parades, displays of flags and emblems, and the place of paramilitary murals, reveals the virtually unchanged effect of regulating these displays and the uses to which they have been put, by various actors, as part of resisting or destabilising the peace process.

While the research and government publications draw back from putting it in such explicit terms, the evidence points to a consistent pattern of Loyalist-Unionists employing symbolism and a surrogate form of political action in parading and using the Union and paramilitary flag displays in public spaces in their response to the unwelcome developments of power-sharing and a rights-based approach to governance. As if to mirror this, Republicans have, to the dismay of most Nationalists, exploited flags, emblems, culture and tradition more as conduits of triumphalism than expressions of protest. Where there is violence and protest, from non-unionists, it tends to be an attempt by dissident Republicans to undermine the position of Sinn Féin in government. For unionists the sense of loss in the peace process is long-standing and now entrenched in their political discourses and protests about loss of culture and identity.

John Hume famously said *you can't eat a flag* but many people have waged symbolic struggles in their use, just as some have made a career out of flags. So, this is nothing new in Northern Ireland.

## The historical context of flags and emblems

Hennessey speaks of *an ethnic conflict between two national communities*. For him embedding peace needs *considerable sensitivity* regarding displays of symbols, flags and emblems in the public space. The Belfast Agreement recognised that symbolism had a central role in the conflict and retained the potential for future disputes. Paragraph 5 of the *Rights, Safeguards and Equality of Opportunity* Section confirms an all-party acknowledgement of

> *the sensitivity of the use of symbols and emblems for public purposes, and the need in particular in creating the new institutions to ensure that such symbols and emblems are used in a manner which promotes mutual respect rather than division. Arrangements will be made to monitor this issue and consider what action might be required. (20)*

The origins and history of Northern Ireland were Unionist, partisan and anti-Catholic. This created entrenched division played out by electoral gerrymandering and discrimination in employment and allocating social housing, in a one-party state, and this partiality was enacted symbolically in control of displays of flags and emblems. For instance, under the Flags and Emblems (Display) Act (Northern Ireland) 1954, the display of all flags and symbols, except the Union flag, was regulated. One single Irish Tricolour flag set in the Republican Party Office window on the (mainly Catholic-populated) Falls Road in Belfast, led to rioting in 1964. The power of symbolism was integral to sustaining the bitter and violent sectarian divisions on which both state and society in Northern Ireland rested, which were then exacerbated in thirty years of conflict, and which have continued to create disputation and antagonism during the peace process.

Flags function to communicate strong if occasionally ambivalent messages. They have always sustained sectarian division and violence in Northern Ireland (Jarman, 2003). They *are associated with allegiance, loyalty, territory and authority* and *can be used to challenge another group, to assert dominance or to seek a confrontation* (Bryson and McCartney, 1994: 10 and 26). Displays of flags on street furniture such as lampposts are almost exclusively in working class housing estates, and on main roads in urban areas. They assert the dominance of a particular political allegiance – and, more often than not, paramilitary presence – and threaten confrontation with those who differ. Displays of flags, emblems and symbols at public events express exclusive possession rather than civic or shared ownership. For example, in Northern Ireland, flying the Irish Tricolour in St Patrick's Day parades and the Union flag in the Twelfth of July Orange parades are powerful symbolic messages of exclusion, and sustain bitter divisions and hostility between factions.

Displays of flags reflect strongly polarised politics in which *people across the political spectrum are looking for ways to assert themselves* so that, in the context of Northern Ireland, they are *political artefacts. This element of the debate is often not articulated, but it is often understood* (Bryson and McCartney, 1994: 130 and 184). It is precisely because this is well understood and needs no articulation, that disputes over flags, emblems and symbols continued to be violent and had to be addressed, after the peace settlement. Flags and emblems mark territory as dangerous to live or work in. Painted pavement curb stones articulate the 'chill factor' by warning 'outsiders' and delineate whether Unionists and Nationalists can safely travel in these areas (Darby and Knox, 2004: Shirlow, 2006). Their absence in socially deprived areas may signal where people of ethnic minority or in mixed-religion relationships can live without threat.

Challenging displays of flags and emblems in workplaces carries considerable risk and people have been subjected to threat, death or injury for removing such symbols (Robinson and Nolan, 1999; Goldie, 2021). Flags, emblems and murals are used to mark territory and intimidate 'the other' in overtly sectarian ways. Insofar as these are expressions of 'identity', such displays are claimed as being about the sovereignty and constitutional status of Northern Ireland; despite the fact that this was settled by the Belfast Agreement and Northern Ireland Act (1998). And, the convenient equating of constitutional issues with 'culture' and 'identity' has served political purposes, for some political parties and all paramilitary groups. Flags, emblems and symbolism are visible manifestations of segregation. Shirlow (2006) emphasises the importance of this for politics and peace-building.

> *Given the nature of residential segregation and the impact that has on spatial mobility it is argued that the capacity for normalised social relations remains, in the short to medium term, unlikely. ... segregation influences the localised nature of the politics of territorial control and resistance, and where the imperatives of communal difference, segregation and exclusion still predominate over the politics of shared interests, integration, assimilation and consensus. (227)*

Symbolism was contested in Northern Ireland as long ago as the late 1940s and again in 1953 with the Queen's coronation, when Nationalist-dominated Councils, such as Newry and Strabane, refused to display British flags and emblems (Palley, 1972). This had led the Stormont government to enact the Flags and Emblems (Display) Act (N.I.) 1954, which was not repealed until the Public Order (N.I.) Order 1987. This legislation gave special protection to the Union flag and prohibited the symbolic expression of any form of Irish Nationalism. Yet, the 1987 repeal of this Act did not settle debates on the symbolism of sovereignty and specifically the Union Flag and the Irish Tricolour. National flags and associated symbolism express *the structures and beliefs that underpin a particular aspect of politics* (Jarman, 1997: 21). Expressing political and national 'identity' remained bitterly contested throughout the conflict and into the peace process. Government management of public displays of symbolism sought to *offer the possibility of developing public spaces that allow community celebration and commemoration without intimidation* (Bryan and Gillespie, 2005: 5). Yet policy, practice and public sector delivery around this remain confused, sometimes contradictory and ultimately improved nothing.

Until well after the 2007 return to devolved government, the reality of public displays of flags and emblems marked clear segregated *boundaries through both symbolism and force* (Shirlow, 2006: 227). And progress in the peace process was often largely determined, and seriously limited, by the use and meanings of flags.

Post-1998 regulation and politics of flags and emblems

In May 2000 the peace process was apparently progressing well, with declarations on weapons decommissioning from both the Provisional IRA and the Secretary of State for Northern Ireland. At that very point concerns were raised about the flying of the Union flag on public buildings. This had become a matter of political leverage for the First Minister and leader of the UUP, David Trimble. This matter was elevated to the equivalent status of the proposed reforms to policing in Northern Ireland, which changes were very unwelcome to Unionists. However, Trimble's opportunistic equating of flying the Union flag on public buildings with policing reforms appears to have been little more than an irritation to the Secretary of State – and one he was determined to resolve.

> *Mandelson looked to the restored Executive to address the issue; but if the Executive could not reach a consensus the Secretary of State would take the power, by Order-in-Council, to provide a legal basis for the regulation of the flying of flags. Mandelson did not want this issue to become a 'running sore'. (Hennessey, 2000: 213)*

The SDLP regarded this as Unionist stalling after weapons decommissioning had allegedly been settled. The Deputy First Minister, Seamus Mallon criticised the Ulster Unionists and the First Minister David Trimble.

> *For two years we had a problem. The problem was decommissioning. One half-hour after the decommissioning issue was effectively resolved then we had two more issues on the table. (Hennessey, 2000: 214)*

The flying of flags remained hotly contested in local government long after the issue was regulated for central government buildings. Under the Flags Regulations (Northern Ireland) Order (2000) central government could only fly the Union flags on or in designated public buildings on 17 (later 18) designated days. Yet the 'running sore' would not be healed as this legislation neglected to include local government. Although policy on flying the Union flag on government buildings was challenged by Sinn Féin, the court upheld the decision of the Secretary of State that it could be flown on the legally designated days (Murphy's Application for Judicial Review [2001] NI 425). Policy on flying of flags on Council property was strongly disputed. Councils sought legal advice, but did not get firm answers or determinations from the Equality Commission for Northern Ireland until June 2006. Before that the Commission advised that the matter was one for each Council to decide, leaving open the space for continued argument.

The legal status of publicly displaying flags is clear. Displays of the Union flag in public places are not illegal, but displays of paramilitary flags are. Under the Terrorism Act (2000) supporting terrorists by displaying symbols is a crime. However, there are arguments that flying the entirely legal Union flag in public places, such as on lampposts, should be regarded as illegal as these mark territory and are potentially intimidating. The Flags and Emblems (Display) Act (Northern Ireland) 1954 was repealed in 1987 because of its controversial implementation but it took no account of the public disorder implications of displays of flags and emblems, so that a *more equitable* version of this legislation has been considered (Bryan and Gillespie, 2005: 56). Interestingly, decisions on contested parades take public order considerations into account but not the 'custom and practice' of popular public display of flags.

Although law restricts the illegal use of symbols, it cannot resolve political disputes. The limited efficacy of the law in settling such debates is evident as the Poppy (commemorating the dead of Britain's wars) is not considered, in judicial terms, *an emblem of the conflict* whereas the Easter Lily (commemorating the 1916 Easter Rising against British rule in Ireland) is. So, prisoners in Northern Ireland were permitted to wear the Poppy but, in 2004, were banned from wearing the Easter Lily.[13] The Easter Lily

---

13   Queen's Bench Division [2004] NIQB 23 Transcript of Hearing (2 April 2004). A prisoner at HMP Maghaberry asserted his right to wear an Easter Lily to note and commemorate an event of great historical importance to people of his political and cultural background, namely the 1916 Easter Rising. Northern Ireland Prison Service Standing Orders dated 3 July 1997 at para 4.12 states that: *Prisoners may not wear emblems, nor should they be displayed by prisoners in their cells.* The prison governor had allowed the wearing of shamrocks for St Patrick's Day and Poppy for Remembrance Day; *These emblems are non-political and non-sectarian and will, in future, be permitted to be worn at the appropriate time by any prisoners who wish*

remains a potent symbol as is evidenced in the 2011 determination of the
European Court of Human Rights.

> *In its decision in the case of Donaldson v. the United Kingdom (application no. 56975/*
> *09) the European Court of Human Rights has by a majority declared the application in-*
> *admissible. The decision is final. The case concerned the ban on all prisoners in Northern*
> *Ireland wearing, outside their cells, emblems with a political or sectarian connotation.*

This is an exceptional case as, until 2007, discussion on contested displays
of flags and emblems focused largely on the Union flag and Loyalist paramilitary flags and emblems.

Many Unionists considered that ECNI operated on a nationalist
agenda. However, as their determinations emerged, it became clear that
these were not politically one-sided. For example, the decision on Lisburn
City Council flying the union flag (ECNI, 2006) was a landmark verdict,
in that it addressed the implications of that Council's practice with regard
to both Section 75 statutory duties to promote equality of opportunity and
good relations. This was a determination that flags and emblems must be
appropriately displayed by public authorities, and in line with the law for
central government. In this case the emblem was the Union flag, and this
did not please Unionist politicians of any party.

However, ECNI decisions on symbolism and emblems were viewed
in a much more positive light by Unionists with the publication of the
Commission's verdict on Omagh Council's practice (ECNI, 2007) – deter-
mining that the manner in which Omagh Council had dealt with a memorial for the 1981 Hunger Strike by Republican prisoners had been in
breach of its Equality Scheme. This monument had been erected on Council
ground in 2001, and had been the subject of a dispute with Omagh Council
since 2004, before ECNI investigated the matter. The Council were deemed

---

*to wear them.* The prisoner argued that differentiating between the shamrock and
Poppy as non-political emblems and the Easter Lily as a political emblem was not
legal and the prohibition was a breach of the Section 75 (2) duty to promote good
relations, on the basis of judgements made by the Fair Employment Commission it
was decided that the Poppy was *not an emblem of the conflict.* For this reason and a
determination on the proportionality principle in the context, the application for
judicial review was dismissed.

to have actively encouraged the group that erected the memorial to buy the land on which it sat, rather than address any equality and good relations implications. ECNI recommendations provided Unionists with 'evidence' that they might seek redress on concerns of equality and good relations importance.[14] Thus, in 2007 Unionists from Limavady Council were calling on ECNI to investigate the disputed Kevin Lynch monument in Dungiven, erected in memory of the local man who died in the Hunger

14    ECNI, 2007: 13-15 states; This investigation concerns the presence of a Memorial
      to the 1981 I.R.A. hunger strikers on the site of the Old Church grounds and grave-
      yard in Dromore Co. Tyrone, which is owned by Omagh District Council, and the
      subsequent decision of that Council to dispose of the section of the site in which
      the memorial is situated to a group who are believed to have been responsible for
      erecting the memorial. (1) The Investigation Decision was that 'Omagh District
      Council has failed to comply with Section 7.4 of its approved Equality Scheme by
      not conducting a screening exercise in relation to its policies that allowed the un-
      authorised Memorial to remain on its property. Omagh District Council has failed
      to comply with Section 6.3 of its approved equality scheme by not conducting an
      Equality Impact Assessment in relation to its policies that allowed the unauthorised
      Memorial to remain on its property. Omagh District Council has complied with
      Sections 6.2 and 7.4 of its approved Equality Scheme in respect of the screening ex-
      ercise conducted in respect of its subsequent decision to dispose of the land in ques-
      tion.' (14) ECNI Recommendations include; 'Omagh District Council' intends to
      conduct an Equality Impact Assessment relating to its policy 'Disposal of Land for
      the Purpose of Erecting or retaining a Memorial or a Monument'. Application of
      the screening criteria to this policy had highlighted the potentially sectarian nature
      of the Memorial, and that altering this policy might better promote good relations.
      Omagh District Council officials indicated in the course of the investigation that
      a decision had been made in principle to dispose of the land in question, and that
      it would be unlikely that the planned Equality Impact Assessment would consider
      the potential equality implications of allowing an unauthorised Memorial of this
      nature to remain on Council property in the first place. The Commission is of the
      view that a proper equality analysis of the proposal to dispose of the land in ques-
      tion to allow the Memorial to be retained would necessarily need to consider the
      implications, in terms of equality of opportunity and indeed good relations, of a
      policy that allowed the Memorial to remain on the site for the previous 4 years and
      any proposed policies that would permit the Memorial to continue to remain there.
      (14-15)

Strike. After nearly a decade Unionists of all parties were starting to see some value in the ECNI strapline 'equality for all'.

Some commentators regard legislating for such deeply divisive social issues as being questionable and see the aspiration to use symbols to promote mutual respect as *worthy but underplays the significance of such emblems and the opposition they generate*, because such legalistic responses do not ensure popular legitimacy and are even *likely to inspire further conflicts* (Little, 2003: 380). The cogent and more realistic argument is made that some regulation is necessary, without any claim that the state should 'control' the process (Bryan and Gillespie, 2005). This reflects the broadly accepted view among community sector practitioners, officials and many politicians that taking account of local community concerns is essential to regulating the use of public space. ECNI considered such issues as central to implementing Section 75 (2) good relations duty.

> Local councils in particular have made significant efforts to progress good relations through this process; with policies regarding bilingualism, celebratory bonfires, the display of portraits of the Queen, flags and emblems and the flying of flags from council buildings, and community development funding, being subject to EQIAs. (ECNI, 2006c, 4.19: 32-33)

However, having finally recognised the importance of good relations ECNI did not always make the connection between political-sectarian decisions and equality schemes.

## The use of symbols, emblems and flags as a measure of peace-building

While the Belfast Agreement promised that *Arrangements will be made to monitor this issue and consider what action might be required*, this only materialised in the form of academic research funded by the Office of the First Minister and Deputy First Minister and by the Economic and Social Research Council. In this Bryan and Gillespie (2005) argued that the peace process might be, to some degree, evaluated by how the government manages public displays of symbols and symbolic behaviour. Seemingly, symbolic action had by then overtaken visual displays of symbolism as claims to symbolic and geographical territory.

The importance of symbolism is so well established that it has become a received wisdom. Jarman (1998) notes *the place of murals in the symbolic construction of urban space*. Memorials possess similar power. Kenney (1998) and Buckley (1998) have described the powerful mythologising capacity of symbols and icons in Northern Ireland. Two decades ago it could be said with some accuracy that the ethno-political power of the Union flag was so strong in Northern Ireland that it *has acquired an ethnic, Protestant connotation that it may not carry in the rest of the UK* (Wilson, 2000a: 2). And, seven years after the Belfast Agreement this remained a critical problem for government and politics.

> *The display of flags and emblems in Northern Ireland has been a site of contest since the foundation of the state. Many existing public events and most public occasions of public presentation have become sites of symbolic competition. ..... Analysis of the use of symbols must involve an exploration of the way symbols work. The same symbol can be viewed and used in many different ways. There is no innate meaning to a symbol. Human beings give symbols meaning. Thus a flag can simultaneously be the marker of official and legal sovereignty and also the marker of local territory. It can be emblematic of democracy but also the harbinger of fear ... defended as freedom of speech whilst also criticised as intimidation. This is particularly evident in Northern Ireland. (Bryan and Gillespie, 2005: 8)*

This research, *Transforming Conflict: Flags and Emblems* indicates that managing – and hopefully controlling – the use of symbols and symbolic politics was recognised by key senior civil servants, and presumably some politicians, as crucial in the peace-building process. The researchers examined disputes over flying both official and 'popular' flags, and also addressed practises such as graffiti writing, mural and curb stone painting, the erection of arches and bonfires, and the creation of memorials in Northern Ireland.

At a time of continued Direct Rule from Westminster, when the DUP and Sinn Féin were yet to gain the political upper hand, the strategic use of symbolism increased significantly; with a surge in the number and reach of public flag displays and painted pavements, marking out the public space into clearly hostile and sectarian territories. Bryan and Gillespie (2005) noted that flags and emblems served as a proxy for political discussions and activities, and theorised that this was the creation of political capital which is invented, appraised and then either appropriated or destroyed. They cautioned that prohibition or legal restriction could increase the status and power of a symbol. Such was the policy climate that there were no clear statutory responsibilities on government departments, police or local Councils regarding displays of flags and emblems and the management of contested public space. Lampposts along arterial roads throughout Northern Ireland were blanketed with flags; some of them national (legal British and Irish) and others paramilitary (illegal or legally defined as terrorist).

However, this politicised symbolic activity diminished considerably following the success of collaborative initiatives by local government and other statutory agencies with leaders in local communities; many of whom had paramilitary connections and were former (non-state) combatants. So changes occurred rapidly when the post-Agreement era of Direct Rule ended in 2007. The years before 2007 were characterised by profound political uncertainty. Symbolic resistance, particularly on the part of Unionist-Loyalists, was both a reaction to the perceived 'victory' of Nationalist-Republicans in a power-sharing arrangement and an attempt to reinvigorate the former triumphalism of Orange-ism and the Protestant state; as if to restore unquestioned Unionist supremacy, despite the 'new dispensation'. Republican use of flags and emblems, murals and painted curb stones was as much triumphalist as it was a celebration of the right to Irish citizenship and the aspiration to Irish unity. Sinn Féin were not averse to St Patrick's Day being hijacked as 'Tricolour Day' which alienated virtually all Unionists and discomfited the Nationalist SDLP.

The deliberate and strategic use of flags and symbolism as surrogate political capital was an integral part of consolidating the rise of Sinn Féin and the DUP. Their electoral share rose over these years to eclipse the 'centre' SDLP and UUP parties. And, once ensconced in Stormont in 2007, the dominant parties set about working together – albeit usually behind closed doors – and no longer needed the street level hostilities that supported their ascent to political legitimacy and electoral supremacy. The game was still ethnic poker, but it could be played out in a more overtly elite political setting, in 'the Big House'. The ironic result was that, by 2010, mainstream activists and politicians could no longer control events on the streets, as serious rioting on 12th July demonstrated clearly.

Many deprived neighbourhoods remain demarcated as 'Unionist' or 'Nationalist' by flags, symbols and painted curb stones. However, some paramilitary murals had been altered or removed and the BBC reported that the last one in North Belfast was replaced, with community consent, on 30 November 2010. This signalled a significant, if partial, change in the symbolic construction of contested urban space in Belfast.

The historical significance of the use and abuse of flags and emblems deserves attention, because these all-too-public expressions of sectarianism formed a backdrop to political progress in reaching the Belfast Agreement and embedding peace-building during the years of Direct Rule, until recent post-Brexit times. There is little symbolic action in the current 'dissident republican' resistance to Sinn Féin as part of government in a British jurisdiction – although they continue to pose the threat of violence, murder and petrol bombings. Just as the peace-building efforts of David Trimble's Ulster Unionist Party were undermined by DUP 'dissident' Unionism, the intransigence of Loyalist paramilitary factions and hotly contested Loyal Order parades, so dissident Republican groups have sought to outdo Sinn Féin in erecting memorials to the 1981 Hunger Strikers who died, and the appropriation of the Irish Tricolour in combination with the Starry Plough (a powerful symbol associated with the 1916 Easter Rising in Ireland) and other regalia; although with debatable success. The surrogate politics of symbolism remains an arena of controversy, and its relevance to internal splits within Irish Republicanism should not be overlooked.

In the wider public arena, however, the dominant force of symbolic action and display diminished alongside the dramatic decline of political uncertainty as the DUP and Sinn Féin choreographed a sectarian carve-up of 'rights' under a devolved government – although only in the short term. The regulations governing the flying of the Union flag on Government buildings was extended to cover local government property – propelling what can only be described as a pan-Unionist rebellion – as instanced in the 2012 Flags dispute.

# The Commission on Flags, Identity, Culture and Tradition

By December 2021 the much-vaunted Commission on Flags, Identity, Culture and Tradition released its report – which had been completed but not published in 2019. Writing before this very belated public appearance, Waller (2021) saw the entire exercise as futile.

> On June 20 2016, recognizing the need to address these issues the government of Northern Ireland appointed a Commission on Flags, Identity, Culture and Tradition (FICT). The Commission was tasked to produce a report and recommendations on the way forward in regard to a range of symbols-related issues. Its findings were supposed to be released by December 2017. By June 2019, a year and a half after that date and at a cost of £730,000, fict had yet to release any findings. Particularly irksome was that more than half the Commission's cost had been spent on remuneration paid for travel expenses of Commission members. Reflecting the complexity of their charge, particularly in the midst of three years of political paralysis, it would not be until July 2020 that FICT submitted its final report, including recommendations, to Stormont ministers. As of writing the final report has not yet been made public. (Waller, 2021: 220)

After considerable public and media pressure the report was published. The general response was cool at best. One might be forgiven for citing the now familiar adage – *if it's a difficult issue, set up a working group, if it is really difficult set up a committee, and if it is near to impossible set up a Commission* – but in any case delay proceedings and dilute the findings lest there are outcomes.

The Irish Times had a small piece on page four, headlined as *Delayed commission report raises possibility of new civic flag for* [Northern Ireland]. The five column inches ended with: *The report made 44 recommendations but it is unlikely they will be enacted.* Northern Irish press response on 2 December 2021 was more heated and predictably selective – and politicised if not sectarian – in headlines and editorial.

The *Belfast Telegraph* front page announced *Flags report 'an £800k exercise in can-kicking'* and devoted pages 4-5 on the subject. Reporting on the political response it read, Alliance Party Justice Minister, Naomi Long slams *lack of political will to agree an action plan over recommendations* and is quoted as saying: *After 5 years and £800k the least we would expect is the Executive Office to produce an action plan, implement what's agreed and resolve what wasn't.* Sinn Féin and the DUP rolled out the predictable responses and narratives – that Unionists wouldn't respect equality and rights and that Republicans want to erase British culture and Britishness. Renowned columnist and Twitter commentator Allison Morris argued that the *Commission failed to come down on the side of what's right* – under the header, *Pointless fence-sitting exercise a waste of five years and £800k.*

> *FICT findings were presented to ministers in July 2020. But we, the public, were not ready to receive the report at that stage, it seems, and so a working group was set up to look at the document. …. A commission. A working group. Any of this sound familiar yet? … I can only hope those who participated at least got a few decent lunches out of it. Because, after five years and £800k, little else has been achieved.*

On the political right of the DUP, TUV (Traditional Unionist Voice party) leader Jim Allister described the report as a *'complete waste of time' and a 'colossal waste of money'.* The DUP had its own defensive comment. *DUP MLA Christopher Salford claimed the 'weaponisation' of culture and identity by Sinn Féin made solutions 'very difficult to come by' amid what he described as its attempts to 'remove every trace of Britishness'.*

The nationalist Irish News led with the front page story headline *Sinn Féin accuses DUP of blocking flags report plan.* The paper's *Analysis* feature declared that the time and money was futile – *spent on a report that was never going to satisfy the reactionaries.* The Editorial lead with *Flags report exposes dysfunction and division.*

The more unionist editorial of the [Belfast] Newsletter led with a front page headline *SF 'want to remove all trace (sic) of Britishness'.* The inside story was that the *Commissioners could not agree.* And the only newspaper to give the Commission Chair space to make a case, that particular article quoted Dr Dominic Bryan, under the headline *Report author insists: We have moved forward.* He is reported as saying:

> *I hope people will be pleased that all our four main political parties have found ways of talking about cultural rights, for instance. We got agreement through all the political parties on these issues.*

This was not progress by any standard of peace-building. Community relations practitioners and mediators achieved ways of talking about these
issues and considerably more personal and painful subjects – like murder,
bombing, torture and deeply-seated hatred – decades ago. Meaningful
dialogue – essential as it is to stability and peace-building – is neither
new nor sufficient to sustain the Northern Ireland peace process. Sworn
enemies have met and had highly emotional but non-confrontational discussions both in private and public arenas (Goldie, 2008). And, even this
has not anchored 'good relations' or prevented people making divisive
and provocative decisions.

The recommendations of the FICT report would see the light of day
but they would not be implemented, or even put into a time-framed action
plan. However, there may well be alternative avenues for discrete advances
on flags, emblems, bonfires and 'culture' by the actions and efforts of some
politicians. Thus, it is the context rather than the content of the FICT
Commission's report that is worth some attention.

The Commission was established because these issues, like interfaces
and continuous protests around flags and emblems, threatened to destabilise the peace process. In addition to essential constitutional, legal and
policing reforms, and a new equality and human rights agenda, both the
1998 Agreement and the first Programme for Government acknowledged
the need to address polarisation, inter-communal hostility and segregation;
and yet these were to become increasingly problematic. Levels of violent
division and hostility at sectarian interfaces rose in the years after 1998,
stoked by parades-related disputes. There was a pressing need for managing
contested space, and symbolisms that marked out deep division – with the
blatant abuse of displays of flags and emblems, and contentious marches
posing more acute public order issues.

Although the FICT recommendations are in what Brian Rowan might
call *Political Purgatory,* they may well come about through alternative
measures – from government departments, local government and – at
worst – through security responses. Some accommodations may produce
advances on flags, emblems, bonfires and 'culture'. Interestingly, in February
2022 UK regulations on flying the Union flag on government buildings
were changed and the number of designated days for official flag displays

was reduced from eighteen to eleven, and yet this was barely noticed in Northern Ireland until it became a short-lived debate among Unionist politicians (Bradfield, 2022). There were no protests or demonstrations as had happened in the Flags dispute of 2012-2013. In fact, the issue barely registered on the public or media radar.

For those who have the appetite it is worth reading the full FICT Commission report – not for its conclusions but for the many examples of questionable statements and obfuscation. For example, the section *A Historic Overview* is a sanitised and partial description of events and cultural traditions that is almost devoid of political and historical facts.

> 2.26 *The reality however is that our common heritage is diverse, rich and multi-faceted. The influence of English, Irish and Scots on our language, culture and heritage should be allowed to act as connections rather than barriers. And while these influences inform who we are, they are only a part of the wider diversity that exists within our society. This diversity and complexity of culture and tradition, which includes the rich heritage of our migrant and minority ethnic communities, defies placing people and whole sections of our community in boxes marked 'Orange' and 'Green'.*

Dispensing with core aspects of history and constitutional aspirations, the anodyne language avoids acknowledging entrenched and profoundly emotional attitudes and beliefs, and intention to offend 'the other' as the following section shows.

> 2.27 *It reflects the reality that we continue to be a divided society, in which events and the use of symbols that inform our cultural identity can bring people together, but they can also communicate exclusion, or fear to others.*

This is hardly credible. As McKay (2022) writes, *It used to be called triumphalism, this flaunting of Northern Ireland's Britishness. Now it looks more like desperation.* Indeed she quotes an interview concerning the flying of the Parachute Regiment flag on the outskirts of Derry city on the 50th anniversary of Bloody Sunday – in mocking the dead.

> *Those who put up the Parachute Regiment's flag are full of incoherent rage. They believe Protestant civilians killed by the IRA have not been given the same attention as those who died on Bloody Sunday. They want recognition for 'the exodus' that saw many Protestants effectively driven out of the city side of Derry by the IRA during the conflict. They feel*

*betrayed and neglected by unionist leaders who have taken their support for granted and done little to improve their lives. One man told me that those responsible are 'giving two fingers' to everyone else. 'They're saying – we can do this and you can't stop us,' he said.*

As if it would detract from the failure of its deliberations and its final report, and given the continuous destructive use of symbolism, the Commission reverted to an interpretation of Section 75 that is mistaken and rightly much-criticised.

> *3.32 Equality and Good Relations are interdependent of each other and both are essential to building a shared, peaceful and equal society. The Commission wishes to reassert what was recognised in section 75, and contend that the resources and policies required to create a more shared, peaceful and equal society need to have Equality and Good Relations outcomes at their core. In such an approach to policy aims and programme delivery, the Commission discussed a number of models including Equity, Diversity and Interdependence.*

This is the traditional community relations model – in which equity is not equality as defined in law (NIA). Also, the Community Relations Council for Northern Ireland contested the Section 75.1 duty to promote equality of opportunity in the early years of the peace process – using an ill-defined notion of interdependence regarding good relations as equivalent to equality. In 2022 it did rather seem 'tired' and a form of 'pacification' given that it simply did not match up with the evidence on effective peace-building.

On *Leadership for a Shared Society* the report makes the naive if not absurdly coy note that expressions of culture may be 'perceived as' territory marking.

> *4.6 In many cases the expressions of Britishness and Irishness are more prevalent within our society than in the rest of Ireland or in the rest of the United Kingdom. In addition, as these expressions of cultural identity are so deeply connected with political and constitutional matters, their expression can, on occasion, cause offence, hurt and antagonism. Overt expressions of culture, heritage and identity particularly manifest in areas where Nationalists and Unionists live in close proximity to each other. Whether intended or not, these expressions of culture are often perceived as markers of territory.*

There is and always has been an element of intended antagonism in cultural expression, whether in territory marking, triumphalism or blatant threat to 'the other'. Why else would the government establish a Commission on this?

Reading the sections that refer to paramilitarism, the Commissioners' apprehension is palpable. The interconnections between paramilitary, community and political leaders and activists, referred to in 4.14, is worded tangentially and almost with a sense of trepidation.

> *4.14 It is striking that some 25 years after the Mitchell Principles, our society is still faced with the challenge of providing communities with safety and confidence, and of removing paramilitarism. The Commission's view is that this challenge, and the challenges associated with public expressions of cultural identity, are in some cases closely connected. The rule of law and a culture of lawfulness, as described by the IMC in 2006, should underpin our society.*

It is difficult to find meaning in this oxymoron.

The section on Language, Culture and Heritage is indicative of the entire report – avoiding reference to the fact that the DUP refusal to introduce the agreed Irish Language Act was pivotal to the fall of Stormont in 2017. As McBride (2019) notes the Irish language was a key issue on which the DUP was uncompromising. Indeed, in the middle of the political crisis over the Renewable Heat Incentive (RHI) scandal, as Stormont was on the verge of collapse and just days before Christmas 2016, it was a diversionary tactic.

> *Communities Minister Paul Givan axed a £55,000 bursary scheme Líofa, which provided small grants for those from disadvantaged backgrounds who wanted to learn the Irish language. A message conveying the news said it was due to 'efficiency savings' and added 'Happy Christmas and a happy new year'. In Stormont terms it was an inconsequential sum of money and the DUP's lack of enthusiasm for the Irish language was well known. ... Givan- who after an outcry reinstated the fund, but too late to undo the political damage – insisted that the row had been unintentional rather than a cynical attempt to take the focus off RHI. (McBride, 2019: 255)*

The Stormont government collapsed in January 2017 when Martin McGuinness resigned. While the FICT report asserts that the diversity and complexity of culture and tradition ... defies placing people and whole sections of our community in boxes marked 'Orange' and 'Green' the entire future of government in Northern Ireland rested on just such political 'boxes'.

> In McGuinness's resignation letter he had not just demanded that Foster step aside over RHI but had also revived a list of mostly forgotten Sinn Féin demands, including an insistence that there should be an Irish language act. At the launch of the DUP campaign Foster used a phrase which some saw as a gaffe but which may well have been a deliberate attempt to take the focus off RHI. Asked ... if she would agree to Irish language legislation, Foster visibly bristled and said to loud cheers from her candidates: 'I will never accede to an Irish language act ... if you feed a crocodile it will keep coming back and looking for more.' Sinn Féin were delighted at the remark. Hours later, Gerry Adams beamed as he dismissed Foster's animalistic analogy, simply saying 'see you later alligator'. (McBride, 2019: 270)

Writing in 2018, Rowan recorded a conversation in which he was told about *the NIO* (Northern Ireland Office) *fudge* on the Irish language act.

> The NIO official Sir Johnathan Stephens is credited with the formula or fix of trying to advance the Irish language issue alongside two other pieces of legislation – the Ulster Scots and 'Respecting Languages and Culture'. I am told this was first rejected by Sinn Féin in the autumn of 2017 and then accepted. That had not been expected, and then, according to a talks' insider, there was 'consternation' and 'shock' within the DUP. The ball was back in their court. (Rowan, 2021: 130)

It is predictable that the FICT Commission failed to reach consensus on enacting Irish language legislation along the lines of the Welsh Language Act. The 'NIO fudge' of 2018 did *spare the blushes of the DUP. There was not an Irish Language Act but there was an Irish Language Act, except that it was called something else.* (Rowan, 2021: 179). However, by the end of 2021 the Act had still not appeared – and as the May 2022 Assembly election approached the Secretary of State had still not taken this promised legislation forward in Westminster. So it is also predictable that the FICT recommendations include *that the NI Executive recognises the shared heritage of British, Irish and Ulster-Scots within our society,* that these *should command equal respect in our society,* that *public bodies be supportive and generous* and *that the NI Executive, political parties and civil society consider how to increase positive attitudes.* Echoing this, platitudes about education (which has signally failed to make significant difference to sectarian hostilities) the report continues, *education should be central to promoting mutual understanding and respect in our society around cultural diversity.* The intransigence on Irish language of a by-now electorally threatened DUP sits uncomfortably with 'respect' for language and culture.

A viable method of evaluating future trends and progress could have been proposed but the report affirms *the special place of the Irish language and Ulster-Scots language, culture and heritage be resourced appropriately and that this should be audited on the basis of Equity, Diversity and Interdependence.* It is a disappointment that the Commission could not find persons with the expertise or capacity to provide an adequate evaluation instrument – although, since the government has not done so, that was perhaps to be expected.

## Displays of flags on lamposts

Government and the public sector in Northern made attempts at managing division and hostility around displays of flags, emblems and symbolism throughout the twenty-first century – although the two largest parties, SF and DUP, have consistently shown ambivalence, if not electorally motivated resistance to such change. Attempts at policing and introducing protocols on displays of flags proved ineffective. Symbols and 'identity' were and remained no less contentious than in previous years, and, as the FICT report added *the 2005 [flags] Protocol has not been effective* and *statutory organisations faced particular challenges in delivering their obligations* while it bemoaned the lack of *consistent partnership working between agencies.*

The fact that local Councils were not part of the 2005 Flags Protocol was an unfortunate repetition of the Flags Regulations (Northern Ireland) Order (2000) which failed to include regulations on flying the Union flag on local government buildings. An old chestnut, in the proposal of a civic flag, re-emerged. *This would not be a regional flag, but rather a civic*

*flag that would be designed to be representative of the diversity of our society,*
*including our new communities.*

The 'Challenges' are bluntly and succinctly stated:

> *12.23 The various political positions in relation to this issue contain no meeting point.*
> *However, a range of suggestions and options were explored by the Commission in an*
> *effort to identify potential areas for future discussion and negotiation on this issue.*

For all the talk of getting 'beyond the two traditions' thinking, and despite
including political representatives other than the two largest parties, the
FICT report is forged in the spirit and language of two opposing sides –
Orange and Green, Protestant and Catholic, Unionist and Republican.
Therefore reaching consensus could never have been possible. At best the
results and recommendations are anodyne and avoid decisive recommen-
dation, presumably on the understanding that there would not be any
action taken. It is a sad reflection on our governance that lengthy and
expensive Commissions cannot even get past 'Challenges that remain'.
There are other discussions and details about 'remaining challenges' in
the Commission's report. However, for fear the reader may close the book
at this point, discussion will pass on.

## Conclusions

Flags, emblems, identity and culture can all be abused and exploited but
there is abundant law on equality and human rights, and in the substance
of the Belfast Agreement which allow citizens to choose identity, citizenship and to legally express their culture. The very idea that all these
should, or even could be lumped together is little more than groupthink
that fails to tidy up a messy narrative. If anything, it increases confusion
around these phenomena.

Whatever the agreements, negotiations, renegotiations and government policy intended to stabilise the Northern Ireland peace process,
the FICT report ruminations on symbolism were neither persuasive nor

sufficiently authoritative to produce greater social cohesion, sharing or integration. The inability to make any progress on flags, identity, culture and identity – and the continued absence of Irish language legislation until late May 2022 – were indicators of intransigence and an unfortunately predictable outcome. However, in 2022 these issues remained as 'identity' took its place at the epicentre of the Unionist narrative on the Northern Ireland Protocol.

The final shreds of credibility in the New Decade New Approach disappeared, as this agreement, its policy and agenda evaporated with the Executive in early 2022 – just weeks before crucial elections that would see a change in power relations and the party claiming the post of First Minister at Stormont.

CHAPTER 7

# The legacy

This chapter cannot do justice to the complex and painful reality of the legacy of the Northern Ireland conflict. Over 3,700 people were killed, an estimated 40,000 people were significantly injured, some of them very seriously (Daly, 1999) and many more left traumatised, bereaved and unable to deal with the horrors they witnessed. Families were bereft, and left with grief, anger and nowhere to turn; there were virtually no counselling services during the years of conflict. Emergency service workers – police, ambulance and hospital staff – were caught up in the literal stench of death and carnage and expected to simply return to work later, 'as normal'.

Over three decades, the population became numbed by the daily television pictures of death and destruction – so people stopped remembering the last atrocity as the next gruesome story stole the headlines. Republican and Loyalist paramilitaries vied to outdo each other in what was often no more than sectarian murder. The IRA waged a bombing campaign, destroying lives and livelihoods. The Loyalist UVF and UDA murdered Catholics or those mistakenly perceived to be Catholic. They all targeted 'the other side' including some security personnel in organised murders. Intimidation of workers was so widespread that the trade union movement set up an anti-intimidation unit, Counteract. As a life-time trade unionist and Northern Ireland Officer of the Irish Congress of Trade Unions said;

> *A union official from Newry rang because his men were being threatened – if they collected the bins from the police station the IRA threatened violence – if they didn't the UVF had warned 'collect or else!'. That was what it was like. (Goldie, 2021: 8)*

Workers had the vehicles hijacked – often told to drive them with bombs to a designated target. Taxi drivers were shot. Businesses threatened and some business leaders murdered for supplying goods or services the police or army. Members of the police and judiciary were particularly targeted by the IRA. During these years there was sectarian intimidation in housing – both privately and publicly owned – with de facto evictions that increasingly segregated the population. As security tightened around Belfast and other towns and cities, interfaces were erected – some of them to prevent easy access for vehicles carrying bombs. So, this discussion cannot do justice to the lived experience of the legacy that many people still live through. Bew and Gillespie's *Northern Ireland: A Chronology of the Troubles 1968-1999* details the landmark events and death toll of these years. The continuous IRA bombing campaign claimed many lives and left a vast number injured. This, and the results of Loyalist terrorism, continued to poison politics and attempts at negotiating peace.

Forgotten victims and survivors have spoken and had their stories told, in numerous fora, including the Wave Trauma Centre (wavetraumacentre. org.uk) but official recognition has been slow to come, snatched from depths of Byzantine legalistic procedure and political resistance, and too late for those who did not live to see the day. These people, and the all-too-human suffering and degradation they have endured, are not 'collateral damage'. If anything their leadership is the spring of hope for a leap across the fault lines of the peace process.

Aside from the lack of treatment for chronic pain and the absence of significant counselling services until the twenty-first century, those survivors who made it as far as a court hearing for compensation were badly mistreated. Dr Roger Parke was a surgeon and consultant in rehabilitation at Musgrave Park Hospital in Belfast, in the regional unit where the most seriously injured received treatment over the decades of conflict; and since.

> Some of the injured whom we interviewed reported that, without prior information or notice, they had been forced to strip and show their injuries, scars, and visible signs of disability at the High Court. Dr Parke was involved in giving evidence on behalf of many of his patients and concurred with this:
>
> I can verify that that did happen. For many years the case was heard in front of a jury and it was the jury's job – advised by the judge – to decide on the matter of compensation, which was not a good system. And that was changed I think some time in the 90's. I've been present when the litigant has been so asked ... to show the injured leg – to take off the prosthesis on occasions in the court in front of the jury – and I would absolutely

*agree that that was not a good idea. After I had experienced that two or three times, I personally would have advised ... that, if the case did come to Court, there might be this requirement by the judge. So at least I was able to prior warn the patient. If that was not acceptable to the patient, I think that could have been made known to the court via the solicitor. ... More recently we would have retired to the judge's quarters to do that. ... To do that was generally in the plaintiff's interests. (Deiana and Goldie, 2012: 11-12)*

The peace agreement saw a dramatic reduction in violence. However, it did not deal with the legacy and this has been a major obstacle to once hoped for reconciliation. For the seriously injured the 'Troubles pension' would take half a century to appear. For those seeking recognition and redress for state violence in Northern Ireland it would be a fifty-year battle.

In particular, the search for 'truth and justice' has been contested and frustrated because many Unionists could not accept the early release of (mainly Republican) political prisoners. Equally challenging was the fact that many Nationalists and Republicans believed the police and army had colluded with Loyalist paramilitaries in the 'dirty war', and the attendants state obfuscation, 'missing' official records and denial of collusion – now extensively evidenced and documented by Smith (2022).

Although sectarian murders were committed by all paramilitary factions, there is increasing credibility in claims of collusion between loyalist paramilitary groups and the Northern Ireland police, Special Branch and Intelligence, endorsed by the Police Ombudsman's in 2021 and 2022 who spoke of *collusive behaviours* by the (then) Royal Ulster Constabulary (Morrison, 2022a). Echoes of the past reverberate to this day – with press reports in 2022 that *Police handed gun used in Belfast bookies massacre to loyalist terrorist* (Hutton, 2022). This raises questions of the state, which in theory is held to a higher ethical and legal standard than paramilitary and illegal forces. Smith (2022) details the research conducted by the Pat Finucane Centre into collusion, secreted documents and the military response to the IRA – although it's somewhat crude theory is that this is entirely due to Colonialism.

The longest-running battle for truth and justice can be seen in high-profile cases concerning the conduct of British security forces during the conflict such as Bloody Sunday, the Hooded Men and the Ballymurphy massacre. The truth of these events has taken half a century to verify and still 'justice' has not been found. Although these cases involve relatively small numbers of people, they have fuelled deep and bitter distrust of the UK government and its state apparatus ever since.

## 50 Years' wait for truth – and still no justice

It is half a century since events like the 'hooded men', the Ballymurphy massacre and Bloody Sunday happened. Investigations and inquiries took place, and there were even public apologies, but even with truth established there has been no justice in the courts.

Internment without trial was introduced in Northern Ireland in August 1971 and used almost exclusively to imprison Catholic, Nationalist and or Republican men who were suspected of attacks on members of the British army and the Northern Ireland state apparatus – 'suspicion' often being seriously misplaced. Demonstrations and rioting broke out in West Belfast in Ballymurphy. The army response was brutal and ten people died that day. Fifty years later McClements (2021a) reported on the Coroner's Inquest into the killing of *at least nine of the ten* people in Ballymurphy after the anti-internment violence.

As with other cases where British army personnel killed citizens in the UK and further afield, there were official and public allegations as to the 'guilt' or paramilitary membership of the victims, so families had long campaigned to clear their loved ones' names. In the Ballymurphy Inquest the Coroner ruled that *all were 'entirely innocent'* and spoke of the *'abject failure' to investigate at the time*. The determination undermined the UK government claim that after fifty years cases could not be adjudicated.

McClements (2021b) also reported on the Hooded Men.

*The 14 individuals known as the Hooded Men were arrested and interned without trial by the British army in 1971 and subjected to a series of controversial interrogation tactics known as the 'Five Techniques'. These included hooding and being forced to stand in the 'stress position', to listen to white noise, and being deprived of sleep, food and water.*

> *Some of the Hooded Men reported being thrown from helicopters near the ground which they had been told were hundreds of feet in the air.*

The UK Supreme Court upheld the Northern Ireland Court of Appeal ruling that there was sufficient evidence to warrant reinvestigating the case, and that the Police service of Northern Ireland (PSNI) decision in October 2014 was *'seriously flawed'*.

> *The judges also concluded the 'deplorable' treatment to which the Hooded Men were subjected would be 'characterised as torture by today's standards' and that it was 'administered as a matter of deliberate policy by the law enforcemenet agencies of the state'.*

The fact that investigation was still required after fifty years did not diminish the truth of the Supreme Court ruling. The fact that this coincided with the announcement of a planned 'amnesty' by UK legislation on a statute of limitations on all conflict-related murders and crimes demonstrates how peace-building is hampered by state and political interests – and gives the lie to the notion that it is a matter of local community relations.

The killing of thirteen people, and a fourteenth who died from his injuries, by the Parachute Regiment of the British army in Derry in 1972 is known as Bloody Sunday. After two Public Inquiries, an unreserved apology from the British Prime Minister, David Cameron for the atrocity, and rescinding the false accusations made in the Widgery Inquiry about these innocent people, there has been not a single court case for murder. In 2022 the Conservative government declared plans for an amnesty for all conflict-related murders – a move that united every political party in Northern Ireland, and the Irish government in their opposition.

Writing on Bloody Sunday, fifty years on Fintan O'Toole (2022) highlights the emblematic nature of a massacre that intensified the conflict. In protest at the introduction of internment without trial and a ban on all marches and demonstrations, the civil rights movement defied the prohibition on marching – and the army was made ready to respond robustly. *The first Bloody Sunday, the real one, was a moral and human disaster. The second one, the British Establishment's fictionalised and slanderous version, was a political disaster.* He reports the murderous intent on the part of the

1st Parachute Regiment and their commanding officer as they killed those civil rights marchers who had returned to the Bogside in order to avoid confrontation and rioting. *This meant that the whole supposed justification for the operation – the arrest of rioters – had evaporated.*

Despite the fact that the power of the Unionist state would later be undermined by Direct rule, Bloody Sunday served the purposes of those who wanted to go far beyond peaceful civil disobedience – *the combination of atrocity and cover-up, of crude savagery and suave cynicism in the Bloody Sunday story, gave credence to a counter-narrative of war to the death.* (O'Toole, 2022)

The Bloody Sunday commemoration in 2022 attracted thousands, including leading Irish and Northern Irish politicians, as well as mass media, although, as the political temperature in Stormont rose and May 2022 elections loomed, no Unionist politician attended. Indeed, as if there was need of a reminder of the exploitation of flags and emblems, counter demonstration from 'Unionist Derry' was manifest in the flying of the Parachute Regimental flag on the outskirts of the city.

> *Family members of those killed have talked about the pain the flying of these flags causes them. Politicians, including some unionists, and even the Parachute Regiment itself have called it 'unacceptable'. The flag flies because there are some in the unionist community who want to show that not everybody is mourning the dead of Bloody Sunday as its 50th anniversary is marked in Derry this weekend. It is a show of disrespect. (McKay, 2022)*

*The Belfast Telegraph headlined on 31 January 2022, solemn day: Thousands remember lives lost ... and voice their opposition to a proposed Troubles amnesty. Morris, in her opinion column said, We must remember our past for fear of repeating it. Bloody Sunday was one of the darkest days of the Troubles* (Morris, 2022b). This event triggered the most violent year of the conflict – with the greatest number of civilian and military deaths, the suspension of the Stormont government with Direct Rule from Westminster, the introduction of the Diplock courts – a non-jury system of trial. The fiftieth anniversary was a day of united remembrance across the island of Ireland, politically, with one notable exception – Unionists.

> For all the talk of reconciliation, it was evident much remains to be done. Despite the multi-denominational nature of the service – which included contributions from the Jewish and Muslim communities as well as the Protestant denominations- there were no unionist politicians present. (McClements, 2022)

Other instances of unjustified army shootings of innocent civilians have come to light with cases reaching the Coroner's court 30–50 years later. The prospect of these verdicts leading to criminal or civil action drove the Conservative government to announce plans for an amnesty – and specifically to provide immunity for service veterans.

## Amnesty

The Conservative government had stood over the findings of the Saville Inquiry – exonerating all those killed by Paratroopers in Derry on Bloody Sunday – with an unreserved apology. However, as moves to prosecute veteran soldiers got underway reaction in England was not conciliatory and a groundswell of public and political support for an amnesty for veterans gathered pace. By July 2021 Secretary of State for Northern Ireland, Brandon Lewis announced that there was to be a ban on all conflict-related prosecutions by introducing a statute of limitations. The United Nations expressed *serious concern* about this and said this would constitute *a de facto amnesty and blanket impunity* (Burns, 2021). This development would prevent the Police Service of Northern Ireland (PSNI) and Police Ombudsman from investigating legacy cases and prevent judicial progress in both criminal and civil cases. The UN was also concerned that *this would effectively also preclude colonial inquests and victims' claims in civil courts.*

McClements (2021) reported on the challenge to the determination to collapse the criminal case against soldier F for Bloody Sunday murders – seen very differently on either side of the Irish sea. This was quickly followed by the announcement of an amnesty preventing further attempts for justice through the courts.

This was a crude attempt to appease the English electorate and military interests in halting criminal cases where criteria for a criminal prosecution had been met, and in the case of soldier F whose identity had been kept secret in the Saville Inquiry. The Secretary of State justified the move as a way of promoting reconciliation and 'drawing a line' under legacy cases. This did not convince the UN, any political party, any of the victims groups in Northern Ireland, or the trade unions. It drew criticism from Taoiseach Michael Martin (Staunton 2021) and distressed many survivors and victims. Moriarty (2021) noted, *Britain's stance brings more anguish to victims* and quoted the spokesman for the 10 killed by Paratroopers in Ballymurphy in 1971 saying the British government's proposals were *a cynical attempt ... to bring in an amnesty and a plan to bury its war crimes.*

The Stormont Assembly was recalled during the 12th July holiday fortnight to hold a meeting with Lewis, which was described as *robust*, and the proposal was universally condemned. McKay (2021b) was unequivocal in her view that the *bad faith is shameless. Brandon Lewis claimed everyone knew the current system for dealing with the past 'is not working for anyone'. But the reason it was not working was because there was no system.* This echoes decades of evidence that no-one in Northern Ireland ever wanted unilateral amnesty for past conflict-related murders and crimes – whoever was responsible.

Emerson (2021) said astutely, *the North has had a de facto amnesty for a generation* and a *feature of Troubles amnesties is strenuous denial that they are amnesties* – going on to cite a twenty-year litany of legal determinations on pardons, immunity and impunity agreed since 2002.

While the legacy of the conflict is widespread – personally, physically, emotionally, socially and economically – it is fundamentally a political matter. The planned amnesty only heightens the sense of hurt and injustice felt across the generations. The horrendous IRA bombings and murders have scarred the Unionist population in particular – although both civilian and security person casualties were Catholic as well as Protestant. Indeed, Bloody Sunday is not the only event that broke any trust in the British government and its state apparatus.

At the time of writing the British government had reviewed the blanket amnesty with the default of perpetrators escaping prosecution by providing evidence to a proposed truth-and-reconciliation body. However, it was still tinkering with the precise terms of the amnesty and legislation to enact this.

## Legacy issues: survivors and victims

The legacy of the conflict is told in gruesome detail in the list of 3,636 deaths in thirty years of war in *Lost Lives* (Kelters et al., 1999). The estimate is now over 3,700 deaths and over 40,000 injured. Many were left with life-changing psychological as well as physical damage. Survivors and their families have had to live with the traumatic and painful consequences – not some abstract 'legacy' – for decades. They are on the wrong side of any 'drawing the line' and are, at best, forgotten as others 'move on'.

Legacy issues, concerning victims and survivors, have always been divisive for almost all groups, and their political allies siding along ethno-political lines – with a notable exception of those in the Wave Trauma Centre. Some declared themselves 'Innocent victims' denying this to any who had been republican combatants – ignoring the occasional overlap between police and security force veterans and Loyalist paramilitary members. Others were vociferously Republican. In all this wrangling, any proposals for a 'Troubles pension' were overshadowed and then lost. Even granting the objective grievances expressed by the various parties, the result was a stand-off where nobody received recognition, support or redress for their pain, loss and injury. Wave Trauma Centre is inclusive, cross-community and proactive in empowering victims and survivors – among whom were the people who eventually won compensation and a pension.

The long-awaited pension scheme was due to open in May 2020, with powers to pay an annual amount of between £2,000 and £10,000. However, the Stormont Executive would not agree to pay for this, looking to the Treasury in London to foot the bill. The two largest political parties argued over who should be entitled to receive payment – so the scheme was *mired in controversy and delay, and was subject to several legal challenges brought by the victims* (McClements and Erwin, 2021). Although the Northern Ireland Court of Appeal ruled in favour of the victims and gave the Executive four weeks to comply, in February, it took until April and a High Court appearance for the Executive Office to give an undertaking to do that. The scheme did not open until 31 August 2021, a full thirteen years after the campaign began. Several of those who had led the collective campaign had already died.

The history of 'dealing with the past' is a sorry tale of apparently worthy attempts to accommodate the views of 'the two traditions'. It is marked by the government policy of *Cohesion Sharing and Integration* which went to consultation in October 2010 and was adopted – although only in the short term – which made no mention of victims and survivors (Potter, 2010). The following decade saw discussions, conferences, reports and public events which did little to address the needs of the seriously injured, falsely accused, survivors and victims of the conflict. Politicians and interest groups indulged in accusation and counter-accusation showing neither a vision for the future nor leadership in peace-building.

The leadership shown in the campaign for the seriously injured stands out in marked contrast to the prevarication and contestation around definitions of 'victim' and inaction for most of this century. It also reflects poorly on the drive to suppress the truth and all prospects of justice for victims' families and survivors of bombing, hijacking and targeted shootings.

Analysis of the campaign leadership follows a transcript of an interview with Dr Paul Gallagher, one of the seriously injured group at Wave. I met Paul Gallagher to hear his experience of the legacy of the conflict from the perspective of victims and survivors, and to get an insider's view of the long road to recognition and some compensation in the 'Troubles pension'. His experience includes being chair of VAST, the Victims and Survivors Trust that supports people affected by the conflict from all backgrounds. His doctoral thesis addresses both the history and the context of the WAVE Injured group (Gallagher, 2021).

PAUL:   I've lived on the interface all my life and know what it's like and been attacked by the other side – so it's all connected.

I joined the [Seriously Injured] group around the start of 2010. It'd been going [to Wave] since August 2008 but had been going since 2000. It kept collapsing for various reasons. Wave started in 1991, just for widows and then it opened up to widowers, and then children and then the injured people – and they had to keep changing their constitution. Over the years there weren't that many injured people coming along for support services – it was mostly bereaved people. There was the women's, the men's and the disappeared group.

Doing my research I came across a letter they sent out saying they wanted a forum for the seriously injured. There were meetings, agendas set and discussions – 'what do we need?' This was just after the Good Friday Agreement – things were being set up like Bloomfield, the Memorial Fund and so on.

People said we want more than this we were treated badly in the past. Compensation was disgraceful, based on your earnings. Most people weren't earning much, especially in the early days and it was young men a lot of the time. There was also a sense that when you went to the courts for your compensation claim it was very adversarial. People were brought into a small room, sat on a chair, stripped down to their underwear and had barristers poring over their wounds, and stuff like that. It was really degrading. A lot of people just settled. Women were told, 'You don't need to claim. You can go out, meet somebody else and get married again. You're a good looking girl' – things like that.

ROZ: Yes, a consultant at Musgrave Hospital, Roger Parks, confirmed that.

PAIL: They were treated like a piece of meat – weren't even talked to. They were just pored over, and barristers spoke over their heads. People just wanted to get out of there. There was also the fact that it [compensation] was based on their life expectancy. There's one of the members of the group who was paralysed when she was 17 years of age and was told she wouldn't live past her 33rd birthday and she is in her 60s now. So those were the sorts of attitudes then.

The other main grievance was that what was firing up people was that they couldn't get back to work. Most people had been working away then this happened and ruined their lives but back in the early days there was no disability discrimination legislation. People were just left on the scrap heap. Some, who were teachers in the past, or in insurance, asked if there was any chance to come back. The answer was, 'No we can't accommodate you.' So all this discrimination keep people down and kept them back.

The sense was, 'Okay the Memorial Fund was set up but it's very piecemeal.' You got offered white goods – you got offered a washing machine or a TV.

ROZ:     That was really patronising.

PAUL:    It was – it was more a charity. The Fund was set up as a charity, and the people in it were treating it like charity. One of the things that really incensed a colleague [in the Seriously Injured group] around that time, 2000-2001, was a letter sent out. There must have been an underspend or something – so a Christmas card was sent out with a cheque in it for £50. It was like 'Happy Christmas from the Memorial Fund, here's £50'. She ended up phoning Stormont and saying, 'Send somebody up here to take this cheque away. I don't want this in my house.' That really incensed her and she said she nearly had a breakdown as well. She was injured in the early 70s but all this coming up, and the expectation that the Agreement would bring something like a peace dividend for victims, and then nothing happened apart from a bit of charity. I remember getting it but I was young at the time – I was injured at the end of the Troubles in '94. For somebody who went through the whole Troubles injured in the early 70s, losing their home – because they would have got compensation in the early days but then they couldn't afford rates and had to sell their home. And you weren't able to claim benefits at the time because you had compensation. Once that went you were on benefits.

ROZ: So, there was no benefit on balance – financially? What you got was taken off benefits.

PAUL: When you got compensation that was clawed back from any benefits you were getting before the claim – and then you had to live off that as your income.

So when people started coming along to Wave, then, this was the nucleus of what later became the campaign for recognition – but there was only a small handful. The people there at the time had other life-issues going on. One had to leave to look after her mother who had Alzheimer's and others were a bit flakey, so it didn't really sustain itself. It died a death. In 2005 it got another go. One of the outreach workers was seconded but it really needed a project worker and didn't get the impetus to go anywhere. Some of the people asked Alan McBride, a coordinator in Wave at the time, if he'd help out. Wave seconded him to look after the group, have monthly meetings and have a more hands-on feel about it. He had a campaigning head on – sent out letters, organised the monthly meetings, had a bit more camaraderie so people were there to enjoy themselves. The group started to build up a bit of momentum.

This was around 2008-2009 in the middle of the Eames-Bradley Consultation process. They were invited to Wave and met the injured group, who told them their concerns and grievances, saying, 'We want you to do something about this in the report.' And they fully expected to be recognised in the report. When the report came out in January 2009, there were other things that brought it down, but there was nothing there for the injured. Denis Bradley is on record as saying that he did take cognisance of the injured but when you go through it what they say is that the injured really will be looked after by the newly set up Commission for Victims and Survivors – the needs of the injured. But this was only being set up and people wanted something more concrete – it'd probably take about three years before they would even come up with a report – which it was. It wasn't until 2012 that they had their comprehensive needs review. So there was a sense that 'there's nothing in this for us'. The recognition payment was going to be given out to the bereaved families of those who were killed – that brought the whole thing down – but there was nothing there for the injured. It was like 'what happened?' 'What about us?'

That really spurred us into action – we were not recognised by this recognition payment. In those months letters were written to Eames Bradley asking what happened there? We'd a sense that we needed to start a campaign here. We went away for a weekend retreat in a hotel – minutes were drawn up and a plan drawn up on what we were going to do. A petition was one of the things – and getting a proper report done on the needs of the injured with academic research. Marie Breen Smyth was seconded in then. So that was one channel – the petition was the other channel.

There were thirty people at that stage in the injured group going around Northern Ireland – all the different towns and cities and villages – standing on street corners collecting signatures asking for recognition. Within a year or so we ended up getting 10,000 signatures. It was slow to start with. We tried to get signatures from family and friends but it was not enough. We had to go out on the streets in the freezing cold asking people to sign. They'd be looking at you – what do you mean? Some were indifferent. Some were hostile and some were very helpful. It sort of gave us an idea of what was coming down the road when we were speaking to politicians. People were asking questions and we knew we'd have to answer these questions.

We didn't really know what we wanted. It was just that we had no recognition. We wanted recognition and we thought if we go out to the public that will happen – the public say we need recognition. So the petition was launched on the same day when the Marie Breen Smyth report was done [in 2012].

We did the whole bit. The TV cameras were there and photo-journalists. We pushed the wheelchairs up the hill to Stormont, past Carson's statue – the symbolism there. And big posters for the campaign for recognition and all that. The media were there doing interviews. It gave a sense that people were interested and the media were there. Wave were great at putting out press releases for us. People were getting media training as well. There was a sense then – yes, it's going somewhere.

Within a few weeks we went up to Stormont, with the report, and started talking to politicians – saying, 'You've got the petition, now here's what we're after.' That was 2012. The [Breen Smyth] report has twenty-one recommendations and one of them was this notion of a pension for the injured. They weren't able to work and build up a pension or build up savings. They were just left on benefits and moved onto the state pension. It just wasn't enough to survive on. And also something for their carers. So, we took this pension idea – we think it's doable and hopefully they will too.

There was a dilemma in this in that we ended up causing a split in the group and nearly brought the group down. The decision was made to have this pension for people with serious physical injury. That was what the report was about – the seriously injured. And the reason for that was the remit for the research – that had to be tight because of the funding criteria. The cost of doing a massive study across the whole of Northern Ireland to take in psychological injury was prohibitive.

So the sense was, this is a foot in the door. If they can't look after the limbless, the blind and all that, they're not going to look after the ones with psychological injuries. Going by some of the figures in the memorial fund moving into the victim's service it was said to be between 500 and 1,000 people with serious physical injuries. That's doable. They can't argue against that – you're talking about the most seriously injured and vulnerable as well. We thought this could open the door – and once we've set a precedent we'll come in with the rest of them – the ones with psychological injuries.

There were people in the group in wheelchairs – they were to be the spearhead, the vanguard but a lot of the people in the group with psychological injuries felt they were being left behind – saying, 'You'll forget about us and we'll not get anything.' A lot of the ones with psychological injuries left the group and it was just left with the ones with physical injuries.

ROZ: That must have been a heartbreaking and difficult but necessary political and practical decision to make at that time.

PAUL: Yes, it was.

Even with the group of 30 you couldn't bring the whole lot up. Whenever we first went up to Stormont lobbying, some of them (politicians) said this is great we'll be able to do this but they said what exactly do you want? Come back to us with more concrete figures – instead of them doing the research.

So we said, okay we will. There was a trainee barrister who worked in the welfare unit (at Wave) and he came up with a report and a template of what this would look like – how it would be assessed, who it would be for, the costings and all of that. We handed it over and said, 'There you go there's the plan.' The Victim's Commission were handed the same plan and they did their own report – which was basically a copy and paste job of what we'd taken to Stormont. That was great – it was recognition that this was a good plan.

That took about eight months to get done – and it was 2013 then. It was brought back up to Stormont then – The Victims' Commission's plan. It was brought to McGuinness and Robinson at the time and they were like, 'Yeah this is good work – this is doable.' Now the elephant in the room then – which we'd always known – was, 'What about the "terrorists" who blew themselves up? Do they get this – the victim perpetrators – those injured by their own hand?'

A lot of this was done behind the scenes but once it got out we knew it would poison the whole thing.

ROZ:     Was this resistance only from the DUP?

PAUL:    The Ulster Unionists knew it but they weren't at the fore-front (of opposition). There were things said like, 'If I go for this there's going to be a picture in the media or in the next DUP or TUV campaign sheet of handing a cheque to Sean Kelly, the Shankill bomber.'

So there was that recognition (of this problem) but we were trying to find our way through it. The Shinners were totally adamant that everybody should get it. The DUP were saying, 'No we can't do this.' Yet there was still a sense that they could find a way. McGuinness and Robinson were still on okay terms but the well was being poisoned outside as well. You had the Special Advisers Bill, the Flags Protest. The Special Advisers Bill really muddied the waters between Sinn Fein and the DUP. Then there was the Maze-Longkesh thing [a 'museum to terrorism' according to Loyalists and memorial of the conflict to others] and it became poisoned too. You had victims groups coming together with politi-cians and the Orange Order and police widows – and all these groups were coming together to say, 'No this can't happen.' So all these victims' groups were coming in and upsetting the modus vivendi of McGuinness and Robinson. It could have got through.

Yes, we knew – we were in meetings with McGuinness going 'I want to be able to do this for you'. Robinson was the same – 'We need to find a way.' It ended up they couldn't find a way but ... they got the Victims' Commission to do a further piece of research. They spent 50 thousand pounds on this piece of research. There were actuaries, solicitors, everybody else involved in it and this big consultation. This paper projected costs down the line. We could have done it. Anybody could have done it.

To be fair they weren't kicking the can down the road. We were moving at that time too. There was a chance meeting on the Conference circuit. We met a journalist and told him what we were doing. In two days there was a headline on the front of the *Belfast Telegraph*, 'Terrorists may get £150 a week pension' – and [a picture of] a guy with an Armalite and a balaclava on the front page. That just completely poisoned the well. That was July 2014. So the DUP had to come out and say, 'No, we're definitely not going to do this – we're not giving a pension to terrorists. We're going to bring through our own private member's bill.' So the brief was given to Pengelly. She wasn't a politician then. She was Robinson's SPAD, and had been for years.

There was a public consultation which we got a lot of people to go to, but it was framed in ways that the answer they were going to get was predetermined – do you want terrorists to get a pension? I remember at [DUP] party Conference in November that year and Robinson saying they were going to bring through this special pension for the poor innocent victims – 'but we will NOT give this to any terrorists!' A big cheer went up from the crowd.

The private member's bill never really got anywhere – they kept coming back to us and saying what do you think about this and that and we're saying okay, that's fine but it's a private member's bill. It has to come up through the Executive – through the (Stormont) Assembly and you're going to have to get the SDLP on your side. And they were hit badly with the SPADs bill a couple of years before, when they were forced to abstain to let it go through – and they would have had to do the same sort of thing again.

We tried to get different ones in the SDLP and the Ulster Unionists on side – behind the scenes – and said, 'Can this be doable?' It had to go in before the end of the year because the next year was an Assembly election. So it didn't happen and we felt really badly let down. Going into 2016 there was going to another election.

Because that didn't happen we kept the bare bones of another bill written up. A friend of ours here, from Queen's University, Luke Moffett had been working with us for two or three years, on reparations – and he had got funding to write up his own private member's bill. ... I got him on board to help us frame it a certain way and brought him along to meetings with politicians and he was big on human rights. So we were bringing in academics and any experts out there to back us up. Luke was one of them. He brought in a professional draughtsman from Westminster – probably getting £500 a day, like top end – and they designed a bill.

Now what he had to do was design two bills – one that was all-inclusive and one with a review panel. The review panel would look at the hard cases. The name review panel came from the special advisers' bill. There's a review panel tied into the back of that. There are a couple of caveats in that. If you want to be a special adviser and you've done time you have to show contrition. It doesn't exactly say you have to put on sackcloth and ashes and beg for forgiveness but it does say you have to help the police with any enquiries and tell them anything you know. It also says you have to approach the family of the person you harmed and ask for their go-ahead.

When you consider some of the evidence given by the person who brought the bill forward – that even hearing the name of the terrorist who killed her sister traumatised her even hearing the perpetrator's name again. The fact that they were demanding that somebody goes and knocks on the door of their victim, and says, 'Will you forgive me so I can get a job?' would be traumatising in itself. This is written into law. So we were looking at this and saying, 'It's not going to be like that.' This was going to be mainly republicans and loyalists who'd been involved – not the army. Only four of them had ever been convicted of any crime. They'd get a pass through. It was only non-state actors who were being discriminated against.

Within the injured group itself we had to talk these things out and people were coming from different backgrounds. This was a group that was cross-community, injured by all actors. So we had to decide, as a group, what if we get asked this question, what do we say? We chose to be agnostic about it – saying, 'It's not our question to answer it is a political question to be answered. You shouldn't be asking us – we're not there to judge. We have our opinions but why should we tell you in public?' As we couldn't all agree we had to come to a compromise in the group.

The fact is that we're a cross-community group where you have to come to these sorts of compromises. With single identity groups I'm not saying there is sectarianism or bigotry or whatever. I think it's down to the areas they are in, their constituent members.

ROZ:    And in these groups there is a sense of safety, identities in common – albeit exclusive but a common identity and that is part of the safety.

PAUL: Exactly, ex-police and then the other side, Relatives for Justice, the Pat Finucane Centre – and Wave was always cross-community and that was what attracted me to it – even though, at the same time, I was in another victims group in West Belfast which was exclusively Catholic from West Belfast, and I ended up chair of that group.

And there were three or four from in the Victim's Forum the injured group – because all these networks of influence were being built. There was work going on in the Victims' Commission and the Victims' Forum on the needs of victims and our guys were in the forefront of that. So, they were getting access to politicians through the Forum. Wave were getting access – were good at getting access, which is the most important thing – they can lift a phone to a politician where if I lift the phone it's, 'Who are you?' A sort of pyramid with Wave in the middle, us at the bottom and politicians at the top.

Another game-changer was people who were on the board at Wave – one of them was Denis Godfrey who joined Wave in 2013 when we were picking up. He'd been a former Director of Communications in NIO. He had contacts, his black book, and knowledge of the media and how it works. We were a cross-community group and had a good story to tell – visually – you'd stick the wheelchairs out – the visuals. You use all that (for the campaign).

Some of the guys said you had to prostitute yourself a bit for the media and that was just the way it had to be done.

ROZ: That's a lot less degrading than stripping down to underwear to claim compensation in court.

PAUL: You didn't want to be giving this sob story because you weren't a sad victim sitting in the corner but you had to give the public a picture.

ROZ: The group came across as very dignified, not begging for sympathy – just asking for your rights.

PAUL:   The rights thing you mention was an important point be-
        cause we didn't use rights language or talk of reparations – it
        was a dirty word. Robinson said, 'That's Sinn Féin speak –
        rights and reparations.' It wasn't us who did it!' I said, 'Just
        because you're paying for it doesn't mean you are accepting
        responsibility. It's just accepting responsibility for looking
        after your citizens in the aftermath.' So we had to tone down
        the rights and reparation stuff because our main aim was
        shaming them into it. It was a disgrace.

        By this stage it was 2016. Every year we went up there
        (Stormont) from 2012 on there was an election every single
        year – from 2009 right up until 2016 – whether it was
        Europe, Councils, Westminster or the Assembly there was
        always an election. They're always in election mode and can't
        do anything that'll freak the election base out. So, they were
        tied and couldn't do anything behind the scenes because that
        would get out and ruin their election.

        We were savvy enough to know and were told 'come
        back after the election and we'll maybe get it done' – and
        then there's the summer [recess], and the autumn and the
        next thing it's another election coming. It was just all the
        frustration and you were trying to keep your dignity, keep
        your patience and trying to work all sorts of moves to try
        and get everybody on board – different politicians. So when
        the DUP's private member's bill went at the end of 2015 we
        brought our bill to Alliance, SDLP and Ulster Unionists
        asking them to bring it forward with Alliance leading it.
        There were a couple of meetings and we thought that was
        going to be doable. Then RHI [Renewable Heat Incentive
        scandal] hit – that was the whole month of December and
        that was the end of that. In January Stormont went down.
        [Stormont would collapse for three years]. Funnily enough
        we were the last bit of business of that Assembly on the final
        day. We were giving evidence in the Executive Office. It was

only a skeleton crew as most were out on the election trail. Mike Nesbitt was the chair and called us up to give evidence.

This is all in Hansard. We were saying make it all inclusive, give to the guys with guns, give it to everybody – just get it through. Christopher Salford sat back and said, 'If we were to bring that through the way you are asking, we would be crucified at the polls by our political enemies. I stared at him and he stared back for about 10 seconds. Then Mike Nesbitt asked, 'Are there any other questions?' That was it. The political enemy was Jim Allister [leader of the Traditional Unionist Party] – it wasn't Sinn Féin. So that was it – Stormont came down and didn't come back up.

Before all this, RHI and so on, at the end of 2016 we held a press conference in Wave. We had written a letter to all the great and the good. So the heads of the churches, all the politicians obviously, Westminster – head of the Northern Ireland Affairs Committee – House of Lords – as many as we could get and we had Peter Hain doing a bit of work in the background. He was a good friend of Denis Godfrey right back from their days in the NIO when Hain was the Secretary of State, and had kept the friendship going over the years. Hain had asked a few questions in the House of Commons.

We had three or four shadow Secretaries of State come over to us. At that time Owen Smith became shadow Secretary of State under Corbyn. He came over to meet us and he was a good leader for us and advocate within Westminster – and was asking questions, 'What about the Wave injured group? What about this pension?' But when Stormont went down it was a game-changer for us because we'd written a letter saying these people here aren't going to do anything – this needs to become part of the Westminster agenda.

The argument was that the Stormont House Agreement had been written in 2014. We were in that. Section 28 was 'further attention should be given to bringing forward a special pension for the injured'. So we'd got ourselves on that bit of paper. The year before was Haas and O'Sullivan and we got ourselves on that as well. So, we were being recognised, the work was being done and we were in these. Yet, the government in Westminster had control of the Stormont House Agreement and they could bring it through. It wasn't a devolved matter because it had a lot of reserved, security matters and they'd had to bring it through with their legislation – we were in the Stormont House Agreement but we weren't on their legislation.

We had also met Secretaries of State – Owen Patterson, Teresa Villiers, Brokenshire. [Karen] Bradley said, 'This victims and pensions stuff is all devolved – it's nothing to do with us.' We argued that, technically yes, but all our injuries happened under Direct Rule (governing from Westminster) and you were in charge. We're as much legacy as anybody else. In fact, you're talking about bringing in investigations to do with deaths. What about us? You can't just fob us off like roads or infrastructure. We are legacy. We kept using these lines and got the media on the story to shame them into it.

When institutions went down we decided we'd have to go over and they have to take us on board because they are in charge. They said, 'It's great what you are doing but it's devolved' and we said, 'No, you are doing it now. You are in charge.'

We organised to get us all over – sixteen of us, some in wheelchairs. Owen Smith got us the invitation to get into Westminster – us traipsing up and down the halls of Westminster and in the back rooms meeting the politicians – it was great. We were lucky because there were these bills going through Westminster at the time to keep Stormont from completely collapsing – around the Northern Ireland Executive Bill and water rates and so on. All these things had to be done by the Secretary of State, who at this stage was Karen Bradley. We wanted to shame them into it. They were going, 'We just want to get Stormont up and running'. We insisted, 'You're doing it – you're in charge.' In one of these bills that came through Peter Hain had brought forward an amendment, and he'd built support in the House of Lords – old Tory grandees, Tom King and all these other top Tories, Lord Eames, Nuala O'Loan. We'd written to them. And they went, 'We can do something for these people.' Lord Duncan had to beg Hain to take the amendment off because if they had lost the vote the whole bill would be brought down – and caused a constitutional crisis here. He said, 'I promise that we'll do this for you.' The promise was made that they would bring through legislation within six months – updating the 2014 reports and so on.

I was on the forum at that stage so all this pressure was building. Still, it was this Westminster legislation they were afraid of losing, and it was Hain's intervention that did it. The Victim's Commission were slow and things were starting to peter out a bit but the year after there was another bill that had to go through Westmisnter again – to keep the Assembly from collapsing completely. They didn't want to call an election – in fact they still hadn't called an election – and the DUP were calling the shots at this stage [with a small Conservative majority in the Commons DUP support was essential] and they didn't want an election. And Brexit had sucked everything out as well – no other legislation was going through apart from a few including the Stormont bills.

So, this bill comes through and Hain puts in his amendment again. This time it was accepted and it was for a special pension for the severely injured – accepted by the government, with a couple of wee tweaks, went through the Lords and was part of the 2019 Executive Formation Act. Section 10 was the victims' pension. A lot of things were added on it – the Abortion Rights Bill, and Same-Sex Marriage amendment were added on. Those three pieces of legislation that had stalled over here for years.

Then we get into why we had to go to court. That was the summer of 2019. It was the law. We had won. So they had a consultation. In January, six months later, they brought in regulations so it was going to be from regulations rather than a whole new piece of legislation and instructed Stormont to set it up. Stormont was just back up. Julian Smyth had come in as Secretary of State at this stage – and he was one of the best Secretaries of State – and he came out and met us when the regulations were made. He'd still be in touch on Twitter and stuff like that. So the bill was brought through, but to exclude terrorists. It had the review panel that Moffett had proposed. The main exclusion was anybody injured by their own hand. The other caveat to be excluded was if you have a scheduled offence of over two and a half years – they take into consideration your age at the time, and what you have done since. At the end of the day most people should get it. It has a caveat regarding the panel is that the Secretary of State should have the final say if it is going to bring the scheme into disrepute.

All these things were brought in but it was nearly a back-door deal. But in the grand scheme of things we got more than we thought we were going to get. The Shinners were up in arms and other groups were up in arms going, 'This is an exclusionary pension – the Brits done us over again.' In many ways that's what I felt at the time, too. I'd rather have seen a fully inclusive one but I wasn't writing it and it wasn't my call. It had to be the politicians and a Tory government. It was sent back then to Stormont. The regulations stated that the First and Deputy First Minister had to nominate a department in Stormont to take this forward. They had to fund it and administer it. They did not nominate. The Shinners wouldn't nominate anyone. We had Naomi Long lined up, 'If I get asked my department will take it on.' She didn't want to take it on, as it should be the Executive Office, but decided to do it for the right reasons. She stepped up and said, 'I'll do it.' The Shinners said, 'No' so we took a judicial review. Jennifer (McNern) applied for legal aid and got it and made the argument that this was the law from Westminster.

In the initial stages both Foster and O'Neill argued against it. Foster did it for monetary reasons ... the costs were being inflated. The Shinners were the Department of Finance and they were throwing out all these figures, muddying the waters, but it was really about the eligibility criteria which is why the Shinners blocked it. The judge ruled against them and said your arguments are 'arrant nonsense'. Their barristers tried all sorts of tactics.

There was another fellow who came along at the same time, one of the Hooded Men, and he had brought forward a judicial review at the same time as Jennifer. They tried to argue with the judge that Jennifer's case should be thrown out and that his case had higher precedence. They tried to use this tactic as his may have been a weaker case than ours. The judge didn't buy it, saying, 'I'll take both cases at the same time. Jennifer McNern campaigned for this for years – I'm not throwing it out of my court.'

So this was the kind of thing they were trying to pull but we had a top QC – a senior QC, Danny Freidman over from London – taking the case with our solicitors and junior QC – who was brilliant too. So the judge threw it out and in a minute of the ruling O'Neill said we were nominating Naomi Long to take it forward. There was still fighting behind the scenes about the money.

Brian Turley, the Hooded Man, took another case to the
Appeal Court saying the judges ruling didn't go far enough
as it didn't say Stormont should pay. They (Stormont poli-
ticians) were still arguing that Westminster should pay.
They couldn't get out of paying it or slowing it down – as
he wanted it concrete that Stormont would pay. ... The
Lord Chief Justice said, 'Never mind the arguments about
Westminster – you're paying for it.'

The Victims Payment Board was then set up and the initial judge who was in the first case with Jennifer [McNern],
was nominated to take it on – Gerry McAlinden, a brilliant
fellow. He met with us and asked, 'What way do you want
this to go? I want to hear from the victims. I want it to be
victim-centred. I want to do my best for you. I've seen you
come through the court and couldn't believe what I was
seeing.'

So we had the right man in charge of it, the President, and
that's proved to be the case since. Groups like SEFF, RFJ,[15]
Ely Centre and ourselves are now on the panel – working
with the civil servants. SEFF and RFJ came together and
said 'let's make this work'. That's big – that is big! It is amic-
able, it's friendly and business-like.

Now it's done. Had it been the other way round I don't
think you'd have had the unionist groups on board. I think
the nationalist groups are more pragmatic – but that's just
my opinion.

ROZ:   I think that there'd have been opposition to an all-inclusive
scheme – not just from Tories, but also a lot of Labour
politicians.

15   SEFF, South East Fermanagh Foundation is a unionist group where RFJ Relatives
for Justice is republican.

PAUL: It just wouldn't have happened. In fact, even in the week it was going though the Sun newspaper put up an article saying Jeremy Corbyn wants to give pensions to terrorists. Jeremy Corbyn wasn't even there but that was what they were saying! And various Tory tweets saying this was all done under the cover of Brexit – nonsense.

At the end of so many years struggling to get a scheme up and running there are problems.

Even to this day, to get payments into the hands of our members it's dragging on – those of old age. Up to now there have been two people paid out. It started in September (2021) this is February 2022. It's taken a long time to get through but more will be coming. A completely new scheme had to be drawn up out of nothing and a whole new department set up. We were frustrated that it has taken so long but looking behind the scenes they have really done well – the panel of judges, officials and so on working to get the victims' payment board running.

The massive problem was – even when I spoke about the split in the group in 2013 about psychological injury – the 2014 paper that came down from the Victims Commission and the Executive Office said that you couldn't just give it to the physically injured, you had to give it to the psychological as well. We accepted that. The issue was going to be how do you assess psychological? We had put in grading systems for physical, using the Industrial Injuries compensation scheme. It was harder for psychological, but there were systems in place for psychological – but this held up progress for about a year as they brought in psychologists and assessors. It started in September last year, so we're just waiting for the money coming down.

ROZ: It may be delayed but it will be paid retrospectively, won't it?

PAUL: Whenever we were going through the design stage, when the regulations were being set out, we were saying – as it was in Marie Smyth's original paper – that the pension should be back-dated to the Good Friday Agreement (1998). That was 2012 so she was arguing for a back date. We said, what about back-dating it to the Good Friday Agreement which was twenty years ago? That was out of the question so we said what about the Stormont House Agreement – that was the first time the two governments and five parties agreed to pay – so it's backdated now to December 2014.

Payments are going to go out at between £2,000 and £10,000 a year. £10,000 is 100% at the top of the scale – for someone like myself, paralysed. Somebody with the loss of two fingers would probably be 20%, but they're getting £2,000 a year backdated. If you're over 60 you can ask for a lump sum, so you can take a 10 year lump sum – that £100k if you're at 100%. A lot of people in their 60s, 70s and 80s will probably take that up front.

ROZ:     Looking at what sums of compensation are awarded by the courts, this is modest. And it's so long fought for.

PAUL:    Yes, it is modest.

ROZ:     Can you say a bit about leadership?

PAUL:    We're all leaders. And with the media we all knew what to say. We were all drilled – Peter (Heathwood), Alec (Bunting), Jennifer (McNern). I did a lot of the media stuff, especially the morning radio. They only give you a few minutes but they are important. And on TV you're only given 30 seconds – you talk for 5 minutes and they use a clip of 10 or 20 seconds. So you have to rhyme it off – no rambling. Yes, I was skilled-up but we all had different contributions.

The BBC came in and a guy called Moore Sinnerton did a documentary series – a three-parter on survivors and some of our group were in it. Then he did these six 4-minute shorts with us in the injured group and just gave it to us. They were on the i-Player for about a year. We brought them to Westminster – we brought them with us twice. We also had this photographic exhibition and brought that to Westminster – and had a room there – Jimmy Nesbitt spoke at it.

It's done now. They were happy to get it done but people are tired now. It was long.

ROZ: I get the impression the Campaign was part of a wider project for you – your work, your writing and research.

PAUL: It became a part of my life. It became a part of their lives too. In fact it was therapeutic to be involved in it. The guys now would speak of post-traumatic growth (as opposed to PTSD) when I ask them questions. When I was interviewing them they were still distant before Stormont went down and Westminster stepped in. I asked, 'If this doesn't happen has this all been a waste of time?' And they're saying, 'No, this has been great for me – we have got the needs of the injured on the top of the agenda. We feel human again.'

Peter (Heathwood) said when he asked, he couldn't get a job again – he was in insurance ... that there were times he felt like giving up. In 2018 it was the 20th anniversary of Omagh and he felt he had to go on and speak for the people who couldn't speak for themselves.

We went through all the bullshit and the pats on the head – wee cup of tea and sandwiches and stuff. We've been patronised enough. So we had to stick it out – that's what the sense was.

There were times, like during the split, when I felt like walking away from it and I think others did too – the hassle, the grief and the bitterness.

ROZ: That is the burden of taking leadership and responsibility – of saying this is doable despite the split and we have to leave them behind in the campaign. That is a very tough decision.

PAUL: And it was tough too. I was saying to Jennifer (McNern) that we have to keep going and basically it was, 'We have to

get this through. it can't be put off – it has to be done.' You
need to be pragmatic. ... Wave didn't tell us what to think or
do – they had a responsibility to their members who were
aggrieved by the thought that terrorists who'd killed their
family member would get a pension. Wave was representing
so many people. We were in favour of all-inclusivity but had
to be cognisant of Wave as well. I was one of the main pro-
ponents of the all-inclusive option and got myself ... not into
trouble but I sometimes went beyond the brief in media
interviews – but said, 'This is my personal view.'

On talk shows people question, but I see it as a reconciliation thing. If I can say I'm okay about the guy who shot me
when he got injured – I can but not everybody was on the
same page.

## Leadership in the campaign

Dr Paul Gallagher is now full-time Trauma Education Officer at Wave.
His account of the Injured Group's long campaign exhibits the key leadership capabilities set out by Chambers et al. (2010). While he was by no
means the only one to show leadership qualities, he was able to harness
those talents and was key to driving the campaign.

Even a sketchy analysis shows these qualities.

Sense-making is clearly present, as the group found and used information and numerous people to help consolidate the case for a pension.
Starting with a virtually blank sheet they sourced data and involved others
in the process, such as the lawyer Luke Moffett from Queen's University,
politicians at Stormont, Westminster and the House of Lords, and engaged a
top barrister in their legal battle. They developed key relationships, through
support and contacts at Wave – who were *good at getting access, which is
the most important thing – they can lift a phone to a politician where if I lift
the phone it's, 'Who are you?'*

And there was strong visioning. Having identified the needs of the seriously injured and the demands they wanted to make, they brought in *academics and any experts out there to back us up. Luke was one of them. He brought in a professional draughtsman from Westminster – probably getting £500 a day, like top end – and they designed a bill.* That was no mean feat for a group of people who started with no qualifications, political-negotiating skills or media training, and who were subjected to treatment that was almost universally patronising, if not actually humiliating. Paul Gallagher and the other members of the group were successful in what Chambers et al. call *creating new ways of working together, including the processes and structures needed to make the vision a reality.*

This leadership was also characterised by Peacebuilding Entrepreneurship (Murphy, 2020). Social commitment to conflict transformation is evident in Paul Gallagher's statement: *On talk shows people question but I see it as a reconciliation thing. If I can say I'm okay about the guy who shot me when he got injured – I can but not everybody was on the same page.* They are a cross-community group and they understand that *you have to come to these sorts of compromises.*

Exercising political skill was a crucial element in the campaign from the arena of local sectarian politics through to the House of Lords. To repeat from the interview:

> *The rights thing you mention was an important point because we didn't use rights language or talk of reparations – it was a dirty word. Robinson said 'that's Sinn Fein speak – rights and reparations. ... McGuinness and Robinson were still on okay terms but the well was being poisoned outside as well. You had the Special Advisers Bill, the Flags Protest. The Special Advisers Bill really muddied the waters between Sinn Fein and the DUP. Then there was the Maze-Longkesh thing [a memorial which was dubbed a museum to terrorism by Loyalists and many Unionists.*

There was also the exercise of professional, reputational expert or positional capital (*We're all leaders. And with the media we all knew what to say. We were all drilled*), and the cultivation of intra- and inter-organisational networks of support. Securing the right to a 'Troubles pension' required all of these.

The two years since 2020 saw the Covid-19 pandemic uproot much of 'normal' life. The repercussions of Brexit and the Northern Ireland Protocol have been used as threats to undermine stability in the peace process. The lack of political leadership from the restored Stormont Assembly is in sharp contrast to the courage, strength, dignity and forbearance of leaders such as Paul Gallagher and others in the Wave seriously injured group, who provide practical examples of how leadership is possible. It is not some miracle or mystery but it demands honesty, integrity and a genuine will for the collective good.

# CHAPTER 8

# Brexit and the Northern Ireland Protocol

In the referendum on the UK leaving the EU, Northern Ireland voted to remain. Brexit went ahead regardless and the UK government negotiated the Withdrawal Agreement over a protracted period. Aside from the necessary and complex trade and financial arrangements between the UK and EU, the British exit from Europe presented a serious problem in deciding where the new borders were to be drawn outside mainland Great Britain. While Northern Ireland was outside the EU, the Republic of Ireland was still a member state and the possibility of reinstating a hard border between the two jurisdictions became a central issue. The Belfast Agreement – like the Withdrawal Agreement – was bound by international law, and assured that there would be no hard border on the island of Ireland. European states and the USA stood firmly by the terms of the Belfast Agreement, much to the displeasure of the Johnson government in London who had pressed for a harder Brexit than was previously expected.

The primacy of the peace agreement and stability in Northern Ireland won the day – and the net result was the Northern Ireland Protocol which permitted free trade from Northern Ireland to mainland Britain and the EU, but which had some restrictions on trade coming from Britain to Northern Ireland. As the Irish sea border became apparent the political temperature rose and rhetoric replaced reason and fact. Protest demonstrations and interface violence followed in April 2021.

The Unionist and Loyalist narrative was unambiguous, asserting that the Protocol and the Irish sea border diminished their Britishness, threatened the constitutional status of Northern Ireland and had to be resisted at all costs. However, the fact of the matter is that the legal rights (and obligations) which secured the Belfast Agreement were not altered, as the Northern Ireland Human Rights Commission (NIHRC) makes clear.

> *Under the Ireland/NI Protocol to the Withdrawal Agreement reached with the EU, the UK Government committed to ensuring that the protections currently in place in Northern Ireland for the rights, safeguards and equality of opportunity provisions set out in the chapter of the same name in the Belfast (Good Friday) Agreement will not be reduced as a result of the UK leaving the EU. (nihrc.org)*

In their Short Guide NICHR set out these guaranteed rights:

- *The right of free political thought*
- *The right to freedom and expression of religion*
- *The right to pursue democratically national and political aspirations*
- *The right to seek constitutional change by peaceful and legitimate means*
- *The right to freely choose one's place of residence*
- *The right to equal opportunity in all social and economic activity regardless of class, creed, disability, gender or ethnicity*
- *The right to freedom from sectarian harassment*
- *The right of women to full and equal political participation*
- *The right of victims to remember as well to contribute to a changed society*
- *Respect, understanding and tolerance in relation to linguistic diversity*
- *The need to ensure that symbols and emblems are used in a manner which promotes mutual respect rather than division (https://nihrc.org/uploads/Brexit-YourRightsShortGuidedigital.pdf)*

This being the case, it must be asked how so much violence and political turmoil was engineered during 2021 and still threatened in 2022.

Indeed, returning to the riots in 2021 at the Lanark Way interface, the question must be, what does Brexit and the Northern Ireland Protocol actually mean? Is the Irish sea border actual and inevitable? Does the protocol diminish the constitutional standing of Northern Ireland? For answers we need to look beyond the general noise of local politicians and press coverage to some expert legal and academic literature. To start with, there is a hefty work, edited by Christopher McCrudden (2022a) which examines the various aspects of the Protocol.

McCrudden (2022a) gives an overview of the EU-UK Withdrawal Agreement, showing how, after the peace agreement, Northern Ireland presented fundamental problems – and required the most amount of negotiating time.

> *What became critically important in determining the content of the subsequent WA (Withdrawal Agreement) was an EU–UK political agreement, early in the summer of 2017, that the withdrawal negotiations would focus on four main issues only.*
>
> *One issue concerned the EU budget and the UK contribution to it. A second issue was the complex question of how EU states should treat UK citizens resident in the EU, and vice versa, after the UK had exited. The third concerned how best to sequence the UK's departure, and in particular the form of any transition period. The fourth issue identified was the one on which most time was spent, and became the make-or-break issue in the negotiations, namely, how to handle Northern Ireland. In addressing each of these issues in the negotiations, the question of trust (or, rather, the lack of trust) was a recurring theme. (McCrudden, 2022a: 9)*

There had to be a border between the EU and the post-Brexit UK. A hard border on the island of Ireland would have been a simple answer and one that would have caused little concern to the Johnson government. However, that option would have destabilised Northern Ireland and contravened the terms of the Belfast Agreement. So, when the combined leverage of the EU and US ensured that this did not happen, the Irish sea border was the solution. Indeed, the Brexit deal included engagement with the Court of Justice of the European Union (CJEU), and *an overall obligation on the UK and the EU to apply the provisions of the WA 'in good faith'* (McCrudden, 2022: 10). Yet, Johnson's government declared the UK was beyond the reach of CJEU and as early as 2017 EU trust in the UK government was running out.

> *Many of the features of the Protocol indicate the lengths to which the EU side went in attempting to guard against backsliding by the UK government after any agreement was concluded, in particular the emphasis placed on the need for effective domestic enforcement mechanisms, and the role given to international governance arrangements, including a role for the CJEU [Court of Justice of the European Union], in resolving disputes, interpreting the agreement and imposing sanctions in the event of an unresolved breach. (McCrudden, 2022a: 10)*

The British Prime Minister was determined to *get Brexit done* with scant regard for the implications of the Northern Ireland Protocol. This included no hard border between Northern Ireland and Ireland while maintaining the integrity of the EU single market and protection of the

Belfast Agreement 'in all its dimensions', including 'no diminution of rights' and maintaining 'the necessary conditions for continued North–South cooperation' (McCrudden, 2022a: 11). The scale of political embarrassment for the DUP, which had been the most robust of persuaders for Brexit, was and remained potentially disastrous.

The Protocol set up the Irish sea border, and was *a result of an imperfect compromise – an attempt to consolidate a range of requirements which, to a large extent, were contradictory* (Jerzewska, 2022: 207). These arrangements were far from the frictionless trade Boris Johnson had pledged at a DUP annual conference.

> *It created a situation where there is a de facto customs and regulatory border going through the territory of the UK's customs territory. What is in place is a most unusual, asymmetric and one-sided border: asymmetric as it does not work the same way for movements in both directions; and one-sided as the customs formalities are applied on only one side of the border. (Jerzewska, 2022: 209)*

The finer points of the economic fallout have been lost in the 'No Irish sea border' demonstrations and rhetoric – a rhetoric at times reduced to hysteria about embargos on the importing of British sausages to Northern Ireland.

The Northern Ireland Protocol was agreed but the frictionless trade promised was not the result.

> *Prime Minister Theresa May was willing to accept such regulatory alignment, since it would facilitate the frictionless trade that she sought. When Boris Johnson became Prime Minister, he made clear that his stance towards the trade negotiations was markedly different. (Craig, 2022: 37)*

The Trade and Cooperation Agreement makes for an increased separation between Northern Ireland and Great Britain on EU rules and standards, though McCrudden notes that the implications are far from clear.

> *The Protocol involves juxtaposing the 1998 Agreement, Brexit, devolution, the WA (Withdrawal Agreement) and the TCA (Trade and Cooperation Agreement), leaving aside the unprecedented idea of a region being, in effect, in two single markets and customs unions simultaneously. When this complexity is combined with a significant*

*element of political toxicity because of the choices made by the political actors, disputes could be predicted with some confidence. (McCrudden, 2022a: 15)*

The reality of the Irish sea border for trade coming from Great Britain to Northern Ireland is a huge regulatory system of paperwork which has resulted in many businesses refusing to ship their wares across the Irish Sea. Large businesses like Tesco and Marks & Spencer have overcome this hurdle – and there were always companies who would send products to GB but not NI. Shortages of medicines have generally been avoided by 'grace periods'. The political toxicity of which McCrudden speaks is another matter. This was underpinned by a mixture of fear and opportunism on the part of both Sinn Féin and the DUP about the political implications of the Protocol, in the run up to the May 2022 elections.

As regards the constitutional implications of the Protocol, Harvey (2022) is clear that it does not alter the conditions and arrangements set out in the internationally agreed Belfast Agreement:

> *The constitutional core of the (Belfast) Agreement contains a formula for dealing with the right of self-determination and the principle of consent. Respecting the Agreement requires that the only way that a change will take place in the constitutional status of Northern Ireland, as a constituent part of the UK, is by way of a process that involves an exercise in concurrent consent by voters North and South, with the outcome to be determined on a simple majority vote in each jurisdiction. If people vote for change, then there is a 'binding obligation' on both governments 'to introduce and support in their respective Parliaments legislation to give effect to that wish'. The Protocol is explicit that it is 'without prejudice' to these provisions of the Agreement, and that it 'respects the territorial integrity' of the UK. (Harvey, 2022: 24)*

This is explicit. The Protocol is not a threat to the constitutional status quo in which Northern Ireland remains part of the UK, and under the terms of the Belfast Agreement also assures *the close relationality among the different parts of 'these islands', and the connection to the EU that was clearly contemplated in the Agreement* (Harvey, 2022: 24).

However, there are other issues, potentially as crucial to stability in the peace process, because *the Belfast Agreement has not been incorporated in its entirety into the domestic law of either Ireland or the UK* (Harvey, 2022: 27). The Protocol – and many of the statements on post-Brexit Northern Ireland from the White House – make reference to the Belfast (or Good Friday) Agreement.

> *Debate continues on whether the (Belfast) Agreement has been faithfully implemented in domestic law in the UK, and the absence from the (1998 Northern Ireland) Act of some key concepts is often noted. The fact that the Protocol consistently refers to the 1998 Agreement, rather than the NI Act 1998 is, therefore, significant. (Harvey, 2022: 28)*

The oversight and enforcement of the Withdrawal Agreement – and hence the Protocol – falls to the Joint Committee and the Specialised Committees, and the Specialised Committee on Ireland–Northern Ireland (INISC), which requires EU-UK agreement (Hayward, 2022). This has proven to be problematic.

> *The Joint Committee cannot act if either the UK or the Commission is not in agreement. … Informal meetings between the co-chairs remained important in the first few months of implementing the Protocol, especially against the backdrop of a UK–EU dispute. (Hayward, 2022: 44-45)*

There were sufficient press leaks to provide some detail of formal meetings, showing amongst other things that the DUP and Sinn Féin junior ministers were included in the Joint Committee. This increased the importance and weight of private meetings and obscured the working of the Specialised Committee on Ireland–Northern Ireland (INISC).

> *This had the effect of sending the work of the INISC deeper into the echelons of the Cabinet Office and Commission, and making its formal meetings less frequent than they might otherwise have been. This only intensified the difficulties for Northern Ireland civil servants charged with keeping up with the work of the INISC. Officials from the Northern Ireland Civil Service are present at official INISC meetings at the invitation of the UK government; whether they are kept informed of the background work of the INISC officials is rather more ad hoc. When asked (amid growing political and public tensions over the Protocol implementation in Northern Ireland) in April 2021 for an update on the engagement by the UK and the EU with Northern Ireland stakeholders, including the Executive, and on formal consultation mechanisms to ensure their full participation in the WA institutions, Lord Frost replied that 'representatives of the NI Executive attend the JC and the Specialised Committee' – meetings that had happened four to eight weeks earlier. (Hayward, 2022: 52)*

As a result, civil servants in Northern Ireland, who were tasked to implement the Protocol, were left in the dark. In terms of process, leadership and effective administration this was a perfect storm. Hayward's conclusion states this clearly.

> *A House of Lords European Union Committee Report concluded that the effectiveness of the UK–EU committees established under the WA 'will depend on the frequency of their meetings, the flexibility of their remit, senior political representation on both sides, and a mutual commitment to effective communication, appropriate powers, and full accountability'. The operation of the UK–EU bodies during the transition period and in the first few months of 'Brexit proper' after the transition period ended has revealed chronic inadequacy in all these areas. This marks an inauspicious beginning for these important new UK–EU institutions. (Hayward, 2022: 54)*

Such a vacuum in governance would only increase uncertainty throughout trade, industry and the public, and provide opportunities to obfuscate if not mislead – feeding the frenzied No-Irish-Sea Border narrative and protest demonstrations.

Wouters (2022) describes the two mechanisms for settling disputes about the Protocol. These are the Court of Justice of the European Union (CJEU) and an arbitration process.

> *This system presents a rather unique combination of, on the one hand, continued jurisdiction of the Court of Justice of the European Union (CJEU) and, on the other hand, an arbitration procedure. As has been rightly observed, these are two very different enforcement mechanisms. The former (the CJEU) relies on an existing supranational court which monitors respect for the EU legal order, works together with national courts, and allows some measure of access to individuals. The role of the CJEU is controversial: its case law and jurisdiction were one of the political drivers of the proponents of the withdrawal of the UK from the EU. The latter (arbitration), in contrast, represents a much more traditional public international law method that is new and available only to the parties of the Withdrawal Agreement (WA). (Wouters (2022: 55)*

Given the UK's total rejection of CJEU in negotiations after WA, this system poses a dilemma – and one that will take time to resolve. This leads to a more fundamental problem, exacerbated by the justifiable lack of trust in the UK government in both negotiating and implementing the Protocol.

Weatherill (2022) notes that the *Protocol is written with what one might generously describe as calculated ambiguity, or, less charitably, outright evasion.* He continues:

> *What the Protocol does is not what it says. ... the approach to drafting the provisions of the Protocol is the same: in each case the Protocol is written in a way that understates the nature and the extent of the commitments made on the UK side. ... Life under the Protocol has, however, been regrettably infected by a persisting disregard for and misrepresentation of its terms by members of the UK government. (Weatherill, 2022: 69)*

The effect of the Protocol is economic rather than constitutional and the problems are the result of Brexit rather than the Protocol – which necessarily separates the internal markets of the EU and UK, leaving Northern Ireland with a different regulatory system.

> *The Protocol represents the unavoidable post-Brexit choice among three objectives: no hard border between Northern Ireland and GB; no hard border between Northern Ireland and Ireland; and regulatory autonomy for the UK (or GB). Only two of these can be achieved. (Weatherill, 2022: 78)*

Weatherill notes an already pre-existing blatant disregard to the outworking of the Protocol in the UK government's actions.

> *It seems painfully clear that the Protocol was a device to 'get Brexit done' as part of a strategy that secured a General Election victory in December 2019 and that the UK government sees no further value in it. The same people who campaigned for Brexit with no regard for its consequences on the island of Ireland are now, having agreed the Protocol, showing disregard for its terms. (Weatherill, 2022: 79)*

This has fundamental consequences for international relations because, as McCrudden (2022b) points out, the UK agreed to the principles of *Good Faith and Sincere Cooperation* in the Withdrawal Agreement. Both had been tested to destruction leaving a profound distrust of the UK within the EU – even before rumours of proposed UK legislation on NI protocol. British government moves to legislate to remove Articles 5-10 of the Protocol in late April 2022 and subsequent tabling of legislation were in bad faith, given the Withdrawal Agreement and the workings of an international treaty. *Such a move would be a more aggressive step than triggering*

*Article 16 of the protocol and would be in clear breach of Britain's treaty obligations and international law* (Staunton and McClements, 2022).

The motivation behind this is uncertain – although the media did not flinch from describing it as a distraction from the fallout from Partygate and the (then) Prime Minister being fined for breaking the COVID lockdown and social distancing rules that he and his cabinet introduced during the pandemic. The result was a strong and credibly critical response from both a former Irish ambassador to London, Brussels and Rome, Bobby McDonagh, and a former senior Stormont official, Andrew McCormick. McDonagh gets to the core of the matter, saying that *one can dismiss out of hand the stated reason that the intention is to protect the Belfast Agreement* (McDonagh, 2022).

Of at least as much importance is the publication of what had previously been in-house information on the Protocol.

> *Responsibility for the Withdrawal Agreement of 2019 and the Protocol lies fairly and squarely with the UK government*, Dr McCormick has written in an article for the Constitution Society. ... *There is little credibility in any argument that the UK government either did not anticipate the implications of what it had agreed, or was constrained and unable to choose any other option. The facts and choices had been spelt out clearly over the whole period from 2016 onwards and the detail of the provisions (notably most of the applicable EU law contained in Annex 2 to the Protocol) were known at latest in autumn 2018. And the time constraint to 'get Brexit done' was entirely self-imposed. Indeed, as some have pointed out, the UK government could not explain the Protocol without having to explain properly the wider consequences of Brexit.*
>
> *Dr McCormick retired last year as Director General of International Relations for the Northern Ireland Executive Office. Between 2017 and 2020, when the North's institutions were suspended, he regularly attended UK ministerial meetings, and until May 2021 represented the Executive during meetings of the EU-UK Specialised Committee on the Protocol.* (Connolly, 2022)

This contradicts claims to the contrary and further undermines the credibility of the DUP and Johnson administration on the subject of the Protocol. The rationale for the Unionist-Loyalist protests – that the Protocol threatens the constitutional status of Northern Ireland – is simply not factual. Until the May 2022 election, which saw Sinn Féin gain political ascendancy to becoming the largest party in Stormont, the leverage in this campaign was little more than the threat of Loyalist paramilitary violence. This was graphically demonstrated when the UVF hijacked a vehicle containing a hoax bomb at a Belfast peace centre – causing the hurried evacuation of Simon Coveney, the Irish Minister Foreign Affairs.

Although 'mass protests' were planned, these did not materialise and the gulf between unionist feeling on the ground and the political and para-military elite was evident.

> The Protests of Lurgan had spoken, eloquently, by not turning up. Perhaps 1,000 people ... a small fraction of the envisaged 10,000, and even that would have been a feeble echo of the flag protests a decade ago and the vaster throngs that protested against the Anglo-Irish Agreement. ... There is a disconnect between unionists and unionist parties. Most pro-union voters favour marriage equality and abortion rights, while unionist parties are more socially conservative. (Carroll, 2022)

Not only was support for protests much weaker than DUP and TUV politicians suggested, but the results of a 2022 survey had already clearly shown that education, health and the economy were greater priorities than constitutional issues for most voters in Northern Ireland (Institute of Irish Studies, 2022).

The UK government position on the Protocol, and legislating against it, had wider implications than domestic politics in NI or Britain and the fate of Prime Minister Johnson who resigned in July 2022. As McDonagh points out, the UK would not be trusted in relation to the war in Ukraine or EU matters, and that such action may undermine future trade negotiations.

> it would gratuitously challenge western unity in the face of Putin's outrages. It will certainly not be appreciated in the US where the complexities of the Belfast Agreement are well understood. ...such behaviour would undermine the UK's standing to lecture Putin, or anyone else, on the rule of law. Britain's international reputation and influence would suffer. ... reneging on a binding treaty would further undermine relations between the UK and its natural partners in Europe. Finally, and most importantly, it would further unsettle the delicate situation in Northern Ireland by moving the real and unavoidable challenges of dealing with the consequences of Brexit back to square one. (McDonagh, 2022)

On 27 April 2022 Lord Frost, the former chief negotiator who was key to negotiating the Protocol, stated in the House of Commons – without evidence to support his assertion – that the Protocol seriously threatened the Belfast Agreement. This was little more than misinformation and scare-mongering which contradicted the evidence-based opinion of professional, diplomatic and academic legal experts.

## Conclusions

By way of final observations, it is evident that UK negotiations for the Withdrawal Agreement and the Northern Ireland Protocol were settled with the full knowledge of the implications. There was no doubt that there would be an Irish sea border, and the promise of 'frictionless trade' was duplicitous. And there is no basis for the assertion that the Protocol undermines the Belfast Agreement – which is no more than a media spin used by the DUP and the UK government – echoing the stance of Loyalist paramilitary factions.

The high-risk poker game of scrapping key articles of the Protocol, and thus breaking international law and reneging on an agreed international treaty, has yet to be played out. Nothing in this will necessarily destabilise the Northern Ireland peace process. However, it bodes ill for the future of dealing with paramilitary Unionism – as negotiating with 'Loyalist Command' lacks political certainty and eradicating the various factions is unlikely – leaving Northern Ireland no more than a pawn in the GB brexiteers' game.

# CHAPTER 9

# Equality: Too big an ask?

This chapter concerns equality. It briefly examines the legislation on this and what is called 'the equality agenda' that was intended in extensive re-forms to embed a rights-based peace process.

Discrimination and inequality were major factors contributing to the Northern Ireland conflict – and key to Republican attempts at legitimising violence. Demonstrations in protest against inequality, discrimination and electoral gerrymandering, notably organised by the Northern Ireland Civil Rights movement, were brutally suppressed. In January 1969 the student-led People's Democracy march at Burntollet Bridge was attacked by a Loyalist mob, including some off-duty B Specials, while some of the attendant Royal Ulster Constabulary stood by. However, as O'Toole (2021) has noted, there was an ambiguity, in that the movement had dual goals. So, was the desire to reform or destroy the Northern Ireland state? It seems it was both. In response Unionists were defensive and Nationalists now open to the belief that Northern Ireland was beyond reform.

> The violence, however, was two-sided. There was the violence of a Protestant sectarian bigotry that need [sic] little excuse to assert itself. And there was the side that O'Brien most feared – the long history of armed, conspiratorial, revolutionary nationalism. In organizational terms. It had withered into irrelevance. ... But what that leadership did not know then was that Northern Ireland was about to implode with extraordinary rapidity. [182]

Thus, an automatic antagonism to 'equality' was integral to Loyalism and Unionism from before the beginning of the conflict, if not for the entire existence of the state – and indeed the Conservative party view of the Northern Ireland state has always been equivocal. As Kenny and Sheldon note, Brexit merely exposed an underlying ambivalence with the existence of

*two distinct modes of thinking about Northern Ireland co-exist within the party's col-*
*lective mind: the notion it constitutes a 'place apart' from Great Britain, and the belief*
*it remains integral to the UK. The circumstances of 2018–19 meant Conservative MPs*
*were forced, reluctantly, to choose between the implications of these ultimately incom-*
*mensurable perspectives. (Kenny and Sheldon, 2021)*

This equivocal view of Northern Ireland blinded London governments
to the dangers of the gross inequalities and injustices which ignited
'the Troubles' – although, despite retaining that contradiction, the UK
became co-guarantor of the peace agreement.

Equality and human rights were central to the peace negotiations,
the settlement and the Belfast Agreement – after which both rights and
statutory obligations were enshrined in the 1998 Northern Ireland Act.
Securing peace was therefore much more than a matter of an IRA ceasefire and disarming.

The arrangements for a devolved power-sharing Stormont Assembly,
the reform of policing and fundamental changes in public administration
were all part of a comprehensive change in governance. This embraced
the inclusion of human rights and equality in public service delivery at all
levels and set up the Equality Commission for Northern Ireland (ECNI).

These new rights to equality were mandated in Sections 75 and 76 of
the 1998 Northern Ireland Act.

## Sections 75 and 76 – two aspects of equality

Where Section 75 of the 1998 Northern Ireland Act (NIA) mandates
a duty on public bodies to promote equality of opportunity and good
relations, Section 76 is the law that prohibits discrimination by public
bodies. There is an important difference between these two aspects of
equality legislation – and this is intentional.

Section 76 is specific and clearly states that it concerns *Discrimination*
*by public authorities.*

*(1) It shall be unlawful for a public authority carrying out functions relating to Northern Ireland to discriminate, or to aid or incite another person to discriminate, against a person or class of person on the ground of religious belief or political opinion.*

*(2) An act which contravenes this section is actionable in Northern Ireland at the instance of any person adversely affected by it; and the court may– (a) grant damages; (b) subject to subsection (3), grant an injunction restraining the defendant from committing, causing or permitting further contraventions of this section.*

This would cover cases of where public services are discriminatory – such as in unfair allocation of housing, health or education. It adds to the existing employment equality legislation in the Fair Employment and Treatment (Northern Ireland) Order 1998.

Section 75 is more complex and was, in its time, the most advanced equality legislation in Europe. Its states:

*75 (1) A public authority shall in carrying out its functions relating to Northern Ireland have due regard to the need to promote equality of opportunity-*

*a) between persons of different religious belief, political opinion, racial group, age, marital status or sexual orientation;*

*b) between men and women generally;*

*c) between persons with a disability and persons without; and*

*d). between persons with dependants and persons without.*

*(2) Without prejudice to its obligations under subsection (1), a public authority shall in carrying out its functions relating to Northern Ireland have regard to the desirability of promoting good relations between persons of different religious belief, political opinion or racial group.*

Schedule 9 of the Act also requires a designated public body to assess and consult on the likely impact of policies adopted or proposed to be adopted on the promotion of equality of opportunity, that is, to carry out an equality impact assessment (EQIA) on new and existing policy (ECNI, 2003a and 2003b).

Critics argue that the Agreement, and thus key aspects of the NIA, is flawed because it rests on liberal discourses such as equality of opportunity, 'tolerance' and 'diversity'. Zapone (2001) and O'Cinneide (2004) note the paucity of equal opportunity because it does not deliver equality of outcomes – that is, it does not change substantial and systemic socio-economic inequalities. Others saw merit in the finely crafted Section 75 (1) as advancing beyond any other equality legislation and was the *fourth generation equality laws, based on a positive duty to promote equality, rather than simply to refrain from discriminating* (Fredman, 2002: 122).[16]

However, the weakness of the Section 75 equality duty, as a means of tackling deprivation, was important. At the time it was the most far-reaching equality legislation and was intended to ensure that there would be positive changes in policymaking and the delivery of public services. It may now seem rather meagre in failing to address socio-economic disparities but it was a hard-won advance in the peace negotiations.

Although the equality agenda was central to reaching the 1998 political settlement, Section 75 equality regulations and duties (such as equality impact assessment) came as somewhat of a shock to Ulster Unionists, according to a special advisor to the Ulster Unionist Party (UUP) leader during the negotiations, interviewed in 2007.

> [It was] *something that was just there, that would cause a lot of people a lot of unnecessary work – all very pc* [politically correct]. *... Everybody knew that it* [the equality agenda] *would be made bigger after the Agreement was settled. Equality and human rights were like dandruff – just there – pc rhetoric like 'duty of care'.*

UUP negotiators, like all the parties in the negotiations, had input and an important influence on the content of the Northern Ireland Act but they did not draft the legislation.[17] Nor did they officially have sight of it prior

---

16    Fredman argues for a value driven approach, which challenges liberal assumptions of state neutrality and individualism, claiming them insufficient to promote equality.

17    Legislation such as the Northern Ireland Act (1998) is drafted by civil servants, who interpret what politicians and government meant and wanted, albeit with strong direction from Special Advisors. It is then examined for matters of law by lawyers and, when complete, submitted to the Parliamentary scrutiny committee. Source of information is a former Northern Ireland Civil Servant.

to its appearance in Westminster.[18] The full implications of the Section 75 obligations, especially the positive equality duty with its requirement for time-framed equality schemes and equality impact assessments of policy, turned out to be stronger than supporters of Unionism expected, and more thoroughgoing than Ulster Unionist politicians had imagined during Parliamentary debates (Hansard, 1998a, 1998b, 1998c, 1998d).

Section 75 required radical changes in the process of policy making. It was initially regarded by many in the public sector as *an enormous administrative burden.*[19] Although ECNI expected resistance to implementing Section 75(1) in 2001-2002, there appeared to be a general willingness by central government departments, if not all of the public sector, to implement the equality agenda (McCrudden, 2004: 41).

Besides administrative considerations, the equality agenda was seen as a nationalist 'win' and thus a unionist loss (Hayward and Mitchell, 2003). This discourse on equality and rights has continued and been reproduced by unionist politicians and their fellow travellers ever since. This was clear in Paul Gallagher's comments on political dimensions of the campaign for a Troubles pension, when he said,

> *The rights thing you mention was an important point because we didn't use rights language or talk of reparations – it was a dirty word. Robinson said 'that's Sinn Fein speak – rights and reparations'.*

Furthermore, the meaning and scope of the two duties in Section 75 have been hotly contested since the days when it was debated in the House of Commons. The attempt to address sectarianism – and racism, if only as an afterthought – in Section 75 (2) immediately became a bone of contention. This was a compromise reached when the Republican demand for parity of esteem (between those of British and Irish citizenship in the jurisdiction) was more than Unionists would accept. The concession was

18  A party advisor to the negotiations reported that, given the consultation on equality policy preceding the Agreement, all parties understood the likely outcome and *probably saw some draft legislation.*
19  The Chief Executive of the Northern Ireland Chief Executive's Forum used these words in an interview in late 2003, adding that it was *feared that the good relations duty would bring the same.*

the duty to promote good relations, which turned out to be grounds for an ideological if not overtly sectarian battle. So, on one hand Unionists detested the equality agenda and, on the other, Republicans took issue with the duty to promote good relations. It remains a source of sometimes acrimonious debate and so is worth some discussion.

## Contested views and the 'conflict' between the Section 75 duties

The relationship between the two Section 75 duties has been constantly disputed, with claims that they conflict. Republicans had pressed hard for *parity of esteem* with equal status for Irish and British citizens, so Section 75 (2) was a huge disappointment. It was seen as *a sop to Unionists* (McVeigh and Rolston, 2007) and a victory for what they regarded as discredited community relations practice. In contrast, community relations practitioners argued that promoting equal opportunity would provoke antagonism and sectarianism, which they claimed created a conflict between the two duties.

As then-Secretary of State, Mo Mowlam, stated in the House of Commons on 27th July 1998 there should be no conflict between Section 75 (1) and (2).

> On the points made by the hon. Member for South Down (Mr. McGrady), it would be helpful if we accepted amendment No. 193 and withdrew Government amendment No. 183. I ask the Committee to resist amendment No. 180 because we regard equality of opportunity and good relations as complementary. There should be no conflict between the two objectives. Good relations cannot be based on inequality between different religions or ethnic groups. Social cohesion requires equality to be reinforced by good community relations. The provision will create a clear statutory obligation on public authorities to have regard to the desirability of promoting good relations between persons of different religious belief, political opinion or racial group. The Government amendment would strengthen that and bring it into line with the obligation to promote equality of opportunity. I repeat that we see no conflict between those two objectives. (Hansard, House of Commons, Official Report, 27 July 1998, Vol. 316, col. 109.)

Although this statement might seem to settle the matter, arguments continued. Clearly the positive equality duty has primacy. Yet, some claimed that Section 75 (2) could be used to undermine it. Commentators, such as McVeigh (2002), asserted that the equality agenda is undermined by promoting good relations because it derives from community relations, stating:

> *The continuing hegemony of the community relations paradigm threatens to remove this commitment to equality and replace it with what is little more than the latest version of a tired and fraudulent pacification programme. (44)*

For McVeigh, attempts to achieve sustainable peace by promoting good relations are fraudulent. *Pacification* implies a conspiracy to deny the legitimate aspirations of Irish Nationalists and Republicans. Given these were copper-fastened in the 1985 Anglo-Irish Agreement, the 1998 Belfast Agreement and the NIA, this perspective is outdated if not irrelevant. The Review of Section 75 – written by a key architect if not author of Section 75 – raises this point, asserting that no conflict exists between these duties.

> *The idea that community relations is in some way in constant tension with equality is a dangerous notion. It is either an attempt to retain the status quo with respect to existing levels of inequality or it is an attempt to retain policy making and administrative turf, neither of which is a suitable way of dealing with the problems. (McCrudden, 2004: 22)*

To say that positing this conflict is *dangerous* is appropriately strong language. The tension, perceived to exist, derives from the drafting of Section 75 and the politics of implementing the Agreement. According to the late Professor Elizabeth Meehan, who was involved in the peace negotiations, influential academics, key amongst whom was Chris McCrudden, and voluntary-community sector leaders, were emphatic that the equality duty in Section 75 (1) should be as robust as possible. They were backed by members of Parliament from Northern Ireland and England and the then Secretary of State, Mo Mowlam, who amended the legislation to make Section 75 (2) subsidiary to the equality duty – asserting the (politically essential) primacy of Section 75 (1). The community relations lobby lost out as influential actors in the legislative process understood that promoting equal opportunity had to trump promoting good relations.

The alleged tension between the two duties is not necessary. However, arguments that it exists were strengthened when subsequent government policies failed to connect promoting good relations with promoting equality.

In comparison with Section 75 (1), Section 75 (2) is weak. Section 75 (1) requires that a public body must have *due regard to the need to promote equality of opportunity* in its operations. The obligation includes obtaining approved Equality Schemes, making five-yearly reports on these, submitting mandatory annual equality reports, and EQIA on existing and new policies. Failure to comply with these obligations results in an ECNI investigation and, if unsatisfactory, reporting to the Secretary of State. The words *due regard* accentuate the force of this duty. In contrast Section 75 (2) only requires *regard to the desirability of promoting good relations*.

The pre-eminence of Section 75 (1) was intentional, as the debates in the House of Commons make clear. Government amendment No. 183 would have altered the *wording 'desirability of promoting' to more obligatory terminology* (Vol. 316, 105). However, Eddie McGrady MP tabled amendment No. 193 and was supported by Kevin McNamara MP. This amendment, it was argued, was meant to ensure the predominance of the equality duty in Section 75 (1) lest the good relations obligation should be used to undermine it. That argument won out and the then Secretary of State for Northern Ireland, Mo Mowlam, accepted it – though with the clear statement that there was no conflict between the two duties.

> On the points made by the hon. Member for South Down (Mr. McGrady), it would be helpful if we accepted amendment No. 193 and withdrew Government amendment No. 183. I ask the Committee to resist amendment No. 180 because we regard equality of opportunity and good relations as complementary. There should be no conflict between the two objectives. (Vol. 316, 109)

The third reading of the Bill, in the House of Lords on 17 November, had only one mention of Section 75 (2) and this was to clarify that the duty was exclusively in relation to matters within the jurisdiction of Northern Ireland, as opposed to elsewhere in the United Kingdom. Lord Dubs said,

> *It brings Clause 75(2) into line with Clause 75(1) in making clear that it bites on public*
> *authorities in carrying out their functions relating to Northern Ireland. We are not of*
> *course seeking to regulate in the Bill what an authority with a remit extending elsewhere*
> *in the United Kingdom does outside Northern Ireland. (Vol. 594, 1,212)*

A senior Civil Servant at that time and Advisor to the Secretary of State in 1998, who was centrally involved in writing the White Paper *Partnership for Equality* that preceded Section 75, recalled the debates and key questions around Section 75 between June and the passing of the Act in November of that year.

> *A hierarchy had to be established because of the 'danger' of the equality duty being under-*
> *mined. ... There were influential academics – Chris McCrudden – and 'the equality*
> *lobby' – NICICTU (Northern Ireland Committee of the Irish Congress of Trade Unions),*
> *NICEM (Northern Ireland Council for Ethnic Minorities), Disability Action – making*
> *the point that the good relations duty might be used to dilute the power of the equality*
> *duty. ... They had influence with Mo and Kevin McNamara. Mo had made an election*
> *promise that PAFT would be put into legislation ... The model for equality schemes was*
> *in the Welsh Language Act. ... There was the 'community relations' lobby, with academics*
> *and CRC arguing that government could introduce into policy a proactive good rela-*
> *tions duty ... the 'shared future' agenda. Good relations ... was explicit [with the three*
> *categories] in the white Paper 'Partnership for Equality'.*

As attempts to mainstream Policy Appraisal for Fair Treatment (PAFT) in the public sector in Northern Ireland had failed dismally, New Labour was determined to legislate and accepted the Civil Service advice to be explicit and name the nine equality categories, require Equality Schemes and processes such as Equality Impact Assessment – despite some *fears that this might lead to endless Judicial Reviews.* The legislation also named the three good relations categories, but the 'equality lobby' won out and had the wording of Section 75 (2) altered to include the prefix *Without prejudice to its obligations under subsection (1)* rather than *more obligatory terminology* (Hansard Vol. 316, 105).

The predominance of Section 75 (1) is further evidenced in the fact that ECNI did not in 2000-2002 require Section 75 (2) considerations to be taken into account in Equality Schemes. Nor did they ask questions about Section 75 (2) until 2003, and even then, it received scant attention. Clearly the good relations duty was not then a priority for ECNI, and therefore was seen as less important to public bodies – as was stated publicly and accepted by Commission officials at a consultation on the draft document *Promoting Good Relations in Practice: A Guide for Public Authorities* at which the author was present.

Interestingly, Section 75 (2) is not mentioned in relation to EQIA guidance, which is central to implementing key aspects of the Agreement and Section 75 (1). On this evidence it seems that the duty to promote good relations was only considered enforceable when it is an explicit part of an organisation's Equality Scheme that a public authority fails to implement; and a senior ECNI official confirmed this fact in the above-mentioned public consultation meeting.

Beyond this, and reflecting a widespread misunderstanding of equality of opportunity, Mowlam's comments infer that the equality lobby was pressing for more than was possible from Section 75 (1), given the content of the Belfast Agreement.

> I had thought that our new amendment would achieve what people wanted, but there is clearly still a degree of dissatisfaction. We shall do all that we can over the summer to satisfy those folk who feel that more should be done. As I said at the beginning, we are listening carefully and we shall do everything possible to add where we can to the settlement Bill, but, however important equality issues are to us all, we shall be in difficulty if we go further than the Good Friday agreement, as I am sure hon. Members understand. (Hansard, House of Commons, Official Report, 27 July 1998, Vol. 316, Cols. 110-111)

There were over-optimistic hopes of equal opportunity and Social Democratic and Labour Party (SDLP) MPs pressed for anti-poverty measures that were well outside the ambitions of the New Labour government. Section 75 (1) was not about tackling poverty and deprivation and perhaps also because the broad Unionist family would not have been party to the Belfast Agreement had that 'socialism' been integral to the settlement. And yet there has been a constant complaint that Unionist people have not seen a peace dividend. This misunderstanding, sometimes deliberate and for ulterior motives, explains the poor practice and disregard for equality in planning reported by Murtagh (2017), O'Neill and Murtagh (2021) and the Review of Planning.

The Unionist – one might say pan-unionist – opposition to anything called equality struck at the heart of the Belfast Agreement. The international treaty was signed, but without the engagement or full endorsement of Loyalists and their dependent DUP (who had boycotted the peace negotiations). Protests against policing determinations on parades such as Drumcree, democratic decisions on the flying of the Union flag, and recently the Northern Ireland Protocol, show a pattern of resistance to change and the implementation of the peace process.

This, besides matters such as reproductive rights, equal marriage and the long-agreed Irish Language Act, would appear to paint a picture of recalcitrant Unionism battling the spirit if not the letter of the peace process. Add to this the failure of the planning system, the farce of the FICT Commission on Flags, Identity, Cultures and Traditions, and the ECNI struggling to grasp the new positive equality duty and there is a perfect storm. The Belfast Agreement was settled but implementing the law on equality was too big an ask.

It is all fine and well to propose and draft legislation – though it should be noted that the Belfast Agreement is enacted in legislation only insofar as the 1998 Northern Ireland Act goes (Harvey, 2022). Nevertheless, it is crucial that there is a match between statutory obligations and the capacity of an administration to understand, implement and enforce such law.

This brings us back to the most credible overview of post-conflict studies and (de)stabilising peace (Meehan, 2018). The Belfast Agreement was an elite bargain – disputed from the very start – and hence the constructive ambiguity of the wording, and the complexity of the law that enshrined it. Northern Ireland's peace has constantly been destabilised by what Meehan calls embedded and permissive violence. It requires a decisive and comprehensive response, and one that goes far beyond groupthinking on 'the problem' being simply a matter of sectarian attitudes.

## Sectarian attitudes are not the issue

An unfortunate instance of groupthink and outdated ideas about sectarianism can be found in a 2019 report entitled *Sectarianism: A Review*, authored by Ulster University's Duncan Morrow and supported by the Sir George Quigley Fund. Its terms of reference were:

> *To understand and identify the continuing and changing nature of sectarianism in Northern Ireland, its extremely negative impact on economic, social and cultural life, together with opportunities for its replacement by a concerted process of reconciliation throughout society. 'Reconciliation' is understood as meaning a general willingness on the part of people throughout the community to tolerate and respect the rights of other law-abiding people to hold views at variance from those which they hold themselves.*

The report concluded, correctly, that sectarian division and hostility remains a defining feature and has significant economic costs. The proposed solution, however, was predictably facile and politically illiterate.

> *Concerted, consistent and determined action on the part of the whole of society will be necessary to eradicate sectarian attitudes and support reconciliation, tolerance and mutual respect. There is evidence that a large proportion of people would welcome this.*

Indeed the 2022 election demonstrated the growing support for 'middle ground' non-constitutional politics. However, electoral support was not about attitudes – it was about public service provision and signalled impatience with political deadlock at Stormont. The report was cogently criticised by McVeigh (2019).

> *We were concerned that the report provided a fundamentally flawed blueprint for addressing sectarianism. We felt it reverted to past community relations approaches and missed out key strategic issues, including any seeming reference to the sectarianism in decision-making that contributed to the collapse of power sharing in 2017. The report also seems to position intervention against sectarianism outside the framework of well-tested human rights standards. (McVeigh, 2019: 3)*

Thus a battle of ideologies continues – with the community relations putting attitudes first and the rights lobby prioritising rights and actions.

The former is buoyed up by decades of government peace-building policy in Northern Ireland. That policy has been inadequate if not derisory – from *A Shared Future* through *Cohesion Sharing and Integration* to *Together: Building a United Community*. In these policy terms it seems that almost any cross-community contact can be described as promoting good relations – but without any proof of positive outcomes.

The equality and rights agenda was central to negotiating the Belfast Agreement, stabilising the peace process and remains at the core of how the EU and US regard peace-building. In Northern Ireland the Republican equality and rights narrative has included Irish language rights and the (now internationally accepted legitimacy of) potential for constitutional change. The Unionist narrative is both constitutionally traditional and reactive. As Sinn Féin edged towards political dominance in large parts of local government and in the Stormont Assembly, Unionism reacted with both a constitutionally defensive mantra and a parallel and implacable re-sistance to agreed changes on Irish language, reproductive rights and equal marriage – all of which were eventually established through Westminster.

There is an irony in this and not least as the two jurisdictions of Ireland have, historically, been profoundly sectarian and a mirror image of each other. As O'Toole (2021) has commented on the sectarian state of the Republic of Ireland since its inception and the need for fundamental reform of the church-state relationship – arguing that the realities of the 1950s and 1960s in 'the South' were not too far from the Northern Ireland Unionist notions of a priest-ridden 'backward' state. Moreover, referring to Ireland in the late 1950s, he deftly and elegantly depicts the existential and politico-social realities.

> So many of its real stories were hidden, occluded in shame and secrecy, that it had to have vast official fictions: the beacon of spiritual values, the oppressed nation moving inexorably towards its destiny of unity and freedom, the poster child of economic global-ization. Ireland was not to be expressed. It was to be asserted – in political rhetoric, in public piety, in cruel violence, because the complexities were unendurable, reassurance could be found only in such grand and hollow simplicities.

> The same logic applied north of the Border. Northern Ireland, too, was a polity built against an undesired future, a redoubt of Protestant hegemony that would keep at bay forever the threat of annexation by a Catholics state. But this, too, required a culture

*of pure assertion. Because its sense of itself was embattled it had to be constantly embel-*
*lished. It demanded an excess of definition, an inflated identity that could not include*
*minorities, its dissidents, its actual complexities. If it did not constantly proclaim itself, it*
*would vanish. That exaggerated and exclusive self-image mirrored the one on the other*
*side of the Border. But it also solidified, within its own borders, a minority counterimage*
*with the same fear of annihilation and thus the same need for overstatement, the same*
*craving for sharp-edged definition. (O'Toole, 2021: 569)*

Six decades on, these two jurisdictions have progressed in both social and
political terms. Indeed, were it not for the constitutional question – triggering the old *fear of annihilation* – Northern Ireland might well have embraced new rights and diversity as the Republic has done. Unfortunately,
Northern Ireland has lagged behind. Where the later-to-be first woman
President of Ireland, Mary Robinson started that process and faced the
concerted vitriol of the Church and political elite in Ireland (O'Toole,
2021: 242-245) no such progress emerged in Northern Ireland – until
forced by Westminster in 2021 and 2022.

Whatever the misunderstandings or failures in Northern Ireland's
public authorities, as regards the equality duty, none came near to the
complete lack of understanding in the Home Office. The DeSouza case
exposed a level of basic ignorance of the post-Agreement arrangements for
Northern Ireland citizens in the context of immigration. Although Sinn
Féin did not get the legislative endorsement of parity of esteem for which
they had strongly argued, the Agreement and legal outworking provided
for parity in terms of citizenship – with the right for people in Northern
Ireland to choose to be British or Irish. In the wake of Brexit this had implications, as Irish citizens were EU citizens for the purposes of immigration.

In London the Home Office decided otherwise. Emma DeSouza from
County Derry and her US-born husband fought a lengthy legal battle to
allow him to remain in the UK while she retained her Irish citizenship.

*The UK Home Office had rejected the couple's application on the basis that Ms DeSouza*
*was British, and requested she either apply for residency for her husband as a British*
*citizen or renounce her British citizenship and apply as an Irish citizen.*

*Their case was listed for the Court of Appeal in June, but did not proceed after the Home Office conceded and changed its rules so that everyone born in Northern Ireland would now be regarded as an EU citizen for immigration purposes. (McClements, 2020)*

The case made news headlines as they launched a crowdfunding appeal to help with their legal bill of over £80,000. Emma DeSouza asked the reasonable question as to why ordinary people of limited means should have to fight such legal battles. The UK Home Office had clearly not taken much if any account of the Belfast Agreement.

## Conclusion

The challenges of embedding the process asked a huge amount of a Northern Ireland government and an administration that had emerged after decades of Direct rule from London. The positive equality duty and attendant EQIA seemed to be difficult for some of those public authorities tasked to implement it, although the duty to conduct Environmental Impact Assessment does not appear to have caused similar such trouble. It also gave the new ECNI a new and altered enforcement role as overseeing this statutory duty required skills beyond policing anti-discrimination law. This proved more than was possible in the early years, with implications that can be seen in the planning system – with a sorry lack of vision and leadership. More worryingly, it took the UK Home Office over twenty years to adjust to the negotiated terms of the peace agreement. This is indicative of the somewhat hands-off approach taken in London to this part of the UK.

At a more strategic level, a lesson may be that there is a chasm between the drafting of legislation and implementation that reaches the intended outcomes. ECNI were enforcers of fair employment so that the difference between anti-discrimination and the Section 75 duty was a conceptual and practical leap that took time to actualise. Good community and race relations were a necessary afterthought – and not included in scrutinising

Equality Schemes. Perhaps those who construct and draft law might take more cognisance of the methods necessary to their implementation?

Nevertheless, faulted as implementing Section 75 has been in certain respects, it has been a vital part of securing the peace process as the Belfast Agreement intended. And, while accepting this move towards equal opportunity has been too big an ask of many Unionists and Loyalists, these legal requirements have been tolerated if not welcomed. Equality, like the Northern Ireland Protocol, has been a contingent factor – not imagined but remade to suit a time-specific political narrative.

# CHAPTER 10

# Stability, terrorists and inertia in peace

Republicanism has no overt or immediate military project now that Sinn Féin has secured the political high ground – although the party has not ditched its implicit references to this. Security issues are, nowadays, most commonly discussed and estimated in terms of the actions of the dissidents. The degree of security threat, as assessed by MI5, was reduced from 'severe' to 'substantial' in 2022, after more than a decade. However, the Police Federation for Northern Ireland were still on alert, issuing a press release: *Dissidents still want to kill us, warns police body as threat level reduced* (McCambridge, 2022).

The UK government was sufficiently concerned, and apparently more focused on Loyalism in its attempts at keeping the peace on the streets of Northern Ireland, when they met a Loyalist delegation. In mid-May 2021 Brexit Minister Lord Frost and Northern Ireland Secretary Brandon Lewis met members of the Loyalist Communities Council (LCC) while visiting Northern Ireland – with the LCC asserting *the need for significant change to the NI protocol to bring it back into consistency with the Belfast Agreement and to remove the clear change in the status of Northern Ireland that has occurred due to the imposition of the protocol.* They told Lord Frost of *the efforts they had to make to try and calm the wider unionist community* – which was somewhat disingenuous as the press had reported claims from various sources, including the police, that Loyalist paramilitaries were orchestrating the riots of the previous month. They also spoke of their intention to bring their message to the then European Commission vice-president Maros Sefcovic.

Two days later the LCC appeared before the Northern Ireland Affairs Committee in Westminster stating that the Protocol was *a fundamental breach of democracy*, that there was a *seething anger* at the broken promise of unfettered GB-to-NI trade access, and that that violence might be used as a *last resort*.

The LCC was set up in 2015 in response to the perceived neglect of working class loyalists, representing Loyalist organisations, including the paramilitary Ulster Volunteer Force (UVF), the Ulster Defence Association (UDA) and the Red Hand Commando – all of which are illegal. This was the British government *engaging widely* by meeting a delegation of terrorists.

Skelly discusses the interrelationship of terrorism and diplomacy as a labyrinth – with all the complexities, uncertainties and potential dangers which the term implies. For the British government, it was diplomacy but perhaps without the understanding of its limits. Writing with reference to the IRA he states:

> *Ultimately, if talking to terrorists can be said to have had some success in Northern Ireland, this was only when the terrorists had come to accept the rules of the game and agreed to abide by them in the search for a settlement. ... Above all, there is a crucial difference between talking to terrorists who believe that their strategy is succeeding and those who have been made to realise that their aims are unattainable by violence. (Skelly, 2021: 610)*

When they held secret and then low-profile talks with the IRA in the 1990s, the British government strategy of negotiating peace had been to agree on the need for radical reform in Northern Ireland – and would only succeed because IRA 'representatives' had *come to accept the rules of the game*. In 2021 the LCC had not come to that position. They were threatening a *last resort* – of violence – and a year later the UVF publicly stated it no longer backed the Belfast Agreement. Not only was the LCC short on accepting the rules of the game but, more importantly, no negotiation could reverse the rise of democratic political Republicanism, the possibility of a border poll and a future that beckoned a united Ireland – albeit likely to be a very long-term future.

The LCC stance had echoes of the situation fifty years ago when, in February 1972, the former Northern Ireland Minister for Home Affairs, William Craig set up Ulster Vanguard *as an umbrella movement for the right wing of unionism*. This was in response to 'soft' tactics of Stormont and London in the Sunningdale talks. A month later Craig addressed a crowd of

60,000 in a Belfast park saying *if and when the politicians fail us, it may be our job to liquidate the enemy* (Bew and Gillespie, 1999: 46). By the end of 1973 agreement had been reached to form an executive at Stormont under London rule, replacing the old Parliament, and talks on re-establishing a Council of Ireland to stimulate cooperation with the Republic of Ireland. In defiance at the outcome of the Sunningdale Agreement, and seeing no other means of changing the new arrangements, the newly formed Ulster Workers' Council emerged to orchestrate the 1974 Ulster Workers Strike – when, for two weeks, Loyalist insurgency brought Northern Ireland to its knees, out-manoeuvring British authority in Northern Ireland.

The language, the nomenclature and threats of 2021 echoed those employed in 1973-1974. Indeed there also seems a parallel in the fluctuating support for mass Loyalist protest. In 1977 an attempt at replicating the 1974 Ulster worker's Strike failed to attract sufficient support to get underway – something very similar to the spring 2022 protest rally against the Irish sea border which attracted hundreds rather than the tens of thousands predicted by its organisers.

Nevertheless, with or without mass popular support, as 2021 drew to a close the underlying threat was sinister. Allison Morris (2021b) reported *Loyalist graffiti claiming 'war is needed' appears in Newtownards.*

> *Threatening graffiti that has appeared overnight in a Co Down town has been condemned as a 'sinister and orchestrated development'. The graffiti, signed by the Protestant Action Force, a group previously used as a cover name by the UVF and UDA appeared close to the town centre in Newtownards.*

It would not take many people to create such graffiti in such a Unionist area, but it had a definite chill factor for all to see. Shocking as it was for many viewing this from a distance, such visual threats are not the work of psychological deviants – they are normal.

> *But, in considering causation, it is worth stressing also that, across the universe of terrorist cases past and present, it is the psychological normality of its practitioners and supporters that is striking. ...Repeatedly crucial also in the generation of terrorist violence has been the large effect of small numbers of enthusiasts, zealots, initiators and entrepreneurs. ... (English, 2021b: 652ff)*

The importance of such paramilitary threats is political, if less than nu-anced. In 2021 the Loyalist threat of widespread violence throughout Northern Ireland was enough to gain the LCC entry to top-level talks in Westminster. By 2022 the DUP had been eclipsed by Sinn Féin at Stormont, and had finally recognised that the British government was neither informed nor interested in Northern Ireland's issues about Brexit arrangements – or anything else, short of outright violence.

The DUP was stirring up popular Unionist fears, afraid of a border poll and the prospect of a united Ireland – neither of which were on the imme-diate horizon, and neither of which would necessarily favour Irish unity, as survey findings confirm (Institute of Irish Studies, 2022). More urgently they faced the ignominy – as they saw it – of accepting the democratic vote and taking their position in Stormont with a Deputy First Minister rather than First Minister. The Northern Ireland Protocol, which was 'fixable', was a convenient fig leaf to cover electoral defeat. Victory for Sinn Féin was perhaps a threat to the peace process – not because it augured Republican violence but the opposite, with the prospect of Loyalist-Unionist reaction in the form of terrorism. As if to mirror protests in the 1970s, and ongoing resistance to reform in Northern Ireland since 1998, Unionist-Loyalist op-position to change was to threaten a return to terrorism.

> *If one legitimate criticism of much current debate on terrorism is its short-term or even amnesiac quality, then historians might seem to have something particularly valuable to offer. In terms of terrorism's causation, its varied duration and its various endings, long-term frameworks are essential. ... Indeed, when we consider in detail some of those previous experiences of terrorism, we see that much that has recently been presented as new should more accurately be read as a new version of historically familiar behaviour. (English, 2021a: 8-9)*

It is within just such a long-term framework that the UVF – formed over a century ago – and its political allies, should be seen. Of course, the IRA have a long history of armed struggle, and are usually 'prime suspects' when there is trouble in or from Ireland. The politico-military difference for British governments has always been whose 'side' each supports but their causes – complex and contingent on contemporary events – are mirror images of each other.

> *So, contrary to some suggestions, we actually know a significant amount about why people turn to terrorism. Its practitioners evince complex, tangled motivation at group but also at individual level. Ideology or belief system, suffering and grievance, individual and group desire for revenge or retaliation, the influence of mentors or of influential friends and family, support or encouragement from external sponsors or actors, tactical imitation and inspiration, organisational and other inherent rewards – again and again in the past these elements have variously combined to make terrorist violence seem justified and necessary for the tactical pursuit of various strategic objectives. (English, 2021b: 651-652)*

Unlike Republicanism, which had *strategic objectives*, Unionism-Loyalism sought only to maintain the supremacy of the union with Britain, against any and all democratic change. The perception of an increasingly precarious status quo was what drove the LCC and its political allies in 2021-2022. Not only was Northern Ireland no longer an Orange state where Unionism was triumphal, but the future of the jurisdiction looked increasingly green – though lagging behind in most global issues, green did not signify environmentally cognisant but Republican-Nationalist.

The expected demographic change, predicted in the twentieth century, that was feared by Unionists to herald a Catholic, and therefore Nationalist-Republican voting majority, did not happen. However, voting preferences changed. Ulster Unionism as a once single dominant party splintered to the right and far-right with the expansion of the DUP and the formation of the TUV. A parallel haemorrhaging of an increased Nationalist vote for the SDLP saw Sinn Féin take seats – in local government, Stormont and Westminster (where they refuse to sit) over two post-Agreement decades. At the same time, but slowly, the centre ground Alliance Party built its electoral base taking around a fifth of Assembly seats in the 2022 election.

So, against such a democratic backdrop, with a devolved government – albeit in suspension again – surely the peace process was secure? Why would there be a need for terrorism? Had it not served its purpose by 1998? To coin the phrase used by Gerry Adams, former President of Sinn Féin, in relation to the IRA, they *haven't gone away.*

> *Some observers in Northern Ireland and the Republic of Ireland have decried another shortcoming of the peace process: it has enabled Sinn Féin and loyalist parties to camouflage their continuing links to terrorists. In 2015 the Police Service of Northern Ireland and MI5 concluded that 'All the **main paramilitary groups operating during the***

*period of the Troubles remain in existence*, which includes the Provisional IRA. *(English, 2021b: 615) (My emphasis)*

## A new civic Republicanism?

As it gained electoral strength on both sides of the Irish border Sinn Féin presented itself as a 'normal' political party – with a civic rather than military purpose – as it progressively diluted its historic agenda of a thirty-two-county socialist republic. By 2022 they were the largest party in the Northern Ireland Assembly and had gained substantial political ground in the Republic. As they gained electorally, they took on the seemingly inevitable hubris that accompanies power. In Derry they had taken seats in the European parliament and Westminster in a constituency that had been the SDLP crown. Nemesis, however, came hot on the heels of the party's self-aggrandisement.

Martina Anderson – the only person convicted of the Brighton bombing, released under the terms of the Belfast Agreement – went on to top the poll in the 2012 European election and became an MEP. Yet, by 2019 she was only re-elected on the fifth count. After Brexit took effect and she was no longer MEP, she replaced Raymond McCartney as MLA for Foyle. After *an internal party review of recent election results* in Foyle, on 13 September 2021 she was stood down by the party alongside Karen Mullan MLA (Hutton, 2021). Mullan's reputation had been tarnished by a Tribunal finding that her evidence in an unlawful discrimination case *lacked credibility*. Both Mullan and Anderson alienated many loyal Republicans in the constituency by abusing their power, by exercising rank favouritism and showing blatant arrogance.

Anderson's cousin, Elisha McCallion, also Sinn Féin, took the SDLP crown as MP for Foyle, following years of Westminster representation by party leaders John Hume and Mark Durkan. In 2017 she won with a majority of 169 votes, only to lose to SDLP leader Colum Eastwood who gained a majority of 17,110, amounting to 36.3% of first preference votes in 2019. Her star waned, with her reputation, when in October 2020 she resigned from her seat in the Irish Senate after accepting she should have acted sooner to repay an erroneous UK government Covid-19 small business grant for her Westminster office after accepting she was responsible for the bank account. She no longer serves as an elected public representative in any capacity.

A Christmas 2021 video from Gerry Adams singing, referring to the IRA 'our day will come' was likened to the hugely offensive online 'humour' about a mass murder that cost Barry McElduff his seat. It appalled all but the staunchest of Sinn Féin. After it was taken down, neither the party President nor the leader in Northern Ireland would apologise – although one brave member of the party did.

So, as press reports stated, *they haven't gone away*, and 'they' are seen as dictating at least some Sinn Féin strategy and policy – including in police opinion, North and South, that they orchestrated the funeral of veteran Republican Bobby Storey – an even more egregious flouting of lockdown regulations than Boris Johnson's party gate.

It goes without saying that Sinn Féin has not been alone in the arrogance stakes – as DUP political posturing and scandals such as the Renewable Heat Initiative have clearly shown – although this did not diminish their electoral support in every constituency. However, the nepotism in Foyle challenged even the strongest party discipline in Sinn Féin, its 'solidarity' and eventually cost them seats.


## Official moves on tackling terrorism


The Northern Ireland state inherited terrorist groups with its formation, in the form of the IRA and UVF. While the definition may upset those who ally with paramilitary groups, these organisations have used and retain the capacity to use terrorist tactics.

The Northern Ireland Executive produced its plan, *Tackling Paramilitary activity, criminality and organised crime* and set up a *four member Independent Reporting Commission (IRC)* which reported in 2021. However, the findings and worthy recommendations are unlikely to produce the desired outcomes. This IRC report would indicate that, after *a total of £50 million over five years 2016-2021* provided by the UK government and the Northern Ireland Executive, the core problems remain. It might have been a different story had there been similar investments in education and the youth service over two decades – as indeed the IRC report recommends – although that is also unlikely, if only because Loyalist paramilitaries have opposed such learning schemes in the past.

History, research findings and the brute facts lead to the conclusion that a significant transformation, let alone eradication of terrorist groups, is unlikely. Managing, policing and restraining the coercion and criminal activities of these groups, so as to maintain what is considered an acceptable level of public safety, may reach the limits of what is viable.

> *The terrorist groups in which states have most interest are in fact long-term in two senses: they exist for a lengthily violent time (as with the PLO, Hamas, the FARC, the IRA, the UVF (Ulster Volunteer Force), al-Qaida and other major actors), and the political struggles to which they relate have very long roots in the past. Major terrorist organisations themselves recognise the need to prepare for and engage in long-term struggle. It may be less appealing for people to hear that living with and containing terrorism are more appropriate responses than striving to eradicate it completely. But terrorism's long past suggests that the more modest goal here is the more effective, life-saving one. (English, 2021b: 661-662)*

The negotiations that finally came to fruition in the Belfast Agreement were life-saving. However, they were clearly more than Loyalists wanted – despite the fact that they had their *terrorists in government*.

A possible explanation, though hardly a justification for continued references to the IRA/'the war' by Sinn Féin, is the difficulty they had with the peace process and getting total Republican buy-in for the end of armed struggle. Where British combatants got medals and public acclaim, their bombers and fighters got prison – and many who had committed no crime got interned, or assassinated. Others died in the 1981 Hunger Strike. This perhaps motivated naming the Council-owned play park in Newry after Hunger Striker Raymond McCreesh – something hardly likely to promote equality and good relations which ECNI only belatedly noticed. The need to get and keep the reluctant on board may have fuelled ambiguities around discourse, echoing a notorious Sinn Féin 1990s acronym TUAS.

Was it Totally Unarmed Struggle or Tactical Use of Armed Struggle? (Bew and Gillespies, 1999: 306)

It was less clear-cut for Loyalists who were generally discontented with the terms of negotiated peace. What had been waning support on the ground was revived and sustained by the resentment at changes affecting contested Loyal Order marches, attempts at regulating 12th July bonfires, and reform of rules on flying the Union flag. At the same time, that support was ambivalent. It was threatened by opposition to Loyalist coercion at local community level – with people against their intimidation, drug dealing and various forms of trafficking, yet too fearful to give evidence of criminal activity.

Far from the nay-sayers of a *Turbulent* or *Fragile* peace process (Cochrane, 2021; Waller, 2021), relative stability is likely. A viable accommodation is possible – albeit an uncomfortable one, with the episodic violence and rioting that has characterised this century. Such civil unrest is, in no small part, currently fed by the Unionist-Loyalist response to the Northern Ireland Protocol – as they portray it. However, it could be that Brexit has spawned no more than a small monster that international guardians of the peace in Northern Ireland will be able to contain. Were it not for the Protocol, concerns about the immediacy of Irish unity would not have appeared on the political horizon with such immediacy. The EU and US have shown an interest in the peace process signally absent in Westminster – and understood that the Russian invasion of Ukraine has intensified the need for international cooperation and collaboration – which must be conducted in good faith.

## Conclusions

The pervasive ignorance in London about Northern Ireland, including the arrangements of the peace process, caused Lord Putnam to quit the House of Lords – saying the government was *pig ignorant* about Northern Ireland. The DeSouza case epitomised this ignorance.

The refusal of the DUP to take their place in the Stormont Assembly after the 2022 elections, suspending the devolved government, calls into question the mechanisms designed for power sharing. Is devolved government in Northern Ireland beyond saving now that collapsing Stormont – or political purgatory as Rowan calls it – to be a regular feature on the political landscape? These considerations raise some difficult questions for the political elite because, if power-sharing has to be renegotiated, is the d'Hondt system at risk – and what would replace it?

British authority in Northern Ireland has been challenged from the start. The threat to the constitutional status quo has been construed as armed Republican rebellion – notably with the various IRA campaigns throughout the twentieth century. And yet history also records the Unionist insurgency that brought Northern Ireland to a standstill half a century ago with the 1974 Ulster Workers strike and threatened so in 2022. The Northern Ireland peace process has evolved in a quarter century, and fears that its collapse is imminent have ebbed and waned over those years. Blatant sectarian protest, rioting and violence throughout this time, the recurring political vacuum at Stormont, and the entrenched problems of poverty and socio-economic inequality have been explained in terms of identity politics, ethno-political intransigence and materialist theories. And yet, despite the continued existence of terrorist groups, it survives. Destabilisation does not come from Republicanism at this point, but from Loyalism.

# CHAPTER 11

# Concluding comments and more than a glimmer of hope

This book began with a description of the interfaces in north and west Belfast a few days after rioting at Lanark Way in April 2021. Like almost all the interfaces in Belfast, the dynamics of these areas and the war-time architecture have not changed during the peace process – they have not been dismantled or transformed and remain a stubborn accretion of hostility and division. Government policy to have them removed by 2023 failed to materialise, while levels of residential segregation and polarisation increased after 1998 – intensified with each wave of violent protests against the reforms intended to embed peace.

The violence and civil disorder at Lanark Way was represented as a sign that the Northern Ireland peace process was crumbling, attracting a huge media out-pouring to that effect. The questions arising from my tour asked why interfaces persisted, and how the 1998 peace settlement had operated, or not, in areas like urban planning, and public authorities promoting equality – acknowledging the context of continuous violent protest against the reforms, particularly since 1998. How could there have been a peace process that left most of these places unaltered – and still the spaces of ferocious hostilities?

History records that, as an effective government from Stormont only emerged in 2007 and was abandoned from 2017 to 2020, the pace of reform was very slow going. The Review of Public Administration, scheduled for 2002, simply did not happen then. Turf wars between departmental and local government aside, this created a persistent and systematic failure in both government and administration – until belatedly it came into operation in 2015.

Slow and sporadic progress in implementing new equality and human rights legislation, and lack of understanding in these fields, provided

abundant space for contestation around flags, identity, culture and tradition. The assertion of the right to march on the Queen's highway – whatever objections local residents might have – to construct 10- to 20-metre
high bonfires with the attendant anti-social drunken behaviour and risk
to life and property, and the refusal to compromise on flags and emblems
seriously reduced the credibility of the Unionist political narrative. Their
message seemed to continue the 'Not an inch!' of the 1960s and 1970s.

The DUP refusal to implement the agreement to introduce Irish language legislation for well over a decade also discredited Unionism, and
provided Sinn Féin with plausible arguments that nothing had changed
significantly.

Important as the politics and misrepresentations of Brexit and the
Northern Ireland Protocol may have been, they paled into insignificance
compared to Renewable Heat Incentive and other scandals that enveloped
the DUP – which were major factors leading to the suspension of Stormont
in 2017. They were little more than a convenient excuse for the DUP to
collapse the Stormont Assembly in February 2022.

None of these factors can be explained by 'ugly attitudes' of sectarianism that might magically be transformed. Yes, Northern Ireland is a
divided place, and sectarian hatred persists. There is no doubt that the
legacy of the conflict, and subsequent violent disputes, such as Holy Cross,
still open old wounds. However, these are not sufficient, in themselves, to
destabilise the peace process.

The rioting in April 2021 at Lanark Way, orchestrated by Loyalist
paramilitaries, exemplified the post-Agreement civil disorder to which
many Unionist politicians allied themselves – publicly or otherwise. It
was what Meehan (2018) calls *Competitive violence: aimed at destabilising
political settlements*. In 2021 it was aimed at undermining the Brexit settlement and continued a trend of attempting to destabilise the changes
brought by the peace settlement in Northern Ireland. However, it did not
significantly do so.

Democratic Unionist politicians were seduced by the idea of resistance
to the Northern Ireland Protocol but shied away from taking responsibility
for the brute facts of street violence and embryonic insurrection – as indeed
many Unionists had for the duration of the Northern Ireland state. So, when

the leader of the much-depleted Ulster Unionist Party refused to take part in Irish sea border protest rallies, because of the potential for serious and widespread violence, he was publicly denounced as a traitor to the Union at one rally, where a cardboard replica of him was displayed with a noose around his neck. That spark of leadership, reflecting the courage of David Trimble in signing the Belfast Agreement, was extinguished.

Republicans had won enough in the peace settlement, and subsequent elections, to make their struggle a political and symbolic battle where such blatant tactics no longer served their purposes. The fact that dissident Republican elements had continued their attacks for two decades was a problem – but mainly for those, such as the police, whom they targeted. The murder of journalist Lyra McKee who was shot in April 2019 during rioting in the nationalist Creggan district of Derry was disastrous for dissident Republicanism. It led to a combination of amnesty/surrender of struggle for Ogla na Heirann (ONH), falling support for the New IRA, and widespread anger among the wider republican, nationalist and Catholic community. Dissident republicans remained a risk factor but not sufficiently to stop the downgrading of the official security threat level from severe to substantial by March 2022. This downgrading made news for a day but did not resonate with public sentiment. The narrative of security alerts was increasingly irrelevant to most people by 2022.

This again begs the question, is there actually a real threat to peace in Northern Ireland? Certainly there is politically motivated violence. Meehan (2018) notes that *Violence can be due to a lack of a deal or embedded in the deal, with very different policy implications.*

> *Violence may be: (i) a result of a political settlement breaking down, (ii) integral to how political settlements operate; or (iii) able to operate alongside a stable political settlement. Policymakers need to analyse carefully the types of violence they are engaging with. (Meehan, 2018: 6)*

Loyalist violence is very much embedded in resisting the deal that was the Belfast Agreement, because it brought in change and reform they could barely tolerate. In this way their resistance operated alongside a relatively stable political settlement. Yet, peace persists.

As English (2021a) pointed out *terrorist groups in which states have most interest are in fact long-term in two senses: they exist for a lengthily violent time ... and the political struggles to which they relate have very long roots in the past.* These groups still exist in Northern Ireland and are embedded in the social and political fabric of this society. Terrorists don't come from another planet. They are not outsiders.

The often-heard accusation that there are 'terrorists in government' should not be taken as one-sided. Former IRA activists, prisoners, hunger strikers and bombers took their place as elected representatives – in local government, the Assembly and Westminster (where they refuse to sit). However, a similar meshing of personal and political relationships is evident in the DUP, if not all Unionism.

It is on public record that Emma Little-Pengelly, DUP MLA, is the daughter of a Noel Little leading figure in the UDA, convicted of gun running. She is married to Richard Pengelly, the Permanent Secretary of the Department of Justice – the department responsible for interfaces as well as policing and justice. She was Special Advisor to Ian Paisley when he was First Minister of the Stormont Assembly and his successor, Peter Robinson – neither of whom were strangers to Loyalist paramilitary groups and actions – until she became MP for South Belfast.

Northern Ireland is currently part of the UK and will remain so until there is a democratic change. The Northern Ireland Protocol is one in a long series of red lines – like the flying of the Union flag 365 days a year on public buildings – that will be resolved. What matters for the future of a stable and relatively peaceful, if divided and sectarian Northern Ireland, is the degree to which embedded violence erupts as a border poll and the real possibility of a united Ireland beckons. This is not likely to happen in this decade but it may form a decisive factor for terrorists. The *political struggles to which they relate have very long roots in the past* and those may produce the shoots of a new and different but equally destructive conflict – where Loyalists are the protagonists.

Yet there is every reason to be hopeful, as the level of sectarian violence and murder is dramatically reduced, the Northern Ireland Protocol has resulted in the best local economic growth in the UK since Brexit (BBC, 2022), and opinions are less divided than in previous years. As Shirlow reports, life in Northern Ireland is considerably more positive than popular opinion portrays.

> *In measuring change since 1998 fewer than 10 per cent were able to accurately identify that reported sectarian crime has decreased significantly (i.e. by 60 per cent) and less than 10 per cent knew that conflict related convictions fell by 90 per cent. Despite a landscape dotted by wind farms fewer than 5 per cent knew that 40 percent of our electricity is produced by renewable energy – at twice the EU average. Yet, in a terrain of negativity respondents were closer when estimating the levels of poverty. (Shirlow, 2022b)*

And, it is not only economic and public safety considerations that provide a brighter picture. The EU and US have taken a strong interest and determined diplomatic stance on Northern Ireland because they understand these issues. They have led in restraining the UK government from reinstating a hard border between north and south in the island – averting any putative justifications from dissident or other Republican for acts of terrorism. It can only be hoped that those in London and Belfast who possess the appropriate leadership, informed intelligence and capacity to tackle terrorist criminal activity in Northern Ireland will see to its containment and save lives.

The short history of Brexit and the Northern Ireland Protocol reveals the dangers of simple slogans that hide the complexities of constitutional change. Sinn Féin rejected the Shared Island project[20] because it did not include discussion of constitutional change. This perhaps unmasked their desire to avoid the difficult questions that a border poll would bring up. It is not as simple as 'get Brexit done'.

---

20    The Shared Island initiative involves: working with the Northern Ireland Executive and the British Government to address strategic challenges faced on the island of Ireland; further developing the all-island economy, deepening North/South cooperation, and investing in the North West and border regions; and, fostering constructive and inclusive dialogue and a comprehensive programme of research to support the building of consensus around a shared future on the island. The Shared Island Fund was announced in Budget 2021, with €500m in capital funding available between 2021-2025, ring-fenced for investment in collaborative North/South projects. A Shared Island unit in the Department of the Taoiseach acts as a driver and coordinator of this whole of government initiative.

Equally the history of the peace process in Northern Ireland is a lesson in how the best laid plans, legislation and constructive ambiguity are a road map, at best. The clear evidence is that implementing the law, policy and administrative change are considerably more problematic – and require political and administrative leadership. Stopping a military campaign and reaching a peace agreement was the start. What followed, however faulted, was the beginning of a process that will embed and inform future endeavours – even in the context of so many missed opportunities. Terrorist groups remain and Northern Ireland society operates by eliding these uncomfortable truths. Changing these realities and the socio-economic fabric of inequality, deprivation and the living conditions that support paramilitary activities – and lives coerced by domestic and social terrorism – is perhaps more than can be expected in the near future. Leadership and relevance in politics is needed. This book has demonstrated the leadership by local people like Gerry Robinson, officials like Dermot O'Kane and leading representative of the seriously injured, Paul Gallagher. Now there are calls for politicians to follow suit.

Shortly after the 2022 Assembly election results were published, Shirlow (2022a) wrote that the *Assembly must show relevance regarding the NI Protocol* and pointed to the fact that *InvestNI were recording a unique growth in interest in investing in Northern Ireland* and yet politicians failed to respond to such good news. The new arrangements had brought economic benefits and yet the Protocol was being represented as a crisis rather than an opportunity.

> *If such an evidenced benefit is not now deliberated upon opportunity will be lost. ... If MLAs do not take such an opportunity and do not now turn crisis into representative and deliberative democracy then what was the point in voting and why are they ignoring their own voters who want to see enhanced and shared leadership?*

The political leadership of the mandatory coalition in a power-sharing Assembly proved to be shared out in a sometimes blatantly sectarian manner over the years. Where Ian Paisley and Martin McGuinness as First and Deputy First Ministers were dubbed the Chuckle Brothers and appeared to be able to hold power without animosity, the open antagonism between their successors has fed division and hostility among the electorate – seemingly legitimising sporadic unrest, and certainly nurt-uring ethno-political division. The shadow of an adversarial government predated and perhaps pre-empted the shadow of Brexit. Brexit itself dem-onstrated the need for clarity – and like Irish unity is too complex for a simple yes-or-no debate.

It is time for political leaders to step aside from gladiatorial games over language rights, flags and 'culture' and demonstrate the courage and leadership seen in those who won the long battle for a peace settlement and the Troubles Pension, and the acuity of some parts of administration.

Returning to our starting point of the Belfast interfaces and the Grace Family Centre, the mundane realities of living in deprived areas under the shadow of hostility, we can ask, what has changed since 1998? Improvements have faced both political and paramilitary obstacles for sure. However, the administrative system did not change sufficiently quickly to implement the terms of the Belfast Agreement to see outcomes that could have altered the lived experience of remaining under siege during critical periods. And, despite a massive reduction in violence and sectarian crimes, many fewer murders and a reprieve from bombings, the interfaces remain the last pitch for actual battles for the future. Unchanged, they will perpetuate the sect-arian crime seen since the 1920s. This is why the new planning regulations, so vital to peace-building, are to be welcomed – as is the leadership integral to their production.

The essential function of the interface is to block connectivity. The intention in building these walls was to stop bombs being driven into the city and to separate areas where sectarian murder and violence frequently happened. While this created sectarian enclaves, it was welcomed by resi-dents, and to this day many still fear their removal – albeit for misguided reasons. The separation fed distrust, fear and hostility and was expedient for ethno-political entrepreneurs. Interfaces no longer serve any useful function. Belfast needs connectivity (Boujenko et al., 2008) – as well as social housing, employment and sustainable development.

So, to finish the book – but not to end a continuing journey – there is a small but significant sign of new-found political leadership that appeared over the months between September 2021 and June 2022.

Belfast City Council six-party Planning Committee took the comprehensive advice from planning officials and voted to develop a community greenway on the site of the former Mackie's industrial plant. This
25-acre site was designated for industrial use and would accommodate
commercial development, but could also provide open green space. This
promised much increased and necessary connectivity in the west of the
city and would be environmentally beneficial. Both unionist, nationalists
and 'other' councillors voted to include the Mackie site as part of the £5.1
million Forth Meadow Greenway, a 12 kilometre route connecting parks
and open spaces from North and West Belfast in September 2021.

The Council then faced legal proceedings when the High Court
granted leave for a judicial review to challenge the decision, which cam-
paigners said *sidelined housing rights*. Press and media coverage almost
exclusively reflected the fact that the site is in the area of highest social
housing demand in the North of Ireland. Objections were based on a social-
housing-only argument and the case taken by an individual on behalf of a
leading rights project. However, their case was based on outdated strategies
for urban development and seemed to hark back to post-war housing development in the 1950s and 1960s, echoing the well-meant but ill-informed
view that housing equals community, and adequate living services and
space. This vision and strategy won the first legal contest.

The Forth Meadow Greenway proposal is clearly complex, and not
merely a matter of building social housing – urgently needed as it is –
on every available plot of land. The housing-only strategy and building
schemes of the 1950s through to the late 1970s produced dysfunctional
estates, lacking social cohesion and many of the vital elements of the necessary social, educational, environmental and employment facilities that
create good living spaces and places where people can build resilience. Huge
swathes of social housing and high-rise flats were constructed with little if
any inclusion of shops, schools, medical, dental, sports or social facilities.
These failed to provide communities with social spaces and were wide open
to becoming subject to paramilitary coercion. The current thinking, strategy
and planning criteria address these and many other key considerations.

The minutes of the meetings to September 2021 and June 2022 provide full explanations of the advice provided by officials and the constructive way in which the interface and other urban space could best be developed.

> *9.13 The aim of the proposal is to help create new connected shared civic spaces for use by all sections of the community, with high quality, safe, shared spaces and Greenway networks, enhancing linkages between communities and promoting sustainable transport opportunities. These are important material considerations which weigh in favour of the proposal. As well as providing new pathways within the site itself to allow for pedestrians and cyclists, the proposal will enhance and expand the ecology and habitats which exist on the site, such as the Open Mosaic Habitat. This is also an important material consideration.*

> *10.0 Conclusion and Recommendation 10.1 The proposal will support connectivity and linkage between communities and promote health and well-being to the surrounding area, which is to be welcomed. It is considered that the proposal would enhance the character and appearance of the area. There are no objections from consultees. The objections from third parties have been addressed in the report. 10.2 Having regard to relevant policy, representations and other material considerations, the proposal is considered acceptable. It is recommended that planning permission is granted with the final wording of conditions delegated to the Director of Planning and Building Control. (<https://minutes.belfastcity.gov.uk/documents/s101314/ 2020%201959%20Forthmeadow%20Committee%20Report%2027%20June%202022.pdf>)*

The detailed considerations and advice given to the committee included

- principle of development
- impact on the character and appearance of the area
- impact on natural heritage
- access, movement and parking, including road safety
- impact on built heritage
- flood risk
- landscaping
- other environmental matters

The all-party members of the Belfast City Council planning committee were again open to informed advice, and, having withstood an impassioned if somewhat simplistic legal challenge, had shown civic and political leadership in their initial decision[21] and similar vision in their second

21    Meeting of Hybrid Meeting, Planning Committee, Tuesday, 14 September 2021

decision in June 2022.[22] These decisions underpin the drive for social housing in its best context and under optimal conditions and bodes well for future urban development in Belfast. Indeed, it may even signal a willingness in political circles to go at least a little beyond the ethno-political decisions of the past.

It has to be said that the Forth Meadow Greenway site is not electorally contested and there are no longer any discernible political gains or losses involved – so it is a level playing field as far as votes go. Nevertheless, the committee decision demonstrates a civic rather than ethno-political leadership.

Although departmental politics around planning and infrastructure remain at least as much a challenge as the machinations of formal politics, there is hope that the promised oversight and regulatory planning commission will appear and operate to tackle urban development effectively and strengthen the peace process.

In the introduction I cited a comment I made to Lauren Van Metre of the National Democratic Institute that *the shadow of Brexit is the footprint of the constitutional struggle*. The reason Brexit and the Northern Ireland Protocol have been constructed as a source of protest, and the stuff of media headlines, is because London and many unionists have forgotten the terms of the international treaty that was the Belfast Agreement – if they ever understood or entirely agreed with these terms.

In any case, this has created no more than the latest in a long line of dark shadows over the peace process since the 1990s. The Belfast Agreement is firmly grounded and has international guarantors. Reforms and positive changes have been slow but have emerged. So, the peace process cannot be overridden on the whim of an unstable UK government and orchestrated but less than wholly popular paramilitary protests. That provides more than a glimmer of hope under dark shadows.

---

5.00 pm (Item 9f).

22    <https://minutes.belfastcity.gov.uk/documents/s101314/2020%201959%20Fort hmeadow%20Committee%20Report%2027%20June%202022.pdf>.

# A late comment on Brexit and the Protocol

This book had already gone into production when I spoke with renowned historian Lord Paul Bew. He will be involved as the Protocol legislation goes to the House of Lords, assuming that no compromise with the EU can be reached in the interim. Having generously agreed to read my work and comment on its balance – at a time when he had his own publishing deadline to meet as well as his work in the House of Lords – I was ethically obliged to add a postscript acknowledging his opinions.

While he accepted the main part of the manuscript Paul Bew took issue with Bobby McDonagh's article *UK reneging on protocol would unsettle North* – which asserted that *one can dismiss out of hand the stated reason that the intention is to protect the Belfast Agreement* – and pointed to other opinions, referring me to Roderick Crawford's *The Northern Ireland Protocol: The Origins of the Current Crisis* – which notes contributions by Newton Emerson and Andy Pollack on North-South and East-West economic relations. Available online, the report is billed as:

> Crawford's work *is the only existing authoritative chronology of the Brexit negotiations and specifically what went wrong in 2017. It argues that commitments, particularly on the Irish border, in the 2017 Joint Report were "a diplomatic triumph for Ireland and the Commission" but that "failing to secure adequate reciprocal concessions was a staggering failure for the UK." The paper is the story of how the UK got stuck with a protocol that was determined by a one-sided and flawed interpretation of the Belfast Agreement.* (https://policyexchange.org.uk/publication/the-northern-ireland-protocol/)

Lord Frost's foreword admits Tory failure in negotiating Brexit arrangements for Northern Ireland in 2017–18 – and gives further credence to the impression that London was either not focused or ill-informed about the implications for Northern Ireland. On the face of it, it would seem a case of oblivious rather than perfidious Albion.

> *We knew, as did the Irish Government, that this new Protocol would require immensely sensitive handling. We understood that the East-West dimensions of the Northern Irish*

*economy are in any circumstances vastly more important than its "all island" dimen-*
*sions – and that the former not the latter were the economic lifeblood of the province.*
*We knew, as some in the Irish Government would privately concede, that the balance*
*between the three strands of the Belfast (Good Friday) Agreement had been upset by*
*the approach taken in the Joint Report; and that the risk was that the EU's approach*
*to the Protocol would not be consistent with the explicit commitment to protect the*
*Agreement, in all its dimensions.*

Crawford sees this part of the Withdrawal Agreement as flawed. *Shared*
*language masking very different understandings of what each side meant*
*and was committing to was a very serious problem throughout the dia-*
*logue* (9). He argues that the UK position was weakened as Dublin out-
manoeuvred London and that the Belfast Agreement was undermined by
prioritising 'all island/North-South' relations. *The power-sharing devolved*
*government in Belfast is primarily East-West, not North-South: that, apart*
*from anything else, is the nature of devolution* (10). One has to ask why all
three strands were not at the centre of UK negotiating strategy.

Not only were UK negotiators out-manoeuvred but those most politically opposed to the outcome – Unionists, and the DUP in particular –
were apparently not included at this early stage in discussions, 'mapping
exercises' and other preparations in 2017 as Stomont was in suspension.

*The interests and insights of Northern Ireland – especially its unionists – had no insti-*
*tutional channel of their own to engage with London, Dublin or Brussels. The require-*
*ment for the North South Ministerial Council to have its 'views taken into account and*
*represented appropriately at relevant EU meetings', as set out in the Belfast Agreement*
*could have helped inform all the negotiators, balanced the influence of Dublin, and held*
*London to account. This may be one of the most overlooked events of the entire period –*
*the original democratic deficit.* (16)

While this may be true it begs the question, was it Unionist/DUP in-
competence or political dereliction of duty? If there was to be no hard
border on the island of Ireland it could only be in the Irish Sea. However,
Unionist politicians were involved, if only at a later stage, in the pivotal
Specialised Committee on Ireland – Northern Ireland (INISC).

*Officials from the Northern Ireland Civil Service are present at official INISC meetings at*
*the invitation of the UK government; whether they are kept informed of the background*

*work of the INISC officials is rather more ad hoc. When asked (amid growing political and public tensions over the Protocol implementation in Northern Ireland) in April 2021 for an update on the engagement by the UK and the EU with Northern Ireland stakeholders, including the Executive, and on formal consultation mechanisms to ensure their full participation in the WA institutions, Lord Frost replied that 'representatives of the NI Executive attend the JC and the Specialised Committee' – meetings that had happened four to eight weeks earlier* (Hayward, 2022: 52).

As is clear in Chapter Eight of this book, senior officials were informed.

*Director General of International Relations for the Northern Ireland Executive Office. Between 2017 and 2020, when the North's institutions were suspended, he regularly attended UK ministerial meetings, and until May 2021 represented the Executive during meetings of the EU-UK Specialised Committee on the Protocol.* (Connolly, 2022)

According to Crawford, in 2017 Unionists, and especially the DUP which then had a 'supply and confidence' alliance to keep the Conservatives in government, appear to have meekly accepted a situation in which:

*In summary the paper exaggerated the role of the EU, of North-South cooperation and ignored entirely Northern Ireland's integration into and dependence on the UK, including across some of the policy areas it listed under North-South cooperation. The word 'consent' did not appear in the document or its annexes.* (50)

*The key development in this round of negotiations was the commitment by both parties to the six guiding principles set out in the EU's paper of September 2017. By accepting them without amendment and without getting EU agreement on any of the specifically UK principles, the UK effectively put an end to its insistence on the balance of the Belfast Agreement being upheld in all its parts: East-West (including NI-GB) and North-South in particular and taking account of their depth and complexity. Commitments to 'the Belfast Agreement in all its parts' were reduced in the EU paper to ensuring (sic) that the institutions established by the Belfast Agreement would be able to continue to operate; that is far from the same thing and far less than the EU negotiating directives stated.* (59)

London was apparently unaware of the importance of the third East-West strand of the Agreement and saw the implications of a hard border - understanding that it might well stoke the fires of dissident if not mainstream Republican resistance, possibly rekindling an imagined justification for armed struggle. To have given top priority to East-West relations would perhaps have been unwise - though failing to see its importance was equally if not more unwise.

To Crawford the paucity of London's negotiation skills was accompanied by a lack of appropriate administrative preparation. Yet this does not square with the account of Dr McCormick, Director General of International Relations for the Northern Ireland Executive Office, between 2017 and 2020 when Stormont was suspended. And, while statements made in 2017 by Theresa May and Michel Barnier indicated very different understandings of the content, meaning and implications of the Joint Report, neither interpretation is a challenge to the constitutional status of the Northern Ireland jurisdiction.

Crawford concludes:

> *The evidence base put forward to justify the need to maintain Northern Ireland's alignment with the EU was hugely exaggerated and never tested or assessed against the far deeper integration of Northern Ireland in the UK. This failure to accept the balance of the Belfast Agreement and the complex realities of Northern Ireland is at the heart of the current trouble with the protocol, and the fault for that lies in part in Dublin, even if the responsibility must ultimately lie in the negotiating 'success' of Brussels and the UK's failure to successfully challenge already existing assumptions. The defence of the UK government is that it was on the ropes.* (86)

It is difficult to imagine a worse combination of failures. These would render an already inevitable Irish Sea Border more inflexible than was necessary. As the DeSouza case epitomises, London appears ignorant of key aspects of the Belfast Agreement - such as the right of all Northern Ireland residents to hold British or Irish citizenship. So much more so in missing - or ignoring - the need to balance all three of its strands.

As the Protocol legislation makes its way towards the statute book - if the UK does not negotiate with the EU - the UK further risks breaking international treaties, undermining the country's reputation to an even greater degree, and destroying what is left of trust and good faith in the UK. Having signed up to a deal that they now find unpalatable, tearing up the agreement is set to have serious repercussions for the Trade and Cooperation Agreement with the EU.

Ultimately, Brexit is the problem, necessitating a sea rather than a land border. Whether that breaks from the Belfast Agreement's commitment to consent is very much a matter of interpretation. Indeed, as the escalating cost of living crisis looks set to dominate political events in the UK for some time, the politics of Stormont and Westminster will have to adapt.

The failure in UK negotiations appears to have been due to their arrogance, as evidenced in October 2022 when a minister of state for Northern Ireland, Steve Baker – former chair of the virulently Brexiteer European Research Group – apologised for UK arrogance in the Brexit negotiations and stated a need for future 'humility'. That is a more credible account of what is seen as an imbalance.

This book began with a tour of the Belfast interfaces and these remain whatever the issues around Brexit and the Northern Ireland Protocol. The neglect of these sites of violence remains one of the greatest challenges of the peace process – requiring leadership and the political will to transform these places. People like Paul Bew who can transcend political differences could help meet these challenges – but only if there is both the political and administrative leadership to see through the recommendations on crucial matters such as urban planning. At this stage, a return to thirty years of conflict in Northern Ireland is not on the horizon.

# Bibliography

BBC. (2022). *Newsline*, 3 August 2022, Belfast, BBC Northern Ireland.

BBC. (2011). *Radio Ulster News*, 3 September 2011, Belfast, BBC Northern Ireland.

Belfast Interface Project. (2017). Interface Barriers, Peacelines and Defensive Architecture, Belfast. <www.belfastinterfaceproject.org/publication/interface-barriers-peacelines-and-defensive-architecture>.

Bell, J., Jarman, N., and Harvey, B. (2010). *Beyond Belfast: Contested Spaces in Urban, Rural and Cross-Border Settings*, Community Relations Council and Rural Community Network, Belfast.

Bew, Paul, Gibben, Peter, and Patterson, Henry. (2002). *Northern Ireland 1921–2001: Political Forces and Social Classes*, Serif, London.

Bew, Paul, and Gillespie, Gordon. (1999). *Northern Ireland: A Chronology of the Troubles 1968-1999*, Gill & Macmillan, Dublin.

Boujenko, N., Buchanan, C., and Jones, P. (2008, June). Improving Connectivity and Mobility in Belfast, *Discussion Paper VI*. Belfast City Council, Belfast.

Bowman, John. (2021). Who Should Get Credit for the Belfast Agreement? *The Irish Times*, 31 December 2021, 5.

Bradfield, Phillip. (2022). Unionists Debate Decision to Reduce Dates for Flying Union Flag by Seven, *Belfast Newsletter*, 23 March 2022, 11.

Breen-Smyth, M. (2012). The Needs of Individuals and Their Families Injured as a Result of the Troubles in Northern Ireland: Final Report, WAVE Trauma Centre. <http://wavetraumacentre.org.uk/site/wp-content/uploads/2019/04/pdfresizer.com-pdf-resize-15.pdf>.

Brewer, John D. (2022). *Advanced Introduction to the Sociology of Peace Processes*, Edward Elgar Publishing, London.

Brewer, John. (2010). *Peace Processes: A Sociological Approach*, Polity Press, Cambridge.

Bryan, D., and Gillespie, G. (2005). *Transforming Conflict: Flags and Emblems*, Institute of Irish Studies, Queen's University Belfast, Belfast.

Burns, Sarah. (2021). *The Irish Times*, 11 August 2021, p. 5.

Byrne, J. (2006). Interface Violence in East Belfast during 2002: The Mechanisms and Programmes Employed to Limit the Impact on Local Residents, *Shared Space*, 2.

Cameron Report. (1969). *Disturbances in Northern Ireland: Report of the Commission Appointed by the Governor of Northern Ireland*, Cmnd. 532, Belfast, HMSO.

Carroll, Rory. (2022). Future of Unionism Marching on … but to Where? *The Observer*, 24 April 2022, 31-34.

Chambers, I., Drysdale, J., and Hughes, J. (2010). The Future of Leadership: A Practitioner View, *European Management Journal*, 28(4), pp. 260–268.

Cochrane, Feargal. (2021). *Northern Ireland: The Fragile Peace*, New edition, Yale University Press, New Haven and London.

Committee on the Administration of Justice. (2006). *Equality in Northern Ireland: The Rhetoric and the Reality*, Committee on the Administration of Justice, Belfast.

Committee on the Administration of Justice. (2020, January). Initial Thoughts on Rights and the New Decade, New Approach (NDNA) Agreement (S485) Briefing Note, Belfast.

Commission on Flags. (2021, December). Identity, Culture and Tradition, Final Report (FICT Report). <https://www.executiveoffice-ni.gov.uk/sites/defa ult/files/publications/execoffice/commission-on-fict-final-report.pdf>.

Connolly, Tony. (2022). Former Stormont Official Criticises UK Govt's Attitude Over NI Protocol, 27 April 2022: 20.58. <https://www.rte.ie/news/brexit/ 2022/0427/1294751-protocol-andrew-mccormick/>.

Craig, Paul. (2022, January). EU Governance of the Protocol: Legal Structure, Rights and Enforceability, Chapter 3 in McCrudden, Christopher, ed., *The Law and Practice of the Ireland-Northern Ireland Protocol*, Cambridge University Press, 31-39. · Online Publication. Online ISBN: 9781009109840.

CRC. (2009). *The Business of Peace: Working for a Better Future: Community Relations, Stability and the Economy: Policy Development Conference Report*, Community Relations Council, Belfast.

CRC. (2008). *Towards Sustainable Security – Interfaces, Barriers and the Legacy of Segregation in Belfast*, Community Relations Council for Northern Ireland, Belfast.

Cresswell, J. (2010). Towards a Politics of Mobility, *Environment and Planning D: Society and Space*, pp. 117–31.

Cross, Gareth. (2021). *Belfast Telegraph*, 29 April 2021, p. 18.

Daly, Oscar. (1999). Northern Ireland: The Victims. *British Journal of Psychiatry*, 174, pp. 201–204

Deiana, Maria-Adriana, and Goldie, Roz. (2012). Survivors in Peace: Government Response in Meeting the Needs of Survivors of Serious Physical Injury and Sexual Assault during Conflict, as a Legacy for Northern Ireland and Bosnia-Herzegovina, *International Journal of Peace Studies*, 17(1), pp. 1–23.

Department of Justice. (2019). Interfaces Programme: A Framework Document, Belfast. <www.justice-ni.gov.uk/publications/interfaces-programme-framew ork-document>.

DeYoung, Elizabeth. (2016). Lest We Forget: Observations from Belfast's Twaddell Avenue, *Streetnotes*. <https://doi.org/10.5070/S5251029669>.

Donnelly, P. (2006). Interfaces, in *Sharing Over Separation: Actions Towards a Shared Future*, pp. 115–128, Community Relations Council, Belfast.

Emerson, Newton. (2021). There Have Always Been Amnesties. *The Irish Times*, 15 July 2021, p. 12.

English, Richard. (2021a). Current Knowledge and Future Research, Chapter 26 in *History and the Study of Terrorism*, pp. 647–671, Cambridge University Press, Cambridge.

English, Richard, ed. (2021b). *History and the Study of Terrorism*, Cambridge University Press, Cambridge. <https://doi.org/10.1017/9781108556248.026>.

Equality Commission for Northern Ireland. (2007, February). *Final Report of Commission Investigation under Paragraph 10 of Schedule 9 of the Northern Ireland Act 1998: Gerald Marshall & Omagh District Council*, Belfast.

Equality Commission for Northern Ireland. (2006a). *Final Report of Commission Investigation under Paragraph 10 of Schedule 9 of the Northern Ireland Act 1998: Paul Butler & Lisburn City Council*, Belfast, 26 June 2006. <www.equalit yni.org/statutory duty>.

Equality Commission for Northern Ireland. (2006b). *Promoting Good Relations in Practice: A Guide for Public Authorities* (Consultation Document). Belfast, December 2006.

Equality Commission for Northern Ireland. (2003a). *Report on the Implementation of the Section 75 Equality and Good Relations Duties by Public Authorities*, Belfast.

Equality Commission for Northern Ireland. (2003b). *Revised Draft Guidelines to the Statutory Duties*, Consultation Document, Belfast. <http://www.equalit yni.org>.

FICT Report. (2021, December). Commission on Flags, Identity, Culture and Tradition, Final Report. <https://www.executiveoffice-ni.gov.uk/sites/defa ult/files/publications/execoffice/commission-on-fict-final-report.pdf>.

Fredman, Sandra. (2002). *Discrimination Law*, Clarendon Law Series, Oxford University Press, Oxford.

Gaffikin, F., McEldowney, M., Rafferty, G., and Sterrett, K. (2008). *Public Space for a Shared Belfast: A Research Report for Belfast City Council*, Belfast City Council, Belfast.

Gallagher, Paul. (2021). New Social Movement Theory and the Reparations Movement in Northern Ireland: The Case of the WAVE Injured Group and Its Campaign for Recognition in Northern Ireland, PhD thesis, Queen's University Belfast, Belfast. <https://pureadmin.qub.ac.uk/ws/portalfiles/por

tal/265267790/PhD_Thesis_Paul_Gallagher_40097757_27_November_2 021.pdf>.

Galtung, Johan. (1969). Violence, Peace, and Peace Research. *Journal of Peace Research*, 6(3), pp. 167–191.

Goldie, Roz. (2021). *A Dangerous Pursuit: The Anti-sectarian Work of Counteract*, Peter Lang, Oxford.

Goldie, Roz. (2008). The Smaller Peace Process in Northern Ireland: Case Studies of Local Government Promoting Good Relations, PhD thesis, Queen's University Belfast, Belfast.

Goldie, R., and Murphy, J. (2015). Belfast beyond Violence: Flagging up a Challenge to Local Government? *Local Government Studies*, 41(3), 470–488.

Goldie, Roz, and Murphy, Joanne. (2010). Embedding the Peace Process: The Role of Leadership, Change and Government in Implementing Key Reforms in Policing and Local Government in Northern Ireland, *International Journal of Peace Studies*, 15(2), pp. 33–58.

Goldie, Roz, and Ruddy, Brid. (2010). *Crossing the Line: Key Features of Effective Practice in the Development of Shared Space in Areas Close to an Interface*, Belfast Interface Project, Belfast.

Hamber, Brandon. (2022). *It's Official: The Planning System in Northern Ireland Is Broken (in So Many Ways)*, 5 April 2022, on sluggero'toole.com.

Hansard (House of Commons Debates), 1998, 316, pp. 845–846 (1998a).

Hansard (House of Commons Debates), 1998, 317, pp. 1066–1070 (1998b).

Hansard (House of Lords Debates), 1998, 593, pp. 164–230 (1998c).

Hansard (House of Lords Debates), 1998, 593, pp. 1693–1736/1878–1881(1998d).

Harvey, Colin. (2000, March). Governing after the Rights Revolution, *Journal of Law and Society*, 27(1), pp. 61–97.

Harvey, Colin. (2022, January). The 1998 Agreement: Context and Status, Chapter 2 in McCrudden, Christopher, ed., *The Law and Practice of the Ireland-Northern Ireland Protocol*, Cambridge University Press, pp. 21–30. Online Publication. Online ISBN: 9781009109840.

Hayward, Katy. (2022, January). The Committees of the Protocol, Chapter 4 in McCrudden, Christopher, ed., *The Law and Practice of the Ireland-Northern Ireland Protocol*, Cambridge University Press, pp. 44–54. Online Publication. Online ISBN: 9781009109840.

Hayward, K., and Mitchell, C. (2003, September). Discourses of Equality in Post-Agreement Northern Ireland, *Contemporary Politics*, 9(3), pp. 293–312.

Heatley, C. (2004). *Interface: Flashpoints in Northern Ireland*, Lagan Books, Belfast.

Herian, M. N., Hamm, J. A., Tomkins, A. J., and Pytlik Zillig, L. M. (2012). Public Participation, Procedural Fairness, and Evaluations of Local Governance: The

Moderating Role of Uncertainty, *Journal of Public Administration Research and Theory*, 22, pp. 815–840.

Herrault, Hadrien, and Murtagh, Brendan. (2009). Shared Space in Post-Conflict Belfast, *Space and Polity*. <https://doi.org/10.1080/13562576.2019.1667763>.

Hutton, Brian. (2001). Anderson Steps Down as SF Fears Derry Loss, *The Irish Times*, 6 May 2021, p. 6.

Hutton, Brian. (2022). Police Handed Gun Used in Belfast Bookies Massacre to Loyalist Terrorist, *The Irish Times*, 8 February 2022, p. 5.

Institute of Irish Studies. (2022, April). *Tracker and Attitudes Survey 2022*, The Institute of Irish Studies, University of Liverpool, The Irish News Opinion Poll.

Jarman, N. (2004). *Demography, Development and Disorder: Changing Patterns of Interface Areas*, Institute for Conflict Research, Belfast.

Jarman, N. (2008). Security and Segregation: Interface Barriers in Belfast, *Shared Space*, 4, pp. 21–34.

Jarman, N. (2006). *Working at the Interface: Good Practice in Reducing Tension and Violence*, Institute for Conflict Research, Belfast.

Jarman, Neil. (2016). The Challenge of Peace Building and Conflict Transformation: A Case Study of Northern, *Ireland Kyiv-Mohyla Law and Politics Journal*, 2, pp. 129–146. National University of Kyiv-Mohyla Academy. <http://kmlpj.ukma.edu.ua/>.

Jerzewska, Anna. (2022, January). The Irish Sea Customs Border, Chapter 17 in McCrudden, Christopher, ed., *The Law and Practice of the Ireland-Northern Ireland Protocol*, Cambridge University Press, pp. 207–218. Online Publication. Online ISBN: 9781009109840.

Kelters, Seamus, McKittrick, David, Feeny, Brian, and Thornton, Chris. (1999). *Lost Lives: The Stories of the Men, Women and Children Who Died as a Result of the Northern Ireland Troubles*, Mainstream Publishing, Edinburgh.

Kenny, Michael, and Sheldon, Jack. (2021). 'A Place Apart', or Integral to 'Our Precious Union'? Understanding the Nature and Implications of Conservative Party Thinking about Northern Ireland, 2010–19, *Irish Political Studies*, 36(2), pp. 291–317. DOI: 10.1080/07907184.2020.1847418.

Kilpatrick, Raymond. (2010). Drumcree Now a Far Cry from Confrontations of the Past, Monday, *Belfast Telegraph*, 5 July 2010. <http://www.belfasttelegraph.co.uk/news/local-national/drumcree-now-a-far-cry-from-confrontations-of-the-past-14865255.html#ixzz1ByRs3YJG>.

Komarova, M., and O'Dowd, L. (2016). Belfast, 'The Shared City'? Spatial Narratives of Conflict Transformation, in Björkdahl, A. and Buckley-Zistel, S., eds, *Spatializing Peace and Conflict: Rethinking Peace and Conflict Studies*, pp. 265–285, Palgrave Macmillan, London.

Kula, Adam. (2020). Coronavirus: Drumcree Protests Suspended for First Time in 19 Years Amid Pandemic Fears, *Belfast Newsletter*, 7 April 2020.

McBride, Sam. (2019). *Burned: The Inside Story of the Cash-for-Ash Scandal and Northern Ireland's Secretive Elite*, Merrion Press, Newbridge.

McCambridge, Jonathan. (2022). Dissidents Still Want to Kill Us, Warns Police Body as Threat Level Reduced, *Belfast Telegraph*, Belfast, 23 March 2022.

McClements, Freya. (2020). Campaigner Receives Donations of Over £25,000 towards Legal Costs from Public, *The Irish Times*, 8 September 2020.

McClements, Freya. (2021a). Failure to Deal with the Past Bedevils the Present, *The Irish Times*, 12 May 2021, p. 5.

McClements, Freya. (2021b). PSNI Wrong Not to Investigate Claims of Hooded Men Torture, UK Court Rules, *The Irish Times*, 16 December 2021, p. 4.

McClements, Freya, and Erwin, Alan. (2012). Stormont to Fund Troubles Pension Plan, *The Irish Times*, 12 May 2021, p. 3.

McCrudden, Christopher, ed. (2022a). *The Law and Practice of the Ireland-Northern Ireland Protocol*, Cambridge University Press. Online Publication, Online ISBN: 9781009109840.

McCrudden, Christopher. (2022b, January). Good Faith and Sincere Co-operation, Chapter 8 in McCrudden, Christopher, ed., *The Law and Practice of the Ireland-Northern Ireland Protocol*, pp. 92–103, Cambridge University Press. Online Publication. Online ISBN: 9781009109840.

McCrudden, Christopher. (2004). Mainstreaming Equality in Northern Ireland 1998–2004: A Review of the Issues Concerning the Operation of the Equality Duty in Section 75 of the Northern Ireland Act 1998, in McLaughlin, E. and Faris, N., eds, *Section 75 Review*, Office of First Minister and Deputy First Minister, Belfast.

McDonagh, Bobby. (2022). UK Reneging on Protocol Would Unsettle North, *Irish Times*, 25 April 2022, 12.

McEvoy, Kieran, and Morison, John. (2003, April). Constitutionalism and Institutional Dimension: Beyond the Constitutional Moment: Law, Transition and Peacemaking in Northern Ireland, *Fordham International Law Journal*, 26, p. 961.

McEvoy, Kieran, and Shirlow, Peter. (2009). Re-imagining DDR: Ex-Combatants, Leadership and Moral Agency in Conflict Transformation, *Theoretical Criminology*, 13(1), pp. 31–59.

McKay Susan. (2022). It's 50 Years since Bloody Sunday, but Sectarian Tensions Are Running High, *Guardian*, 20 January 2022, p. 7.

McKay Susan. (2021a). *Northern Protestants: On Shifting Ground*, The Blackstaff Press, Belfast.

McKay Susan. (2021b). Erasing the Past Is Not How to Deal with the Troubles, *The Irish Times*, 17 July 2021, p. 15.

McVeigh, R. (2002). Between Reconciliation and Pacification: The British State and Community Relations in the North of Ireland, *Community Development Journal*, 37(1), pp. 47–58.

McVeigh, Robbie. (2019, December). *Sectarianism: The Key Facts*, Committee for the Administration of Justice, Belfast.

McVeigh, Robbie, and Rolston, Bill. (2007). From Good Friday to Good Relations: Sectarianism, Racism and the Northern Ireland State, *Race and Class*, 48(4), pp. 1–23, London.

Meehan, Patrick. (2018). What Are the Key Factors That Affect the Securing and Sustaining of an Initial Deal to Reduce Levels of Armed Conflict? *Literature Review*, UK Government Stabilisation Unit. <https://assets.publishing.serv ice.gov.uk/government/uploads/system/uploads/attachment_data/file/766 069/Elite_Bargains_and_Political_Deals_Literature_Review.pdf>.

Montgomery, Rory. (2021). The Good Friday Agreement and a United Ireland. Inaugural Lecture, George Mitchell Institute, Queen's University Belfast, 27 April 2021.

Moriarty, Gerry. (2021). Britain's Stance Brings More Anguish to Victims, *The Irish Times*, 15 July 2021, p. 3.

Morris, Allison. (2021a). We Must Remember Our Past for Fear of Repeating It. *Belfast Telegraph*, 2 December 2021, p. 8.

Morris, Allison. (2021b). Loyalist Graffiti Claiming 'War Is Needed' Appears in Newtownards, *Belfast Telegraph*, 14 December 2021.

Morris, Allison. (2022a). Informers Linked to 11 Killings by UDA Gang, *Belfast Telegraph*, 8 February 2022, p.1 and pp. 4–5.

Morris, Allison. (2022b). We Must Remember Our Past for Fear of Repeating It, *Belfast Telegraph*, 31 January 2022, p. 20.

Morrow, D. (2019). *Sectarianism – A Review*, Ulster University. <https://www.uls ter.ac.uk/__data/assets/pdf_file/0016/410227/A-Review-Addressing-Secta rianism-in-Northern-Ireland_FINAL.pdf>.

Murphy, Clare, *Irish Times*, 30 October 1999.

Murphy, Joanne. (2021). *Management and Wars: How Organisations Navigate Conflict and Build Peace*, Palgrave Macmillan, Eastbourne.

Murtagh, Brendan. (2017). Contested Space, Peacebuilding and the Post-conflict City, *Parliamentary Affairs*, 71 (2), pp. 1–23.

Nolan, P., Bryan, D., Dwyer, C., Hayward, K., Radford, K., and Shirlow, P. (2014). The Flag Dispute: Anatomy of a Protest, Queen's University Belfast. <http:// www.qub.ac.uk/researchcentres/isctsj/filestore/Filetoupload,481119,en.pdf>.

Northern Ireland Human Rights Commission, NI Human Rights Commission Brexit: Your rights. A Short Guide. <https://nihrc.org/uploads/Brexit-Your RightsShortGuidedigital.pdf>.

O'Cinneide, C. (2004). *Taking Equality Seriously: The Extension of Positive Duties to Promote Equality*, Equality and Diversity Forum, London.

O'Halloran, C., Shirlow, P., and Murtagh, B. (2004). *A Policy Agenda for the Interface*, Belfast Interface Project, Belfast.

O'Neill, Diane, and Murtagh, Brendan. (2017). Equality Law, Good Relations and Planning, Chapter 10 in McKay, Stephen and Murray, Michael, eds, *Planning Law and Practice in Northern Ireland*, pp. 191–205, Routledge, London.

O'Toole, Fintan. (2021). *We Don't Know Ourselves: A Personal History of Ireland since 1958*, Head of Zeus, An Apollo Book, London.

O'Toole, Fintan. (2022). Bloody Sunday, *The Irish Times*, Weekend Review, p. 1, 22 January 2022.

Palley, C. (1972). The Evolution, Disintegration and Possible Reconstruction of the Northern Ireland Constitution, *Anglo-American Law Review*, pp. 1–22.

Parades Commission. (2010). *Draft Public Assemblies, Parades and Protests (Northern Ireland) Bill: A Response from the Parades Commission for Northern Ireland*, Belfast. <www.paradescommission.org>.

Potter, Michael. (2010). *Dealing with the Past*, Research and Library Service Briefing Paper, Northern Ireland Assembly, 20 September 2010. <http://www.nia ssembly.gov.uk/globalassets/documents/raise/publications/2010/ofmdfm/ 12910.pdf>.

Public Account Committee. (2022). Review of Planning in Northern Ireland NIA 202/pp. 17–22, 24 March 2022.

Rowan, Brian. (2021). *Political Purgatory: The Battle to Save Stormont and the Play for a New Ireland*, Merrion Press, Newbridge, Ireland.

Shirlow, Peter. (2022a). Prof Peter Shirlow: Assembly Must Show Relevance Regarding the NI Protocol, *Irish News*, 10 May 2022. <irishnews.com/news/ northernirelandnews/2022/05/10/news/prof-peter-shirlow-prof-peter- shirlow-assembly-must-show-relevance-regarding-the-ni-protocol-2667173/>.

Shirlow, Peter. (2022b). Same Old Same Old Rhetoric Helps neither the Nationalist or Unionist Cause, *Irish News*, 5 August 2022. <www.irishnews.com/news/ northernirelandnews/2022/07/26/news/opinion_peter_shirlow_same_old_ same_old_rhetoric_helps_neither_the_nationalist_or_unionist_cause-2780 840/>.

Shirlow, Peter. (2012). *The End of Ulster Loyalism*, Manchester University Press, Manchester.

Shirlow, P., and Murtagh, B. (2006). *Belfast: Segregation, Violence and the City*, Pluto Press, London.

Shirlow, P., Tonge, J., McAuley, J., and McGlynn, C. (2010). *Abandoning Historical Conflict? Former Political Prisoners and Reconciliation in Northern Ireland.* Manchester University Press, Manchester.

Skelly, Joseph. (2021). Morrison, Into the Labyrinth Terrorism, History and Diplomacy, Chapter 22 in English, Richard, ed., *History and the Study of Terrorism*, Cambridge University Press, Cambridge.

Smith, Michael. (2022). *UDR Declassified*, Merrion Press, Newbridge, Ireland.

Staunton, Denis. (2021). Plant to Bar PSNI from Investigating Troubles Killings, *The Irish Times*, 15 July 2021, p. 3.

Staunton, Denis, and McClements, Freya. (2022). NI Protocol Legislations Being Considered, Says Johnson, *The Irish Times*, 23 April 2022, 8.

Waller, James. (2021). *A Troubled Sleep: Risk and Resilience in Contemporary Northern Ireland*, Oxford University Press, New York.

Weatherill, Stephen. (2022, January). Interpreting the Protocol, Chapter 7 in McCrudden, Christopher, ed., *The Law and Practice of the Ireland-Northern Ireland Protocol*, pp. 69–79, Cambridge University Press. Online Publication; Online ISBN: 9781009109840.

Whyte, John. (1983). How Much Discrimination Was There under the Unionist Regime, 1921–1968? in Gallagher, Tom and O'Connell, James, eds, *Contemporary Irish Studies,* Manchester University Press, Manchester.

Wouters, Jan, Dispute Settlement, Chapter 6 in McCrudden, Christopher, ed. (2022, January). *The Law and Practice of the Ireland-Northern Ireland Protocol*, 55-65, Cambridge University Press. Online Publication. Online ISBN: 9781009109840.

Zapone, Katherine. (2001). *Charting the Equality Agenda*, Equality Commission for Northern Ireland and Equality Authority, Dublin and Belfast.

# Index